Population, Development and Environment

Population, Development and Environment

Edited by
C.M. Lakshmana

RAWAT PUBLICATIONS
Jaipur • New Delhi • Bangalore • Guwahati • Kolkata

ISBN 978-81-316-0942-2

The publication of this book was financially supported by the ICSSR. The responsibility for the facts stated, opinions expressed, or conclusions reached, is entirely that of the author and that the ICSSR accepts no responsibility for them.

ICSSR Consultant: Dr. Rekha L. Sitasawad, (former Sr. Scientist, Central Pollution Control Board), 07, Old Transit House, Dakshinpuram, Jawaharlal Nehru University, New Delhi.

Published by
Prem Rawat for **Rawat Publications**
Satyam Apts, Sector 3, Jawahar Nagar, Jaipur 302 004 (India)
Phone: 0141 265 1748 / 7006 Fax: 0141 265 1748
E-mail: info@rawatbooks.com
Website: www.rawatbooks.com

New Delhi Office
4858/24, Ansari Road, Daryaganj, New Delhi 110 002
Phone: 011 2326 3290

Also at *Bangalore, Guwahati* and *Kolkata*

Typeset by Rawat Computers, Jaipur
Printed at Nice Printing Press, New Delhi

Contents

Section III
Urban Growth and Environment

Contributors

Animesh Roy, Assistant Professor, Raja N.L. Khan Women's College, Vidyasagar University, West Bengal.

Ananya Mitra B., Research Scholar, PG Department of Geography, Jnana Bharathi Campus, Bangalore University, Bangalore.

Anuradha Banerjee, Associate Professor, Centre for the Study of Regional Development School of Social Sciences Jawaharlal Nehru University, New Delhi.

M. Balasubramanian, Assistant Professor, Centre for Ecological Economics and Natural Resources, ISEC, Bangalore.

B.H. Doddahanumaiah, Head, Department of Sociology, Government First Grade College Hosakote Bangalore Rural.

M. Gopinath Reddy, Professor Centre for Economic and Social Studies, Nizamiah Observatory Campus, Begumpet Hyderabad, Andhra Pradesh.

C.M. Lakshmana, Professor, Population Research Centre (PRC) Institute for Social and Economic Change (ISEC) Dr. VKRV Rao Avenue, Nagarabhavi (P) Bangalore.

Mala Mukherjee, Senior Research Fellow (SRF), Jawaharlal Nehru University, New Delhi.

Pravin Kumar Shukla, Senior Research Scholar Centre for the Study of Regional Development (CSRD), School of Social Sciences(SSS), Jawaharlal Nehru University (JNU), New Delhi.

Protap Mukherjee, Quantitative Research Coordinator, Young Lives India, New Delhi.

Rajendra Poddar, Associate Professor, College of Agriculture Bijapur (UAS) Dharwad.

Vyasan R., Deputy Commissioner, Wokha District, Nagaland.

Foreword

M.V. Nadkarni

I am happy that Dr C.M. Lakshmana has brought together twelve selected papers, based on original and serious research, for this book from out of the papers presented at the National Seminar he had organized on the same theme in 2013, namely, 'Population, Development and Environment'. Even though the book is appearing four to five years after the Seminar, its relevance has not at all declined; it has only increased. Though the focus of the book is on India, it should be of interest to other developing countries too.

Perhaps the first person to have given a serious thought to and stimulated thinking on the inter-relationship between population, development and environment was Reverend Thomas Robert Malthus (1766–1834). In his *An Essay on the Principle of Population* published in 1798, he spoke of positive checks on population growth in the absence of preventive checks based on moral restraint. Among the positive checks, he mentioned disease, war and famines. He may not have spoken explicitly of the pressure of population on natural resources and environment, but he had it very much in his mind. Malthus was severely criticized for ignoring the possibility of economic development raising the carrying capacity of the earth to sustain population growth. But with development itself causing an enormous pressure on the natural resource environment, Malthus seems to have staged a come-back with a big bang!

The old paradigm of economic development raising the capacity of the earth to carry more and more population, has now given way to a new paradigm where population growth and economic development together are severely straining the carrying capacity of the earth! The new paradigm emerged because almost all the developing countries, including the populous countries like China and India and countries with fast rate of population growth, have taken the environmentally destructive style of development in their zeal to catch up with the West. To the rate of growth of multiplication of wants based on population growth, we must now add the rate of multiplication of wants due to per capita growth in incomes, to arrive at the total growth of wants, to have a measure of the pressure on the natural resources of the earth due to both factors.

Pressure on land and other natural resources comes both from the size of population and the nature of development process. Industries claim huge amounts of land and water compared to the population engaged in them. Mining particularly devastates both land and forests as well. Poverty of course is also a relevant factor. Thus for agriculture, it is necessary to draw a distinction between pressure on land to raise food production, and the pressure on land to earn a livelihood. Even if enough food is grown to feed a given population, it need not reduce pressure on land to eke out a livelihood. This is so particularly when non-agricultural sectors do not create enough job opportunities to absorb under-employed or excess population in agriculture and other primary sectors. Poverty thus becomes a source of pressure on land, though admittedly development itself also can be an equally strong or even stronger source of pressure on land and other resources. Let us, however, be clear that all the pressure on Common Property Resources (CPRs) and forests is not from the poor. Both the rural and urban elite are more prominent and effective in land grab than the poor. Since land has become an increasingly scarce resource, its ownership can be a source of huge amount of unearned rent. The state machinery often helps covertly in land grab by the elite.

Do we have the consolation that let alone environmental costs, at least human costs are minimized by the style of economic development we have been pursuing? Has poverty declined, has human development improved, following this style of development? India and China have different stories to tell in this respect. Poverty has been declining in India, but is far from being eliminated. Our ranking in Human Development is still very low. Economic development may seem to have reduced poverty to some extent in India, but it appears to have also increased in several pockets due to displacement of hundreds of thousands of people following development projects. These human costs of development are holding back the otherwise declining trend in poverty due to spillover or trickle-down effects. Decline in poverty is slowed down also by the tendency to economize on labour in almost all sectors.

In China's case, it is difficult to know the reality as much as in India, as China does not give the same freedom to the media as India does. Poverty does seem to have substantially declined in China even up to the point of its total removal, and certainly much more than in India. Human development levels are higher as compared to India. But we cannot say that the Chinese have not suffered on account of human costs of development. Displacement of people due to development projects seems to have been pretty significant if not massive in China, and how far displaced people are satisfactorily rehabilitated is not known. The difference between China and India in this respect is that incidents of human rights abuses in India become known almost worldwide overnight, whereas they are hidden in China.

We cannot term economic growth as development as long as it takes place by imposing huge human costs as well as environmental costs. When we pursue economic growth in the name of reducing poverty, we cannot then pursue a path of growth which increases poverty and unemployment, hoping that all will be well in the long run. Environmental costs have an inevitably adverse impact of causing or worsening poverty. That is how, environmental and human costs are inter-linked.

I am not against economic growth as such, particularly in India. But look at what is happening in the name of economic growth! Our mineral resources are literally being looted, bringing no increase in long-term and sustainable employment, but at best providing short term and extremely low-paid jobs in mineral exploitation and transport of mineral ore to ports. Much of this exploitation is illegal and even mafia-dominated. The poor workers employed in this are squeezed dry by mafia. We don't have to close down all the mines, but we have to ensure that mineral exploitation takes place only within law on environmentally sound basis, and that much of it is processed within India creating value addition and jobs in India itself.

It is not often appreciated that caring for environment can create jobs for the poor. If our huge urban wastes are properly recycled, composted or used for generation of electricity, depending on the nature of material involved, it will create value addition and jobs even from wastes, and prevent urban degradation and pollution. The energy-intensity of economic growth and styles of living has to be consciously reduced. We seek to minimize employment, even where energy saving can create more jobs.

Economic development is taking place at huge and unsustainable cost to water resources. Our demand for water has reached unsustainable levels both in industry and agriculture, both in urban and rural areas. Both people at large and the state and local government machinery have to learn ways of making judicious use of water, economizing on it beyond our comfort zone. I feel shocked when I see people using a hose to wash their cars and other vehicles, when a bucket of water and a piece of rag can do the job as effectively. But we want to economize on our work, refusing to go beyond our comfort zone.

Much is talked about our demographic dividend especially in India. A large proportion of people being in the working age group is certainly a rich potential source for growth, but it is only a potential. To realize this potential, we have to raise the levels of human development and assure gainful employment. If a bulk of this working-age population is employed in miserably low-paid and uncertain jobs in the informal sector, or is plain unemployed, this potential can turn itself from being benign into being malignant. It can be a source of unrest, lawlessness and utter wastage of human energy. But using this valuable resource is both a means and rationale of economic development. To be called as development, economic growth has to be made to meet social goals, particularly providing gainful employment, and improving levels of human development. It needs a focus on meeting basic needs in an equitable and sustainable way – food, water, health, education, housing and energy. As much focus is needed on their equal distribution, as on their total supply. Equity is basic to development, otherwise, growth would lead only to plunder.

Let me now turn to the issue of mutual causation between population and poverty. Quite a few have believed in the vicious circle between population growth and poverty on the one hand, and between poverty and environment on the other. Increase in population is said to lead to increase in poverty, leading in turn to population growth. Similarly, increase in population and poverty are believed to lead to more pressure on land, water, forests, grazing lands and other CPRs resulting in their degradation, which in turn would lead to increased poverty. It is like wheels within wheels.

We may not be able to reject the vicious circles theory totally, but the problem with this theory is that it is too simplistic to do justice to the complex relationships and processes involved. First of all, poverty is caused more by social and economic exploitation than by population growth. The character of the economic and social system is a major determinant of poverty levels and nature of poverty. Secondly, though fertility rates are supposed to be higher among the poor than among the middle class, there is now an increasing evidence that even the poor are worried about the future of their children, and they are eager to plan their families if the right kind of facilities are available and safety is assured in contraception. Thirdly, the depletion of Common Property Resources, forests and other natural resources has been much more due to commercial and industrial pressure than due to pressure of the poor for livelihood.

These qualifications are so important that they almost demolish the theory of vicious circles between population, poverty and environment. It is naïve to believe that either the rate of growth of population or density of population by itself determines the levels of poverty and environmental degradation. Some of the West-European countries have very high densities of population but have managed to improve their environmental health. It is ironical, however, that the size of population being a valuable resource for economic development can also turn into a liability as well. This is specially so in urban areas. Much depends upon the strategies of development. An urbanized, elite-oriented, capital intensive and labour – saving strategy of development turns a valuable human resource in to a liability. In a Gandhian approach to development on the other hand, population is a valuable asset, more important than capital.

Economic development takes place both through rural development and urbanization. But between the two, economic development seems to prefer to take the form of urbanization. Urbanization certainly tends to improve the quality of life of people by providing easy access to health, education, transport, electricity, water and other social and infrastructural amenities. What is more, it also reduces the importance of caste identities and differences, and allows more scope to realize one's human potential.

However, large cities with million-plus populations seem to be on the declining side of the benefits of urbanization. Benefits of urban growth seem to rise at first with the increasing size of the cities up to a certain point, after which they seem to rapidly decline, not only in terms of the pressure on the amenities but also in terms of pressure on urban governance, and pressure on urban environment in general. The decline is most conspicuously seen in terms of traffic jams and the increasing time taken in commuting the same distance. A lot of precious time is lost which is available neither to be with family nor for productive work, the commuter being in the unenviable state of a modern *Trishanku* who is neither on the earth nor in the heaven, neither at workplace nor at home. But the decline in benefits is seen in other respects too, reflected in increasing costs of providing housing, water, schooling, and urban waste disposal. The city almost grows on its own momentum with nobody controlling its size. We go away further from nature so much that it is difficult to get a view of a good expanse of the sky!

I feel that it would be rewarding to further research on the optimum size of cities, beyond which the quality of urban life and urban governance declines significantly. The optimum may not be fixed, and may vary depending upon several factors including the nature of the urban economy and even technological development.

A related issue of research would be to study the impact of urbanization on poverty levels. Does urbanization help or does it work against poverty removal? Merely comparing poverty levels between urban and rural areas would not do. The focus should be on the process of urbanization and its impact both within a given city and across cities over a period of time. It may be revealing to see whether and how different rates of urbanization across states or even countries, are related to different levels of poverty and trends therein. Furthermore, is there an optimum point before which urbanization tends to reduce poverty, but after which it tends to increase poverty?

The interrelationships between population, poverty, development, urbanization, and environment, are a fascinating area of research, in which not only demographers but also economists and sociologists can participate. This would clearly require interdisciplinary perspectives. The papers presented in the volume here offer useful insights into the complex relationships involved. Not only researchers, students and teachers, but also policy makers and administrators should find the volume of much interest.

M.V. Nadkarni
Professor (Retd.)
Former Vice Chancellor
Gulbarga University, Karnataka

Introduction

C.M. Lakshmana

Globally, high population growth and continued economic development have been causing serious environmental damage in the Asia-Pacific region. However, in recent experience the pace of environmental degradation is found to be faster in developing countries than in the developed ones. In this context one should know the impact of population, development and its relation with the environment. It is indeed, that the rapid economic growth and expansion of infrastructure development in the recent decades have not been without serious environmental consequences, particularly in the south, north and western regions. But in the east, north-east and central regions of the country, environmental damage has been mainly due to the rapid population growth. In India, rapid population growth and expansion of developmental activities have both greatly aggravated resource depletion and degradation of the environment (Jodha, 1990 and Paul, 2009). The extent of environmental degradation varies across countries and regions of the world (Eakin, and Seldon, 1995). For example, poverty has been the major cause of depletion of natural resources and environmental degradation in Africa (Kalipeni, 1992), but in the Asia-Pacific region both rapid population growth and continued economic development are found to be the major causes of environmental pollution (Duraiappah, 1996 and Dewaram, 2007). On the contrary, in the United States, where population density is much lower than in India, the main cause of environmental damage has been the extremely high per capita consumption of resources and the consequent high carbon emission (United Nations, 1997).

Two factors can be identified as environmental threats, viz: (i) proximate causes such as population growth, poverty, and population density and (ii) ultimate factors, i.e. developmental imperatives like urbanization, industrialization and economic development, all of which, often result in unsustainable use of natural resources and eventual degradation of environment. India's economic development has accelerated in the last two decades. India's efforts to reduce population growth have been impressive as shown by the steady decline in growth rate as well as absolute numbers. This has not, however, been coupled with environmental conservation. The degree of environmental pollution differs across regions in accordance with characteristics such as poverty ratio, size and density of population, etc. Besides, economic development and reduction in population growth have not been uniform across regions and states in India. The skewed development across regions has aggravated regional inequality in socio-economic development, which has grave implications on environmental issues for obvious reasons.

Environmental issues have not received enough attention, apparently due to our preoccupation with economic development. The central, eastern and north-eastern regions of India still have huge populations, which indeed cause higher levels of poverty (40% in central and 35% in eastern regions) and overuse of natural resources like forest, water and land (Scott and Linxiu, 1997). Huge population, low quality of human resources and inadequate levels of socio-economic development are the major challenges in the context of conservation of natural resources and protection of environment in the central, eastern and north-eastern regions of India. On the other hand, comparatively low population growth and higher levels of economic development cause environmental stress in southern and western regions (Kumar, 2001).

The extent of environmental damage in India caused by rapid population growth and increased economic development is well documented (Sharma, 2008). There is also a contribution to environmental degradation from the economic power of different groups – poor, middle and rich income people. For instance, high density of population invariably results in poor environmental quality. But, this does not mean that only the poor contribute to environmental degradation in India; even the middle class and rich groups have also been causing environmental degradation by using higher quantities of energy such as fossil fuels, electricity per capita, etc. In India (as elsewhere), development has caused rural-urban migration, urban poverty and the unsustainable consumption of resources, with increased emission levels of greenhouse gases and other pollution (The World Bank, 2004). There has also been a widespread acquisition of consumer goods by the burgeoning middle and upper classes (Kawadia, Ganesh and Malhotra, 2007).

Diversion of huge tracts of agricultural land for establishing industrial estates and special economic zones (SEZ) has directly resulted not only in the shrinkage of agricultural land but also in the migration of displaced agricultural labourers to non-agriculture activities, particularly in the towns (Lakshmana, 2008). The craze for modern ways of life and the spread of corporate culture seem to have impoverished rural life and decimated rural livelihood systems, in addition to spreading discontent among the

Conceptual Framework of Population, Development and Environment

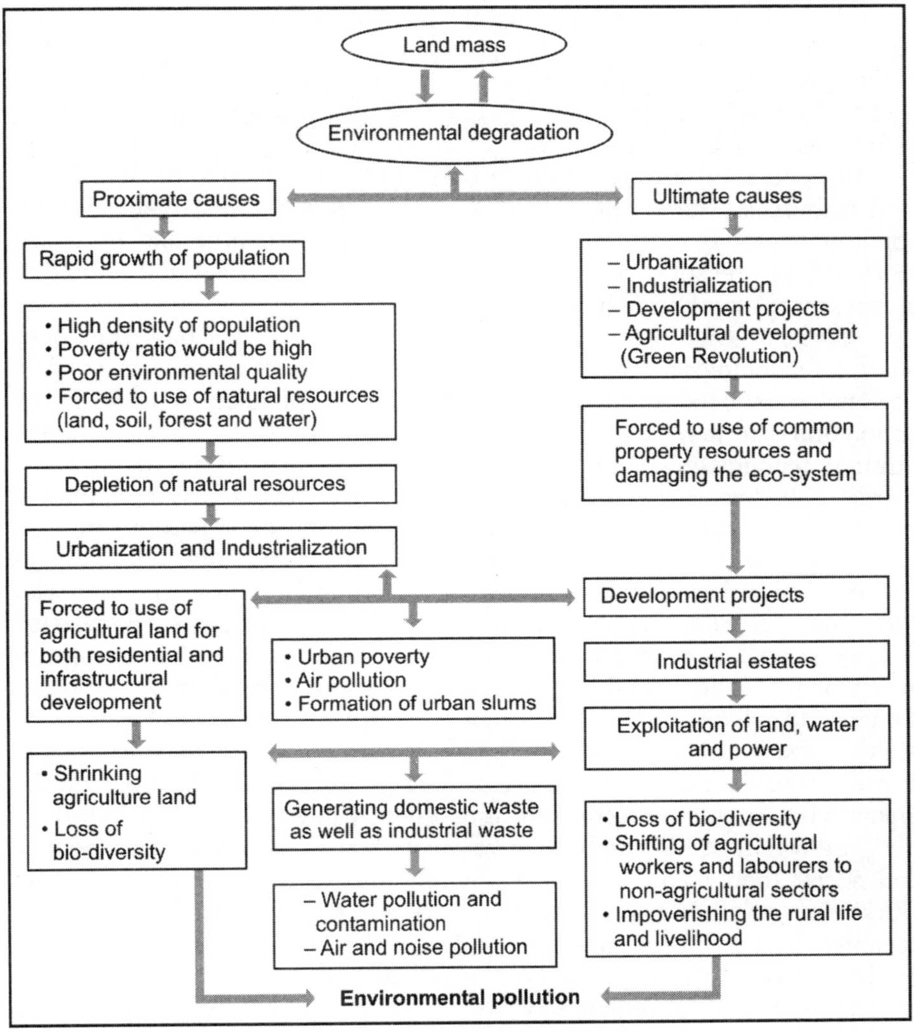

have-nots. However, the relationship of population, development and environment in India can be seen with the conceptual framework that has been drawn in the following:

Theory on Population and the Environment

Malthus versus Boserup

The theoretical framework of population and environment dynamics are limited. Conceptual thinking on population and environment within both the social and natural sciences has, in fact, traditionally suffered from a long-term confinement within 'Malthusian' versus 'Cornucopian' polarities. These opposing points of few have made it, somewhat notoriously, into the popular media through the antagonistic work of the biologist Robert Ehrlich

(1968) and with A. Ehrlich (1990) and the economist Julian Simon (1981 and 1990). However, several demographers, most notably Bilsborrow (1979, 1989 and 1992), have thus, formulated frameworks that integrate Boserupian and Malthusian ideas and account for population impacts on, as well as responses to their environment. The oft repeated central tenet of Malthusian theory (1798 and 1803, republished (1960) is that the growth of human population always tends to outstrip the productive capabilities of land resources. The result is that resources place a direct restriction on population growth and size, and 'positive' checks (famine and increased mortality) or preventative checks (postponement of marriage and limitation of family size) work to reduce population growth.

Malthus has pointed out, that he does not entirely discount the possibility of technological change – since historically important innovations had obviously occurred during his time. Rates of population growth and population size may sustainably increase, according to Malthusian theory, through technological innovation. The core of Malthusian theory, may therefore, be best captured by the 'dependent' role he assigns to population growth in relation to the independent factors of environment and technology. Boserupian theory similarly focuses on the relationships between these three factors: population, environment and technology. Her concept of 'population', in contrast to Malthus, encompasses population density as well as absolute size and growth. Like Malthus, her concept of environment refers mainly to land resources and related factors such as climate and soil quality. It is important to recognize that neither Boserup nor Malthus specifically address 'population', 'environment' and 'technology' per se but rather the topics of land use or food production. Implications on the linkages between these factors are subsequently inferred from their work.

The origin of Boserup's view has historical roots in diverse economic and social theory and may be traced to the work of Smith, Marx and Durkheim as well. In his well-known concept of the economy of scale, Smith specifies the need for a growing population that will permit more efficient production through the division of labour. Marx's concept of 'verkeher' also refers to the need for population growth and a minimal density that allows productive action (Marx and Engels, 1846). Similarly, Durkheim proposes a threshold 'dynamic density' of population that will support the necessary division of labour and more efficient production (Durkheim, 1893). What unifies Boserup with these lines of historical thought is the independent role assigned to population. Smith, Marx, and Durkheim (although strange bedfellows in general) all propose that population growth induces change in the organization of labour which subsequently extends the productive capacity of resources.

Boserup, writing in the midst of the concurrent rapid population growth and technological change which have characterized much of the 20th century, extends population-induced change in the organization of labour to include population-induced change in technology which may similarly extend the productivity of resources. Therefore, a growing population or increased population density leads ultimately to long-term increases in output that outweigh short-term declines (Boserup, 1965). Similarly, she rejects the related assumption that rural population growth inevitably leads to labour surplus and push migration to urban areas. Moreover, the growing population in both urban and rural spheres raised the opportunity for economies of scale or the creation of infrastructure such as roads. This, in turn, allowed the wider transfer of agricultural inputs, stimulating further intensification of agriculture, greater surplus and ultimately further urbanization and industrialization (Boserup, 1990). In her concluding remarks she said that there is much scope for intensification of agricultural production in Sub-Saharan Africa and notes that unlike historical Europe, modern agricultural inputs, such as Green Revolution technologies, exist that are capable of vastly increasing output (Boserup, 1981). On the other hand, she states that current population growth rates are much higher in Sub-Saharan Africa than in historical Europe and that 'agricultural intensification must take place more quickly' (Boserup, 1965).

Reinterpreting Boserup with Malthus: Bilsborrow's Framework of Multiphasic Response

Richard Bilsborrow also attempts to synthesize Malthusian and Boserupian theory but also introduces an empirical dimension in his approach. It draws on evidence from the developing world to construct a conceptual framework that encompasses the array of responses that a growing, rural agricultural population can make in adjusting to resource pressure (Bilsborrow, 1979 and 1992). Davis suggests that a growing population will respond 'multiphasically' or in any demographic way possible to reduce this resource pressure (Bilsborrow, 1992 and Davis, 1963). As Ron Lee observes, 'there are two grand themes in macro-demographic theory: the Malthusian one, and the Boserupian one (Lee, 1986). Boserup's theory and interpretations by others such as Richard Bilsborrow, in fact, provide the only extensively developed alternative to the orthodox Malthusian view of population, technology and resources. However, as recent interpretations of Bilsborrow (as well as Lee) suggest, Boserupian theory may represent not a contradictory but, rather, complementary perspective to Malthus.

However, India has vast extent of land, forest and rich variety of biodiversity. Its wide agro-climatic regions have supported expansion of human and animal populations through ages. Although, economic development in India has been accompanied by certain amount of avoidable environmental damage for want of long-term vision and planning. The rapid population growth and consequent expansion of infrastructure have greatly worsened air and water pollution, not to speak about the carbon emission caused by consumption of fossil fuels by a burgeoning population. Population growth impacts the environment primarily through the use of natural resources and production of wastes, and is generally manifested in environmental stresses like loss of biodiversity, air and water pollution and increased pressure on arable land.

Rural poverty, lack of avenues for gainful employment in villages and consequent ecological stresses are leading to an ever-increasing movement of poor families to urban places. The recent trend of urbanization in India has been changing the urban setting in several dimensions. For example, in the emerging scenario of urbanization in India, smaller cities are becoming bigger cities; bigger ones are becoming metro cities, which are further growing into mega cites. For obvious reasons, infrastructure development in these emerging cities has not kept pace with the increase in population. However, the recent decades have witnessed acceleration in the evils of our unplanned economic development process, particularly the damage to environment. In view of this, the present edited book comprises of 12 research papers broadly highlighting the interrelated aspects of population, development and environment, which helps in policy implications at different levels in order to mitigate the environmental pollution for sustainable development.

Section I of the book 'Population, Poverty and Environment' has four papers which discusses the land use change, migration and industrialization impact on environment; Section II of the book 'Development versus Environment' tries to analyse the development impact on environment. Section III of the book deals with the nexus between urban growth and its negative impact on environment which includes land use and land pattern change and its socio-economic vulnerability on environment and well-being. I hope the present book would be of immense value in order to understand the contemporary issues of population, development and environment with respect to India.

SECTION I

Population, Poverty and Environment

1

Human Capabilities and Sustainable Development Goals

In Search of a Sustainable Framework for Population-Environment-Development Nexus

Protap Mukherjee

> Our society is built not on the joy and happiness of the past, but on the agonies experienced by the long line of our predecessors. Whether or not all the agonies or struggles of the past will emerge into a great future, or will vanish into nothing at all, is likely to be decided in the next few tens of human generations.
>
> – Fred Hoyle on Everyman's Universe in Ten Possible Worlds

The above lines highlighted as a quotation in the initiation of this current paper are told by theoretical physicist Fred Hoyle, founder of the 'steady state theory' which is considered as an alternate of the widely accepted 'big bang' theory explaining the creation of the universe. The very beauty of the steady state theory about the origin of the universe lies in its aesthetic appeal, in which it has been postulated that our universe was neither created in a sudden big explosion nor will it be destroyed in a similar fashion; rather it envisages an eternal homogeneous steady universe existing in an infinite time continuum. Which theories – steady state, big bang or string theory – will be able to answer the most importantly raised philosophical and scientific question about the origin and end of the cosmos, lies in future with further fundamental scientific discoveries and new technological advancement towards solving the mysteries of the extraterrestrial world, and absolutely with human existence.

However, neither the aim of this paper is about the advocacy of the steady state theory over other existing theories on this subject nor it would be in the capacity of the present author, most importantly, to comment on this, even to the least extent. But the real motive of the author here is to start the argument concerning 'sustainability' in this paper can better be started with the very 'origin', which is able to evoke that the earth is the only known planet in the universe that has favourable environment that makes it possible for human beings to live here in the form of shared societies. However, the human civilizations on this shared planet have not progressed uniformly. Human development differs widely from one country to another, even with in the same country; the level of development varies across different socio-economic groups. Economic and social inequality abundantly exists, that leads to widespread hunger, reduced health, untimely mortality and quality living for most of the population on this planet. Moreover, human interference with the environment in the form of consumption of resources for better living does not always go well in harmony; the balance among population-development-environment (P-D-E) has been gravely disturbed and a serious concern has now emerged before policy makers about how this balance could better be restored or be followed without hampering any of the elements of the system, i.e. P-D-E. The opinion on the importance of the 'sustainability' hence received serious attentions in the human development framework, and in international commitments like Sustainable Development Goals (SDGs).

This paper links two issues. First, it deals with the progress of human development, principally in the form of enhancement of human capabilities. Finally, it points towards the pace of human and economic development that goes possibly in harmony with environment, that is, a concern for environmental sustainability. Inequality in human development (for example, education, life expectancy, income and well-being) has been examined as *capability failure* as argued by Amartya Sen. The choice of considering capability approach in P-D-E framework lies in the importance required on the human side. According to Ingrid Robeyns (2005), 'the capability approach is a framework of thought, a normative tool... applying the capability approach implies that we choose the relevant capabilities and indicate how important each will be in an overall judgment'. The present widespread economic and social inequalities in groups of countries and among certain socio-economic groups are actually the results of the basic capability failures, those they should ethically are entitled to have. Many international commitments in the form of programmes and policies have been structuring, monitoring and evaluating to enhance the basic human capabilities to reduce inequalities and vulnerabilities among the deprived population since the last few decades. The eight Millennium Development Goals are such commitments to improve human capabilities.

The Millennium Development Goals Report 2012 highlights several milestones. But despite important achievements like improvement in poverty level and promotion of the various forms of stakeholder participation, the current MDG framework cannot fully address environmental issues like climate change, energy security, loss of biodiversity, disaster preparedness and resilience. The SDGs proposed during the Rio+20 (2012) are expected to address the shortcomings facing MDGs and broaden their goals to interlink economic, social and environmental dimensions as part of a broader framework which can deal with issues like poverty eradication with enhanced environmental considerations.

Sustainable Development Goals is the outcome of the 2012 UN Conference on Sustainable Development in Rio de Janeiro which was the key platform for the agreement of future sustainable development initiatives. SDGs would guide the international sustainable development agenda and serve as a vital contribution to the successor framework to the Millennium Development Goals (MDGs) after they expire in 2015 (Lingan et al., 2012). The SDGs will follow the four principles as the foundations of sustainable human development framework, that is, holistic, inclusive, equitable and universally applicable.

The capability and functionings framework of Prof. Sen provides a rich theoretical framework for evaluating human well-being. Achieving SDGs in all parts of this shared planet would only be possible if the full enhancements of human capabilities are well established, because human capabilities are 'ability to choose the "beings and doings" that are basic to human life'. Hence, a comprehensive examination of the 'population-development- environment' nexus in this paper has been accomplished from the perspectives of 'capability approach' to suggest a final sustainable framework. Presently, those academic literatures which connect capability approach with sustainable human development framework are considered for background study.

Literature Review

Brundtland Commission (1987) in 'Our Common Future' defines sustainable development as 'development that meets the needs of the present without compromising the ability of future generations to meet their own needs'. It contains two key concepts:

1. the concept of 'needs', in particular the essential needs of the world's poor, to which overriding priority should be given; and
2. the idea of limitations imposed by the state of technology and social organization on the environment's ability to meet present and future needs.

The argument is the central theme of the concept of Sustainable Human Development discussed by Anand and Sen (1994). According to their own words (1994), 'A universalist approach cannot ignore the deprived people today in trying to prevent deprivation in the future. The recognition of this need for integration is much in the spirit of the "human development approach" to economic and social progress. The focus of this approach is on the kind of life that all the people – irrespective of nationality, class, race, gender or community – can lead, and this non-sectarianism clearly must apply to generational divisions as well'.

So far, broad perspective of the capability approach is used for a variety of aims, such as poverty or inequality assessment, quality of life measurement, or as an important element of a theory of justice (Robeyns,

2005). 'The capability approach advocates that we focus on people's capabilities when making normative evaluations, such as those involved in poverty measurement, cost-benefit analysis, efficiency evaluations, social justice issues, development ethics, and inequality analysis. Capabilities are people's potential functioning. Functioning are beings and doings. Examples are being well fed, taking part in the community, being sheltered, relating to other people, and working on the labour market, caring for the others, and being healthy'. The difference between a function and a capability is similar to the difference between and achievement and the freedom to achieve something, or between and outcome and opportunity.

But the academic discourse on sustainable development has received little attention from the capability approach (Rauschmayer and Lessmann and Rauschmayer, 2013). But in theory, the high interdisciplinary nature of capability approach allows researchers to evaluate sustainability of development in multidimensional perspectives. The advantages of capability approach in examination of human development in relation to environmental sustainability are manifolds. Firstly, the capability approach can replace the 'needs' in the Brundtland definition of sustainable development with the concept of 'capabilities'. Hence, in this approach, 'sustainable development is development that promotes the capabilities of present people without compromising capabilities of future generations'. This approach enables a better understanding of the development of environmental sustainability with human interferences; a better understanding of 'collective capabilities, norms, intentions, institutions and their link to individual capabilities, norms, intentions, institutions' (Lessmann and Rauschmayer, 2013).

The capability approach of Sen undoubtedly provides a rich theoretical framework for evaluating human well-being. Now, a comprehensive examination of 'population-development-environment nexus' in this paper have been accomplished from this approach to suggest a final framework which links sustainable human development with enhanced environmental sustainability.

Again, the choice of capabilities and other indicators of development and environment are imperative in P-D-E analysis. According to Lutz et al. (2002), 'it would seem obvious that we should explicitly include both population and environment variables and their dynamics of change over time in our analytical model'. Lutz emphasized on selection of appropriate variables of population dynamics and environmental dynamics to be considered in P-D-E analysis. This paper has used many variables/indicators which are able to explain and able to build the P-D-E framework.

Objectives

The specific objectives of this paper are:

1. From 'population' perspectives, to study the population dynamics by examining levels, trends and patterns of relevant population indicators

(TFR, IMR, life expectancy, dependency ratio, etc.), by countries/different economies.

2. From 'development' perspectives, to study the levels of 'human capabilities' or 'capability failure' by countries/different economies (in multidimensional poverty perspective encompassing relevant development indicators).
3. From 'environment' perspectives, to study the levels and linkages among biodiversity, forestry, fisheries, agriculture; environmental system, environmental stress; social and institutional capacity and overall environmental sustainability by different economies/countries.
4. To examine the interlinkages among population, development and environment.
5. Using capability approach, to develop a final framework to establish and explain the interrelationships among population, development and environment nexus in context of achieving SDGs.

Data and Methodology

Data have been used from United Nations Population Prospects 2010, United Nations World Contraceptive Use 2010, Environmental Sustainability Index 2005 and Environmental Performance Index 2010, published by Yale Centre for Environmental Law and Policy (YCELP), Yale University and Centre for International Earth Science Information Network (CIESIN), Columbia University; HDR 2011 and World Bank Data. Data for 144 countries have been included in the analyses.

Levels and linkages have been examined by mean, bivariate cross-tabulation, Pearson correlation and simple linear regressions. For association study, k-means clustering have been carried out.

Population Perspectives

Population dynamics in the region have been shown by trend analysis of four indicators: total fertility rate, natural increase, life expectancy and old age dependency from 1955 to 2050. The trend in all four indicators of population dynamics have been projected till 2050. So, the past performance, present progress and future development can be examined. Graphs show that though the huge gap in levels of TFR has been reducing between less developed and more developed countries in the world, but it will still remain in the future. The less developed countries will have TFR above replacement level and it would be serious concerns for overall development of these countries. Figures 1 to 5 show trend in certain demographic indicators by countries' levels of development.

Regarding the natural increase, more developed countries will experience negative population growth in future, but the rate of natural increase will be very high among least/less developed countries, though the rate of natural increase has been decreasing in these countries since 1990. The levels of life expectancy have been increasing since 1955 in all countries but the rate of increase is different by development level. By 2050, the life

Figure 1
Trend in Total Fertility Rate

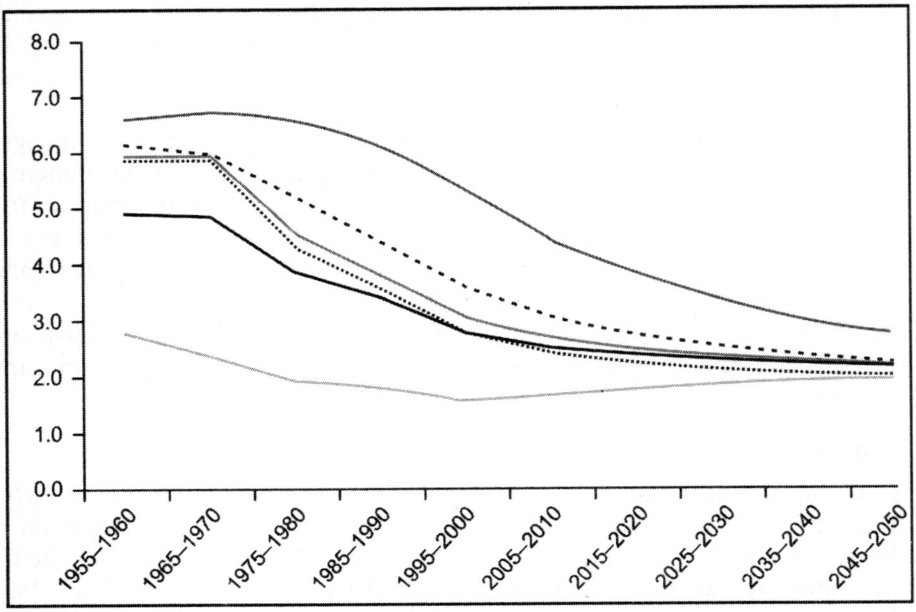

Figure 2
Trend in Natural Increase

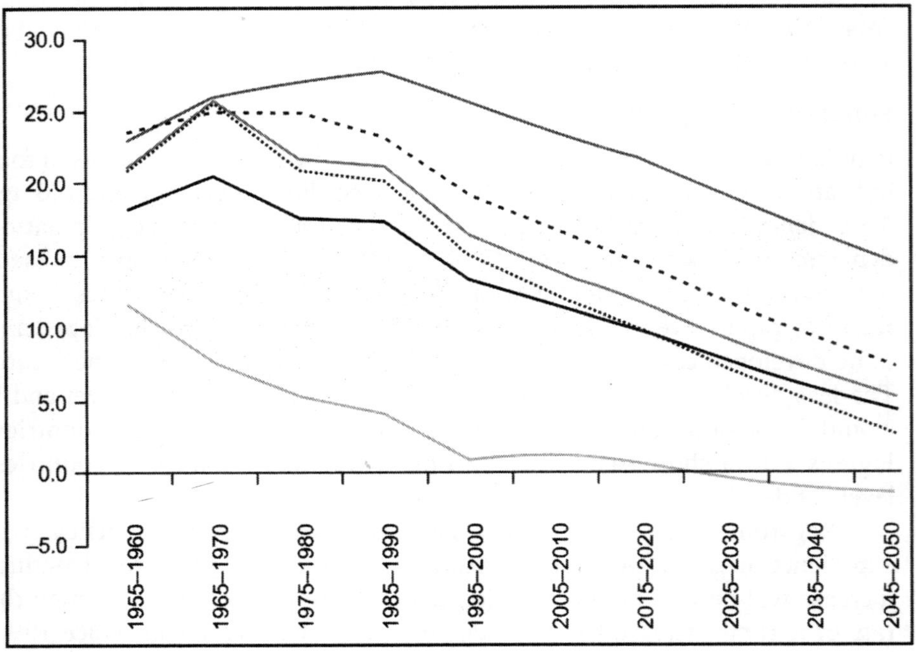

Figure 3
Trend in Life Expectancy

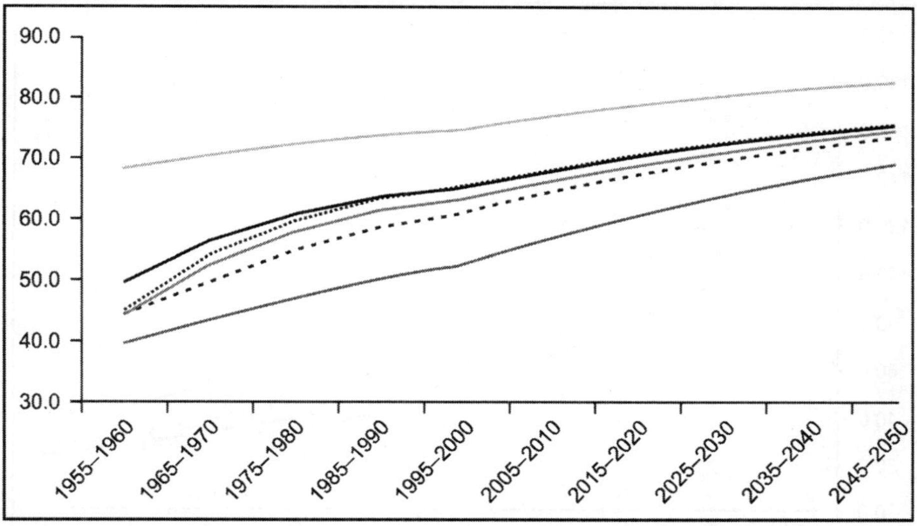

Figure 4
Trend in Old Age Dependency

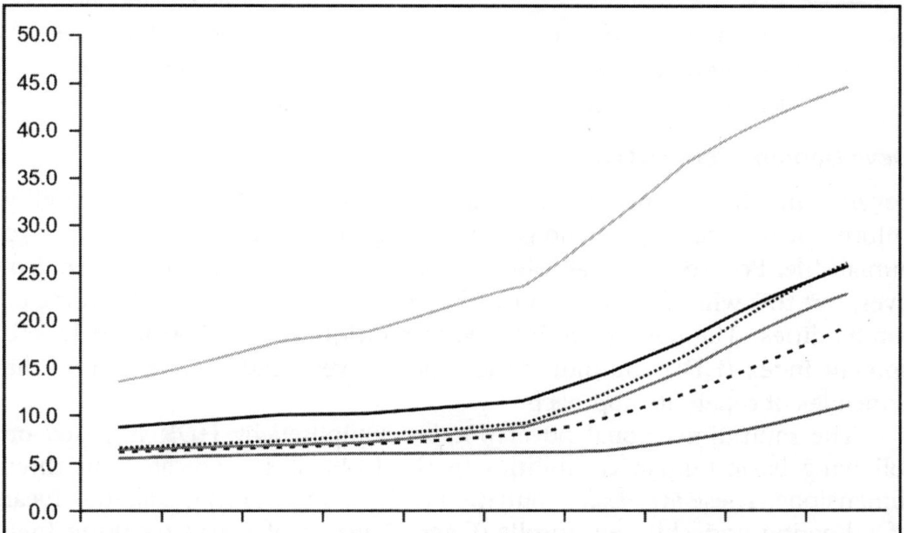

expectancy is supposed to reach at more than 80 years in developed countries whereas life expectancy in least developed countries is supposed to be at around 60 years which would be still lower from the life expectancy achieved by developed countries in 1955. Old-age dependency rate will be strikingly increased in more developed countries and huge gap in old-age population will exist between least developed and more developed countries by 2050.

Figure 5

Trend in Infant Mortality Rate

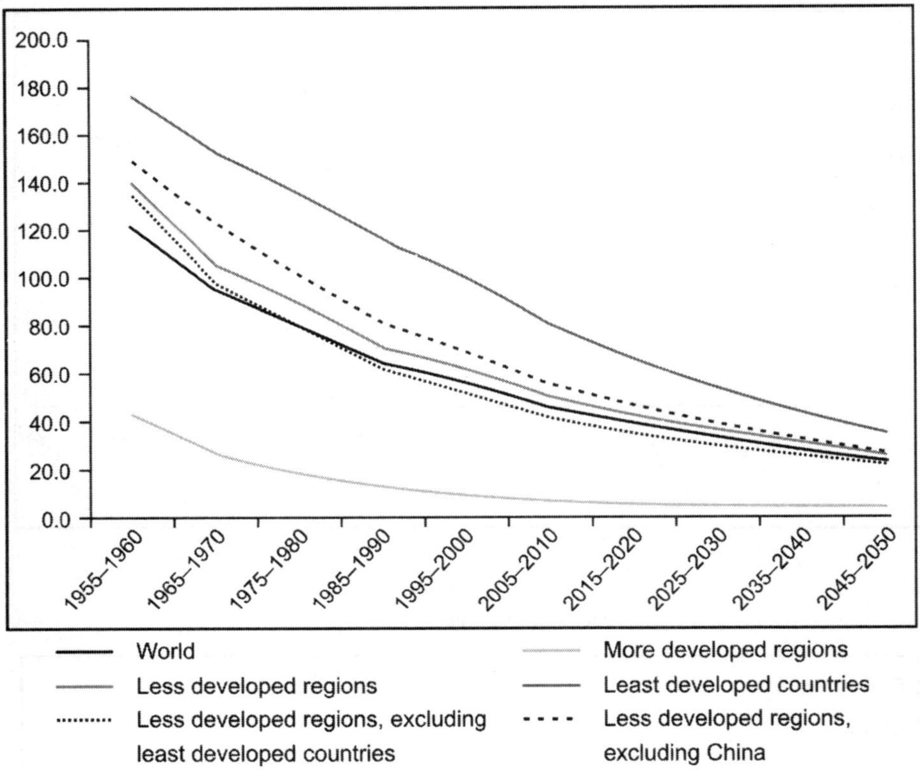

Development Perspectives

Poverty and inequality in the capability framework becomes 'capability failure', or the inability to choose the 'beings and doings' that are basic to human life. Poverty is the absolute inability to pursue one's desired objectives, but this will often be seen in relative terms in the spaces of income or commodities. The concept is inherently multidimensional. Human Development Index (HDI) and multidimensional poverty index are based on the principles of capability approach.

The multidimensional poverty index computed by HDR is based on following basic human capabilities in the form of 10 indicators in three dimensions. These are *Health* (nutrition and child mortality), *Education* (year of schooling and children enrolled) and *Standard of Living* (cooking fuel, toilet, water, electricity, floor and assets).

Table 1 reveals that very high human development positively relates to higher life expectancy, high mean years of schooling and very high GNI per capita, and negatively link with proportion of population living in multidimensional poverty. On the other hand, countries with low development suffer from the reduced life cycle, poor education and lowest purchasing capacity. Moreover, these countries have population of over 50 per cent who suffer in multidimensional poverty.

Table 1

Development Indicators

HDI Groupings	*Human Development Index (HDI)*	*Life expectancy at birth*	*Mean years of schooling*	*Expected years of schooling*	*Gross National Income (GNI) per capita*	*Intensity of deprivation of multidimensional poverty*
Very high human development	0.889	80.0	11.3	15.9	33,352	27.9
High human development	0.741	73.1	8.5	13.6	11,579	38.6
Medium human development	0.630	69.7	6.3	11.2	5,276	43.5
Low human development	0.456	58.7	4.2	8.3	1,585	55.2

Source: Human Development Report 2011.

Amartya Sen, argued that 'the changing agency of women is one of the major mediators of economic and social change, and its determination as well as consequences closely relate to many of the central features of the development process'. Figure 6 shows that high level of human development has the minimum gender gap in labour force participation. Besides, as observed from Figure 7, the capability to basic amenities in low income countries is very poor. Infant mortality is very high in these groups of countries.

Figure 6

Labour Force Participation Rate and Development Indicators of Countries by different Income Group

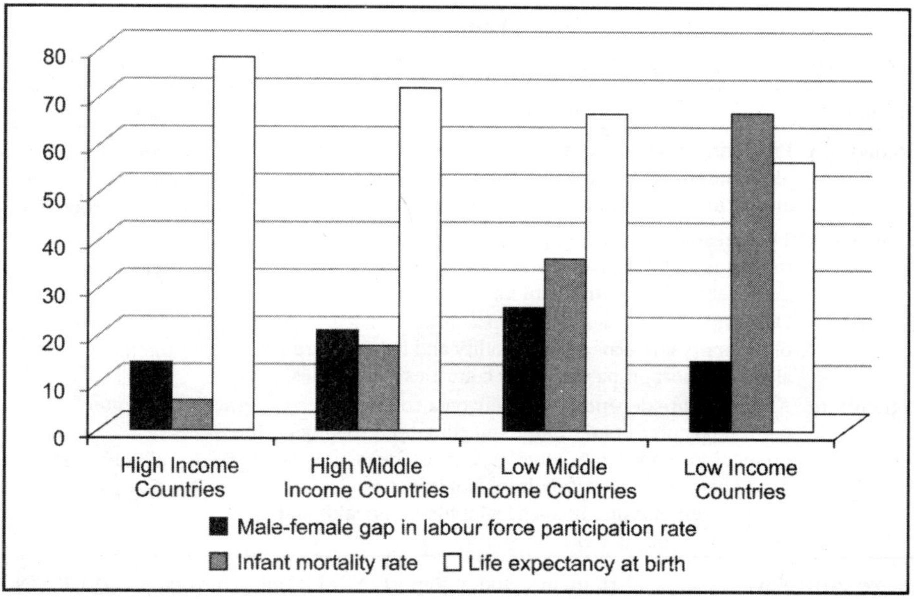

Figure 7
Standard of Living Indicators

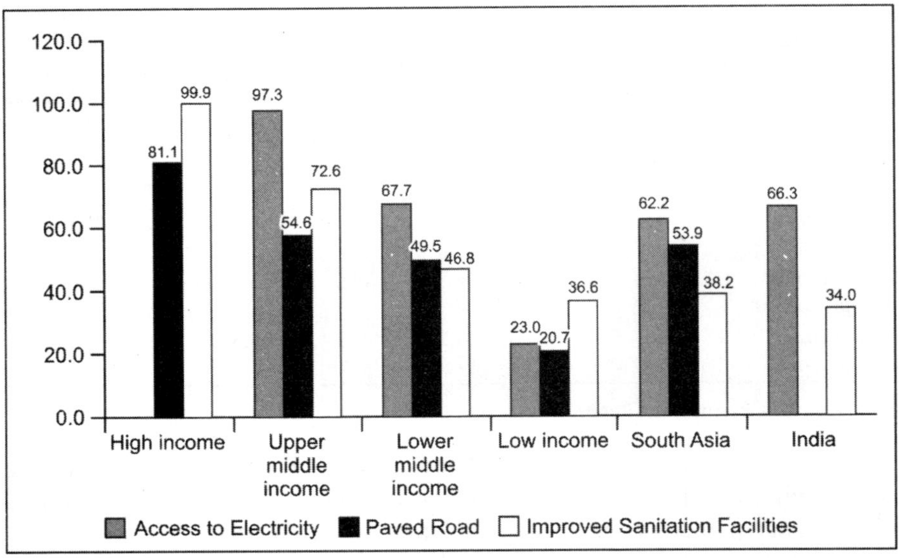

Environment Perspectives

In this paper, environmental sustainability has been examined in terms of ecosystem vitality, environmental systems, environmental stress, reducing environmental stress and overall environmental sustainability index. Ecosystem vitality is a summary measure relevant to the goal of reducing the loss or degradation of ecosystems and natural resources (YCELP and CIESIN, 2005, 2010).

Table 2
Ecosystem Vitality Indicators and their Significance in Sustainability Study

Resources	*Significance*	*Indicators*
Biodiversity	Protecting biodiversity ensures that a wide range of 'ecosystem services' will remain available for current and future generations.	Biome Protection Marine Protection Critical Habitat Protection
Forestry	The forestry metric highlights the importance of forests as a global resource as well as the need for more robust international monitoring efforts.	Growing Stock Exchange Forest Cover Change
Fisheries	Overfishing of species can be disastrous to marine biodiversity and ecosystem stability and fisheries are also an important part of many countries' economies.	Marine Trophic Index Trawling Intensity
Agriculture	As agriculture depends so heavily on a country's natural resources (soil, water and climate), growing populations and changes in diet, increase pressures on productive systems. Agriculture is not just an environmental issue. It is a developmental, health and economic issue, as well.	Agricultural Water Intensity Agricultural Subsidies Pesticides Regulation

Source: 2010 Environmental Performance Index Report, YCELP, Yale University and CIESIN, Columbia University, YCELP and CIESIN (2010).

Table 3 gives a glimpse of sustainability issues by countries with different development levels. The ecological footprints and anthropogenic impact are highest among countries with very high development level and lowest among countries with poor development.

Table 3

Sustainability Indicators by Countries with Different Levels of Development

Countries by Development	*Ecological Footprints Per Capita (Hectares of Biologically Productive Land Required per Capita)*	*Percentage of Total Land Area Having Very High Anthropogenic Impact*	*Freshwater Availability Per Capita in Thousand Cubic Metres*	*Internal Groundwater Availability Per Capita in Thousand Cubic Metres*
Very Highly Developed Countries	5.21	10.35	24.39	5.25
Highly Developed Countries	2.70	3.76	25.99	2.85
Medium Developed Countries	1.71	2.55	43.77	6.61
Lowly Developed Countries	1.02	0.52	18.29	2.79

Source: Author's analyses and YCELP and CIESIN (2005, 2010).

But yet the very highly and highly developed countries still have better reserve of water than poorly developed countries. But it is the medium developed countries which have shown apparently better position in terms of water sustainability. Ecological footprints and anthropogenic impact are lower among these countries in comparison to highly developed countries and also the mean fresh water availability per capita has been found to be highest among this group of countries.

Figure 8 examines the sustainability issues through environmental vitality scores by countries with different degrees of development. Graph shows that high and medium developed countries are relatively poor

Figure 8

Environmental Vitality Indicators by Levels of Development

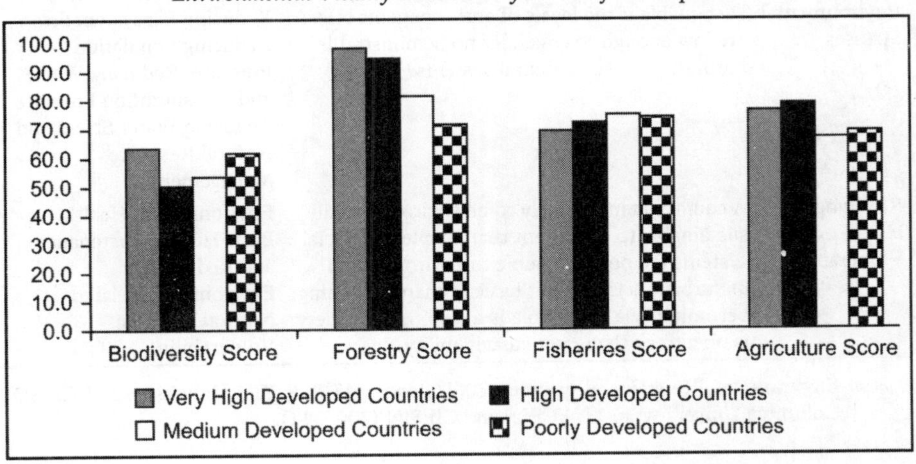

performers in terms of biodiversity scores in comparison with very high and poorly developed countries. Regarding forestry, the scores are negatively associated with degree of development. Poorly developed countries have exploited forest resources heavily and create a serious concern for them. On the other hand, relatively low fisheries score has been observed among very highly developed countries and lowest agriculture score has been found to be among medium developed countries.

Environmental sustainability is complex and hard to define. In this paper, the levels of environmental sustainability has been examined by 'Environmental Sustainability Index 2005' developed by YCELP and CIESIN; the Environmental Sustainability Index suggests that sustainability has multiple dimensions – and distinct challenges for developed versus developing countries. Environmental Sustainability Index is based on 5 components (Environmental Systems, Reducing Environmental Stresses, Reducing Human Vulnerability, Social and Institutional Capacity and Global Stewardship), 21 indicators and 76 variables (Table 4). The Environmental Sustainability Index (ESI) benchmarks the ability of nations to protect the environment over the next several decades. The most important function of the Environmental Sustainability Index is as a policy tool for identifying issues that needs greater consideration within national programmes aimed at environmental protection. 'The Environmental Sustainability Index also provides a way of identifying those governments that are at the leading edge with regard to any particular issue' (YCELP and CIESIN, 2005).

Table 4

Environmental Sustainability Indicators

Sustainability Components	*Significance*	*Indicators*
Environmental Systems	A country is more likely to be environmentally sustainable to the extent that its vital environmental systems are maintained at healthy levels, and to the extent to which levels are improving rather than deteriorating.	Air Quality, Biodiversity, Land, Water Quality, Water Quantity
Reducing Environmental Stresses	A country is more likely to be environmentally sustainable if the levels of anthropogenic stress are low enough to engender no demonstrable harm to its environmental systems.	Reducing Air Pollution, Reducing Ecosystem Stress, Reducing Population Pressure, Reducing Waste and Consumption Pressure, Reducing Water Stress and Natural Resource Management
Reducing Human Vulnerability	A country is more likely to be environmentally sustainable to the extent that people and social systems are not vulnerable to environmental disturbances that affect basic human well-being; becoming less vulnerable is a sign that a society is on a track to greater sustainability.	Environmental Health, Basic Human Sustenance and Reducing Environment-Related Natural Disaster Vulnerability

Source: Environmental Sustainability Index 2005 Report, YCELP, Yale University and CIESIN, Columbia University; p. 11, YCELP and CIESIN (2005: 11).

Figure 9

Components of Sustainability

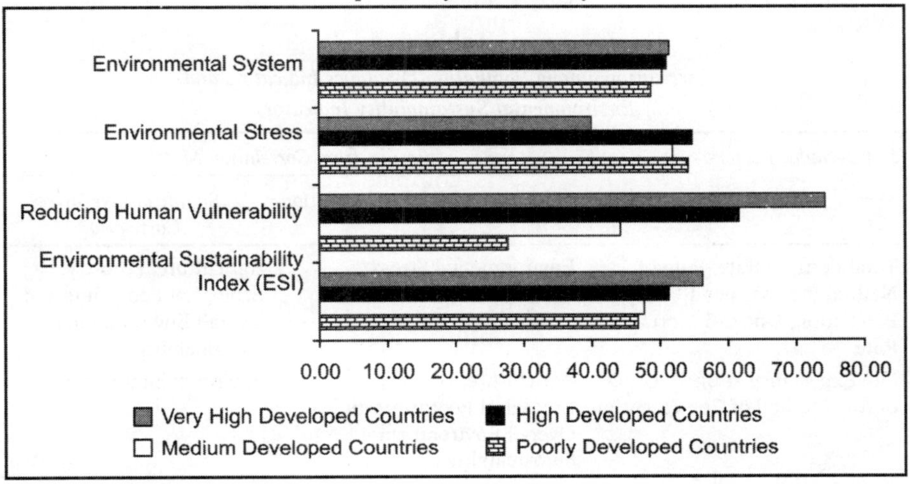

Figure 9 depicts that except for the environmental stress factor, the poorly developed countries will have serious sustainability issues in future. Human vulnerability scores have been found to be highest among this group of countries as well as environmental systems have also been badly maintained. The overall sustainability index is found to be lowest among poorly developed countries. But the concerns for sustainability differ by degree of development. For example, developed countries need to manage the environmental stresses of industrialization and consumption of non-renewable natural resources. On the other hand, developing countries will face the risk of depleting renewable resources such as water and forests.

Population-Development-Environment: Linkages

In this section, the relationships between population and environmental sustainability have been examined. TFR, rate of natural increase per 1,000 population, under-5 mortality rate, life expectancy at birth, usage of any methods of contraception have been taken as indicators of population dynamics. A correlation matrix has been carried out among population dynamics indicators and environmental sustainability indicators to examine interlinkages among the variables. Results show that not all aspects of population dynamics are related in the same way with the environmental indicators. Demographic aspects like total fertility rate, natural increase and under-5 mortality have significant positive correlation with environmental stress and have significant negative correlation with agriculture, forestry, ecological footprints and overall sustainability. These findings establish the fact that higher population growth increases environmental stress, as well as decline the sustainability levels in agriculture, forestry, ecological footprints and overall sustainability. On the other hand, positive (indicator of development) indicators of population dynamics like life expectancy at birth and usage of contraception do have significant positive correlation with resources as well as overall sustainability. Obviously, these population indicators are found to be significantly negatively associated with environmental stress.

Table 5

Correlation among Population Dynamics Indicators and Environmental Sustainability Indicators

Demographic Factors	*Results from Correlation Matrix*	
	Significant Positive Correlation	*Significant Negative Correlation*
Total Fertility Rate, Rate of Natural Increase per 1,000 Population, Under-5 Mortality Rate	Environmental Stress	Agriculture, Forestry, Ecological Footprints and Overall Environmental Sustainability
Life Expectancy at Birth, Usage of Any Method of Contraception	Agriculture, Forestry, Ecological Footprints and Overall Environmental Sustainability	Environmental Stress

Source: Author's Analyses.

The above correlation analysis in Table 5 shows that HDI is positively and significantly related to forestry, agriculture and overall sustainability index. Education is one of the most important human capabilities in the form of means years of schooling (achieved functioning) has also positive favourable impact on forestry and agriculture, that in turn is linked with better environmental sustainability. But the main problems lie in the widespread multidimensional poverty, which not only hinder poor human development, but has a serious threat for unwise resource utilization. Overall environmental sustainability is thus found to be negatively correlated with the intensity of multidimensional poverty (Table 6).

Sustainable Development Goals: Concerns

For interlinkages among population-development-environment, k-means clustering analyses have been carried out to examine the complex associations among these variables. Five different clusters have been identified with distinct characteristics. Each cluster consists of a group of countries. The association among P-D-E in each cluster raises the concerns related to Sustainable Development Goals. Fifteen P-D-E indicators have been used to define the clusters. In Table 7, the basic characteristics of P-D-E indicators in each cluster have been given.

For a better comprehensive understanding of each cluster, cluster profiling has been completed, so that the differences in characteristics between the clusters could be studied. Table 8 represent the summary table of cluster profiling which point towards the gaps that exist in each cluster and points towards the action needed for achieving SDGs. Table reveals that Cluster 1 is the cluster which has maximum number of countries, similar in P-D-E characteristics, mainly composed of highly developed and medium developed countries. Basic human capabilities in these countries have long

Table 6

Correlation among Development Indicators and Environmental Sustainability Indicators

Variables	*Biodiversity*	*Forestry*	*Fisheries*	*Agriculture*	*Environmental Sustainability Index*	*Human Development Index (HDI)*	*Mean years of schooling*	*Percentage of deprived population living in multidimensional poverty*
Biodiversity	1							
Forestry	–0.135	1						
Fisheries	0.205**	–0.164*	1					
Agriculture	0.090	–0.006	0.073	1				
Environmental Sustainability Index	0.284***	0.242***	–0.069	0.330***	1			
Human Development Index (HDI)	0.039	0.503***	–0.100	0.270***	0.477***	1		
Mean years of schooling	0.074	0.425***	–0.055	0.215***	0.450***	0.913***	1	
Percentage of deprived population living in multidimensional poverty	–0.003	–0.427***	0.064	–0.224***	–0.238***	–0.679***	–0.627***	1

Source: Author's analyses, significant at *** 1 per cent, ** 5 per cent and * 10 per cent level.

Table 7

Homogeneous Clusters Associated with Distinct P-D-E Situations, Derived from k-means Clustering Analysis

Indicators	*Cluster 1*	*Cluster 2*	*Cluster 3*	*Cluster 4*	*Cluster 5*
Total Fertility Rate	2.07	5.35	3.19	5.40	5.05
Infant Mortality Rate	15.41	110.66	49.29	84.93	78.64
Maternal Mortality Ratio	39.61	1026.00	261.58	793.75	505.00
Old Age Dependency	15.38	5.01	7.15	6.03	5.57
Life expectancy at birth	74.63	48.95	63.47	51.75	54.31
Any Method of Contraception	65.07	8.36	42.72	20.54	27.13
Mean Years of Schooling	9.27	2.65	5.27	3.63	4.38
Expected Years of Schooling	14.10	8.99	9.59	7.58	9.35
Percentage of Deprived Population	19.12	46.42	40.82	51.66	52.11
Human Development Index	0.77	0.33	0.51	0.38	0.45
Biodiversity	54.73	57.45	55.31	59.66	70.32
Forestry	93.51	60.80	70.17	67.49	79.85
Fisheries	71.90	82.32	69.04	77.50	76.65
Agriculture	76.05	69.50	63.23	66.14	69.04
Environmental Sustainability Index	51.31	44.08	49.09	47.29	47.54
No. of Countries	92	5	19	8	20

Source: Author's Analyses.

been achieved. But these countries will suffer from the problem of old-age aging and regarding environmental sustainability, they have high negative impact on biodiversity and fisheries. Cluster 3 which includes India, among many achievements, suffers from the adverse sign of human capabilities and widespread multidimensional poverty and have a high impact on environment. Custer 2 and Cluster 4 are the clusters of countries that specifically formed by countries with low development. The level of human capabilities and development is lowest among these countries, but the impact on environment is not same in the two clusters. Cluster 2 has adversely affected environment whereas Cluster 4 has a medium environmental impact. Hence, in term of achieving SDGs, these two clusters pose different challenges. The lowest environmental conditions have been observed in Cluster 5, mainly composed of low developed countries, principally from Africa. But these countries have very adverse demographic and development capabilities. The details of challenges needed to overcome to achieve SDGs are presented in Table 8.

Conclusion

The present paper uses capability approach as the base of explaining population-development-environment nexus. With this approach, this paper makes an attempt to bring the problems and prospects of human development in context of future environmental sustainability. The present paper establishes that population dynamics is significantly linked with future environmental

Table 8

Cluster Profiling for Policy Perspectives in Response to SDGs

Clusters	*Country Profile (No. of Countries by Level of Human Development)*	*Demographic Profile*	*Development Profile*	*Sustainability Profile*	*Remarks*	*Countries*
Cluster 1	Very Highly Developed: 30, Highly Developed: 37, Medium Developed: 24.	Below replacement level fertility, low morality, high old age dependency.	Highest life expectancy, highest schooling, least deprived population and very high overall HDI.	High Impact on Biodiversity, Low Impact on forestry and agriculture, high impact on fisheries.	Challenges for SHD: aging population and adverse resource utilization.	UK, USA, Japan, Saudi Arabia, Brazil etc.
Cluster 2	Low Development: 5	Very high fertility, very high mortality, very low old age dependency.	Lowest life expectancy, lowest schooling, high percentage of deprived population, lowest overall HDI.	High Impact on Biodiversity, forestry, medium impact on agriculture, low impact on fisheries.	Challenges for SHD: unfavourable demographic conditions, poor human capabilities and also adverse environmental conditions.	Burundi, Chad, Guinea-Bissau, Liberia and Sierra Leone.
Cluster 3	Very Highly Developed: 1, Highly Developed: 1, Medium Developed: 9, Low Development: 8.	High fertility, medium mortality, medium old age dependency	Higher life expectancy, medium schooling, high percentage of deprived population, medium low overall HDI.	High Impact on Biodiversity, agriculture and fisheries, medium impact on forestry.	Challenges for SHD: adverse human capabilities for substantial proportion of population and high impact on environment.	India, Bangladesh, Ghana, Bolivia, Yemen etc.
Cluster 4	Low Development: 8	Very high fertility, Very high mortality, low old age dependency	Medium life expectancy, low schooling, high percentage of deprived population, low overall HDI.	Medium Impact on Biodiversity, agriculture and forestry, low impact on fisheries.	Challenges for SHD: adverse human capabilities for substantial proportion of population and medium impact on environment.	Mali, Niger, Nigeria, Sudan, Zimbabwe etc.
Cluster 5	Medium Developed: 3 Low Development: 17	Very high fertility, high mortality, very low old age dependency	Medium life expectancy, low schooling, high percentage of deprived population, low overall HDI.	Low Impact on Biodiversity, forestry and fisheries, medium impact on agriculture.	Challenges for SHD: adverse human capabilities for substantial proportion of population but low impact on environment.	South Africa, Kenya, Senegal, Laos, Uganda etc.

Source: Author's Analyses.

sustainability. But the concerns for sustainability differ by degree of development. For example, developed countries need to manage the environmental stresses of industrialization and consumption of non-renewable natural resources. On the other hand, developing countries will face the risk of depleting renewable resources such as water and forests.

The discussions on the linkage among P-D-E in achieving Sustainable Development Goals (SDGs) aim towards meaningful policy implications on capabilities, preparedness and sustainability. For example, high human development (enhanced capabilities) positively relates to sustainability of environment, on the other hand, presence of multidimensional poverty (capability failure) negatively relates to environmental sustainability. In other words, this paper finds the major capability failures and environmental concerns in coming days for a group of countries which must be addressed by SDGs. And SDG framework highlights problems in perspectives that must be linking human capabilities with enhanced environmental concerns.

The present paper speaks for capability approach as the base of explaining population-development-environment framework. This paper directs towards sustainable link between increased human capabilities and achieved functionings with sustainable economic growth which with appropriate regulation advance towards SDGs. From policy perspectives, in nutshell, this paper argues for a freedom-oriented broad-based programme for sustainable human development. But although regarding long-term sustainability, it even raises concerns to maybe shift its focus from the complete freedom to legitimate freedom approach (limits to freedom) as the base of conceptual framework. From these perspectives the problems and prospects of human development in the context of future environmental sustainability can better be formulated and sustained.

References

Alkire, S. (2007). 'Choosing Dimensions: The Capability Approach and Multidimensional Poverty', CPRC Working Paper 88, Oxford Poverty and Human Development Initiative, Chronic Poverty Research Centre, Oxford.

Anand, S. and A. Sen (1994). 'Sustainable Human Development: Concepts and Priorities', Working Papers, Centre for Development and Population Studies, Cambridge, MA.

Brundtland Commission (1987). *Our Common Future: Report of the World Commission on Environment and Development*, United Nations.

Fukuda-Parr, S. (2003). 'The Human Development Paradigm: Operationalizing Sen's Ideas on Capabilities', *Feminist Economics*, 9(2–3): 301–17.

Lessmann, O. and F. Rauschmayer (2013). 'Re-conceptualizing Sustainable Development on the Basis of the Capability Approach: A Model and its Difficulties', *Journal of Human Development and Capabilities*, 14(1): 95–114.

Lingan, J., J. Cornforth and R. Pollard (2012). 'Sustainable Development Goals: Building the Foundations for an Inclusive Process', Bond Development and Environment Group.

Lutz, W., W.C. Sanderson and A. Wils (2002). 'Conclusions: Toward Comprehensive P-E (Population and Environment) Studies, Methods of Analysis', *Population and Development Review*, Supplement to Vol. 28.

Robeyns, I. (2005). 'Selecting Capabilities for Quality of Life Measurement', *Social Indicator Research*, 74: 191–215.

Sagar, A.D. and A. Nazam (1998). 'Human Development Index: A Critical Review', *Ecological Economics*, 25: 249–64.

Sen, A. (2012). *Development as Freedom*, Oxford University Press, Oxford.

——. (2013). 'The Ends and Means of Sustainability', *Journal of Human Development and Capabilities*, 14(1): 6–20.

Sen, A. and S. Anand (2000). 'Human Development and Economic Sustainability', *World Development*, 22(12): 2029–49.

YCELP and CIESIN (2005). *Environmental Sustainability Index 2005: Benchmarking National Environmental Stewardship*, Yale Centre for Environmental Law and Policy, Yale and Centre for International Earth Science Information Network, Columbia University.

——. (2010). *Environmental Performance Index 2010*, Yale Centre for Environmental Law and Policy, Yale and Centre for International Earth Science Information Network, Columbia University.

2

Shrinking Agricultural Land, Food Security and Rural Livelihood in India

Policy Issues

Rajendra Poddar

In India, the post-liberalization economic boom continues to create a voracious appetite for space to meet the demands of industrialization, infrastructure building, urban expansion and resource extraction (Ghatak and Ghosh, 2011). As a result, the arable farm land size in the country has been declining. The total agricultural land in 2003–04 was 183.19 million hectares against 182.39 million hectare in 2008–09, a fall of 0.80 million hectare (Anonymous, 2013b). With commercialization of farming and growing population and changing lifestyles, the cultivated land is shifting towards production of non-food grain products. In anticipation of supernormal profits, predatory investors are investing capital in land grab.

Therefore, before land rush takes heavy toll of food security, social equality and the economy in general, appropriate measures are called for to halt illegal and forced land acquisitions in developing countries and India in particular. A prudent advice would be to keep acquisition of cultivable land for non-agriculture purposes to the minimum. Within the context of 'land grabbing', information on the agro-ecological potentials of current cultivated and additional potentially available land is a critical need for establishing the fair rental/sale value of land. Sound land evaluation methods, combined with participatory land use planning, are key to the principle of sustainable and mutually beneficial land resources development.

Shrinking Agriculture Land

Since land is so central to identity, livelihood and food security of people around the world, a sustainable and equitable land policy is need of the hour as well as for the future. But, the arable farmland has been shrinking over the years across the globe. Given that 70 per cent of the world's food insecure population lives in rural areas, food security cannot be tackled unless the issues of sustainable agriculture and rural development are tackled first (Fischer et al., 2013). In India, the post-liberalization economic boom continues to create a voracious appetite for space to meet the demands of industrialization, infrastructure building, urban expansion and resource extraction (Ghatak and Ghosh, 2011). As a result, the arable farmland size in the country has been declining. The total agricultural land in 2003–04 was 183.19 million hectares against 182.39 million hectare in 2008–09, a fall of 0.80 million hectare (Anonymous, 2013b). This is due to shift in area for non-agricultural purposes such as buildings, road and railways among others. However, it has been suggested that the minimum arable land required to sustainably support one person is 0.07 ha (Myers, 1998), which is a threshold used by United Nations organizations to evaluate the land's carrying capacity. If arable land is less than 0.1 ha per person, it would be difficult to maintain a minimal nutrition level (Uitto and Ono, 1996).

Globalization and liberalization in developing economies have brought new pressures on land from various stakeholders. There has been rush in India for acquiring and retaining land for farming, residential real estate and investment asset purpose (Singh, 2012). In anticipation of supernormal profits, predatory investors are investing capital in 'land grab'. As far as agricultural land is concerned, the per capita availability has declined from 0.48 hectare in 1951 to 0.16 hectare in 1991 and is likely to decline to 0.08 hectare in 2035 (Anonymous, 2012). There is a discernible global trend in declining farmland. For example, farmland in the United States has slowly begun to decrease over the last century. With advances in technology, farmers are able to produce more food with less acres. This may not seem like a problem, but as population increases and farmland decreases, eventually there will not be enough food produced in the United States to feed its population; therefore, it is feared that more food will have to be shipped from overseas (Anonymous, 2013a). Many other countries including countries like Australia too face the same situation and India cannot be an exception.

Land Use Pattern in India

At present India has 23 per cent forest cover, 3 per cent pastures and grazing land, 46 per cent area is under agricultural use, 14 per cent land is barren, 6 per cent land is cultivable waste land and remaining 8 per cent is fallow land (Kushwaha, 2008). As far as agricultural land is concerned there is hardly a scope for further expansion. On the contrary, there has been marginal decline in the crop area due to construction activities on prime agricultural land on account of urban expansion and industrialization, etc.

Several reasons have been identified to be responsible for shrinking agricultural land, some of which are discussed below. While a country moves from the status of developing economy to developed one, land acquisition, land degradation and land encroachments assume greater importance thereby reducing the land available for agriculture and especially, food production.

Land Acquisition

Land use pattern in India is governed by growth of population, its aspiration for development and perception of environment. In India people have a lot of sentimental attachment for their landed property; hence there is a lot of resentment during displacing the communities from their homeland. In the neo-liberal economy the primary sector is neglected and much of importance is given to secondary and tertiary sectors. State is acquiring land in the name of 'public purpose' to create basic infrastructure like roads, industries, irrigation projects, Special Economic Zones (SEZs) and others. Consequences of these development-induced displacement are numerous. Dislocation breaks up living patterns and disrupts their community network. It dismantles existing modes of production, disrupts social networks, causes the impoverishment of many of those uprooted, threatens their cultural identity and increases the risks of epidemics and health problems (Cernea, 1995).

India has invested in development projects, dams, roads, mines, power plants and new cities to achieve rapid economic growth. This has been made possible through massive acquisition of land and subsequent displacement of people. Between 60 to 65 million people are estimated to have been displaced in India since Independence, the highest number of people uprooted for development projects in the world. This amounts to around one million displaced, every year since independence, says a report released recently by the Working Group on Human Rights in India (WGHR). Of these displaced ever 40 per cent are tribals and another 40 per cent consists of Dalits and other rural poor.

Land Degradation

Land degradation will remain an important global issue for the 21st century because of its adverse impacts on agronomic productivity, the environment and its effects on food security and in the quality of life. High population density is not necessarily related to land degradation, it is what a population does to the land that determines the extent of degradation. People can be a major asset in reversing the trend towards degradation. However, they need to be properly motivated to care for the land. In the context of productivity, land degradation results from a mismatch between land quality and land use.

The problems of land degradation are prevalent in many forms throughout India. Degradation is evident in increased soil erosion, decline in soil fertility, waterlogging, secondary salinization and contamination of soils with toxic elements. Table 1 shows that in total type of degradation, water erosion accounts for 68 per cent, chemical degradation 21 per cent, wind erosion 10 per cent and the rest physical degradation.

Table 1

Degraded Lands in India (Million ha)

Sl.No.	*Type of Degradation*	*Arable Land Open Forest No. (Mha)*	*(<40% Canopy) (Mha)*
1.	Water erosion (>10 t/ha/yr)	73.27	9.30
2.	Wind erosion (Aeolian)	12.40	–
3.	Sub Total	85.67	9.30
4.	Chemical degradation	17.45	7.23
5.	Physical degradation	1.16	
6.	Total	104.28	16.53
7.	Grand total (Arable land and Open forest)		120.81

Source: National Bureau of Soil Survey and Land Use Planning (2008).

In a case study, the Soil Use Survey of India has reported that in two sample districts of Karnataka, namely Bagalkot and Bijapur, out of the reported area about 20.51 per cent and 24.3 per cent land has been degraded (http://slusi.dacnet.nic.in/). However, environmental and resource limitations to long-term agricultural growth which were likely to threaten future global food requirements and highlighted land degradation as a serious threat to food supplies in many parts of the world, with some areas under severe risk. From the viewpoint of agricultural land, chemical degradation was much more important, accounting for 40 per cent of the 562 million hectares of degraded agricultural land. Reduction in crop yields, total factor productivity, higher levels of input use, permanent abandoning of land were important potential agricultural impacts of land degradation. The estimates of adverse impact of land degradation emphasized that degradation could be devastating in some continents and subcontinents.

Land Encroachment

Common property resources (CPRs) are an integral part of any community. Many people depend upon it for their life's sustenance. These people are not having any legal rights but they have customary rights over it and their entitlement has evolved over centuries. India is a resource rich country having large tracks of forest, grazing land, water bodies, mineral deposits and others. Common lands in India as throughout much of Asia, have been disappearing over the last several decades, despite the collective benefit that they offer (Nadakarni and Pasha, 1991).

To assess the magnitude of land encroachment in Karnataka a 'Task Force for Recovery of Public Land and Its Protection' was formed in 2009 under the chairmanship of retired Additional Chief Secretary of Karnataka, V. Balasubramanian. The committee found that of the land nominally under the government, the area under encroachment as reported by officers of Revenue, Forest and other departments and statutory bodies is 11.07 lakh acres or about 10 per cent of the total government land. This is obviously an under-reporting because for instance, the Belgaum Division consisting of seven districts is reporting an encroachment of only 49,800 acres and the Gulbarga Division reports 1,25,000 acres under Revenue Departments jurisdiction, while the Mysore Division has 4,47,352 acres and Bangalore Division 3,01,708 acres. As the Belgaum and Gulbarga divisions are larger in area and cattle heads, the community lands under the revenue department should be proportionately higher and so also the encroachments. By a conservative projection, the total encroachments all government lands would be in the range of 12–15 lakhs of acres. This will amount to about 12–15 per cent of the total extent of government lands (Balasubramanian, 2011).

At the national level, in view of the controversies over forcible and illegal land acquisitions, and to overcome many of the shortcomings of the colonial Land Acquisition Act of 1884, the Government of India has proposed to enact The Land Acquisition, Rehabilitation and Resettlement (LARR) Act. The salient features of the proposed legislation are as follows: it significantly increases the minimum compensation payable, but continues to use the market price obtained from recently registered sale deeds from the region as a yardstick. The minimum compensation has been fixed at four times the market price in rural areas and twice the market price in urban areas. Which is a comprehensive Bill on land acquisition as well as Rehabilitation and Resettlement (R&R), subjects all eminent domain acquisitions as well as private purchases of over 100 acres in rural areas and 50 acres in urban areas to a mandatory R&R package, with a host of benefits both for affected landowners as well as livelihood losers. These benefits include annuities, transportation allowance, land for land, a portion of capital gains from resale, and the construction of alternative housing and communal amenities in the event of loss of homestead. In addition to defining compensation parameters, the proposed law also places several restrictions on the exercise of eminent domain, limiting the use of multi-cropped land and tightening the definition of 'public purpose'. Procedural safeguards have also been introduced, including social impact assessment, adequate notification and consent of at least 80 per cent of the affected community. The new Bill provides for compensation at double the market price in urban areas and four times the price in rural areas. Many fear that the proposed land acquisition Bill will greatly harm economic progress through skyrocketing land prices, rewarding speculators while eroding India's global competitiveness. Fortunately, the government has now accepted a suggestion to make long land leases an alternative to outright acquisition.

The shrinking agricultural land and several other factors have contributed to an uncertain situation of food insecurity. Due to various reasons land resources are being acquired, degraded and encroached by the state and by private owners. Fuzzy boundaries, fragmentation of land and undurable demarcations, lack of affordable land rights, no stringent laws, unsuitable and unsustainable agricultural practices, tendency of violation of laws and chance to get away with the punishments have still more worsened the scenario. In the present scenario of population growth, state sponsored development, induced displacement and urban expansion, the extent of agricultural land is bound to decrease in the future. Since the mid-90s, Indian and foreign companies, governments, trusts, and others have been rapidly building businesses – colleges, factories, flats, offices, plants – on land purchased primarily from poor farmers. Consequently, the farmland in India is vanishing at an alarming rate.

A case in point is the allocation of 186 hectares (460 acres) of land by the Gujarat government purchased or leased, at an undeclared price, by the Ford Motor Company of America who will build a new automobile manufacturing factory in 2012. While it is heartening that people will find work at the Ford factory and in ancillary industries, it is disheartening in that farmers have lost their livelihoods and the plough land has been reduced.

An analysis of the following data, provided by the Directorate of Economics and Statistics, the Ministry of Agriculture, India, indicates two disturbing trends. Both the net area sown (Table 2) and the availability of grains (Table 3) have been diminishing.

Table 2

Net Area Sown in India

Year	*2000-01*	*2001-02*	*2002-03*	*2003-04*	*2004-05*	*2005-06*	*2006-07*	*2007-08*
Area Sown in Mha	141.36	140.73	132.47	140.76	141.17	141.49	139.95	140.86
Index	100	99.55	93.71	99.58	99.87	100.09	99.00	99.64

Source: Agricultural Land by use in India.

Table 2 and Figure 1 show that when compared to 2000–01, every year the agricultural land use has been reduced, with the exception of a slight increase in 2005–06 when 141.49 million hectares (349.62 million acres) were sown. Furthermore, when an average of index-row is computed and converted it into an equivalent of base year 2000–01, the results are 139.85. This means that the net area sown has been reduced from 141.36 to 139.85 millions of hectares in eight years or 1,88,750 hectares (4,66,400 acres) every year!

Figure 1

Changes in Net Sown Area in India

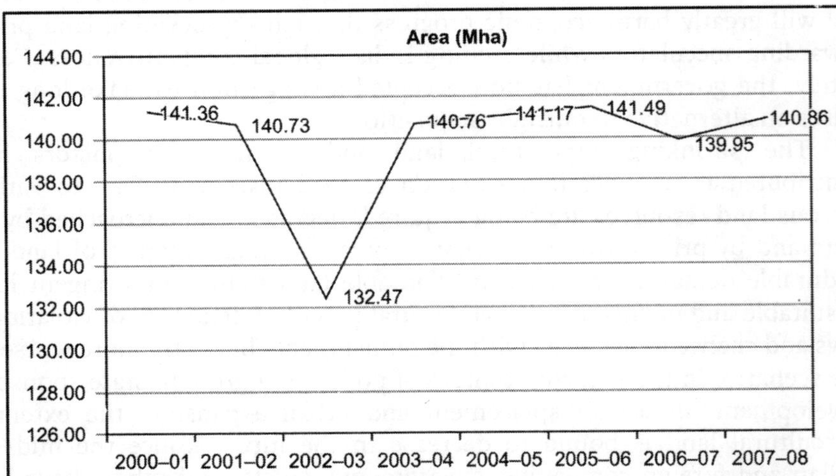

Source: http://mospi.nic.in

Food Security Scenario

Though the term 'food security' would conjure up images of providing access to nutritious and adequate quantity of food to everyone, it is important to understand its meaning in larger, universally accepted terms. Food security exists when all people, at all times, have physical and economic access to sufficient, safe and nutritious food that meets their dietary needs and food preferences for an active and healthy life.

Attainment of self-sufficiency in food grains at the national level is one of the country's major achievements in the post-independence period. After remaining a food deficit country for about two decades after independence, India became largely self-sufficient in food grains production. Food grains production rose from 52 million tonnes in1951-52 to 244.78 million tonnes in 2010-11. As per the second Advance Estimates, production of food grains during 2011–12 is estimated at an all-time record level of 250.42 million tonnes, which is mainly in the production of rice and wheat. The long period growth rate of food grains has been around 2.5 per cent per annum between 1951 and 2006–07.

However, the experience of the last two decades shows that growth rates of production and yield have declined for crop groups/crops during the period 1996–2008 as compared to the period 1986–97. The growth rate of food grains production declined from 2.93 per cent to 0.93 per cent during the same period. The growth rate of production was much lower than that of population in the latter period. Similarly, growth rate of yields of food grains declined from 3.21 per cent to 1.04 per cent. There was also a decline in growth rates of production and yields for cereals, pulses, oilseeds, rice and wheat.

These and many other factors together have resulted in the decline of per capita net availability of food grains from 469 grams/day in 1961 to 443 grams/day in 2007. In other words, significant increase in production of food grains has not been able to keep pace with the increase in population. In spite of efforts in ensuring adequate food supplies, the country suffers from threats of hunger and malnutrition. Malnutrition continues to be a significant health problem for children and adults in India. While there have been some improvements in the nutritional status of young children in several states, nutritional deficiencies are still widespread. There has been an increase in wasting (pronounced loss of body mass), among children under the age of 3 years. Around 23 per cent of children were wasted. At the same time, there has been very marginal change in the percentage of children who are underweight (43% in NFHS-2 and 40% in NFHS-3). NFHS-3 also found high prevalence of anaemia – 70 per cent – in children of age 6-59 months. Anaemia in India is primarily linked to poor nutrition. Women and men suffer a dual burden of overnutrition and undernutrition. One-third of men are too thin, and 9 per cent are overweight or obese. Anaemia is also disturbingly common among adults. More than half of the women in India (55%) are anaemic.

With commercialization of farming along with growing population and changing lifestyles, the cultivated land is shifting towards production of non-food grain products. Further, the cropping pattern in India has undergone significant changes over time. As the cultivated area remains more or less constant; the increased demand for food because of increase in population and urbanization puts agricultural land under stress resulting in crop intensification and substitution of food crops with commercial crops. In fact, it is striking to observe that area under food grains in gross cropped area (GCA) declined by 12.02 per cent mainly due to fall in area under coarse cereals by 13.34 per cent between triennium ending (TE) 1970–71 and TE 2007-08. There is a definite shift from food grains to non-food grains such as fruits and vegetables, oilseeds, fibres, condiments and spices whose share in both area and in value of output has been increasing over time (Kannan and Sundaram, 2011).

Table 3

Per Capita Net Availability of Food Grain in Gram per Day

Year	*2000*	*2001*	*2002*	*2003*	*2004*	*2005*	*2006*	*2007*	*2008*	*2009*
Grain in gm/day	454.4	416.2	494.1	437.6	462.7	422.4	445.3	442.8	436.0	444.0
Index	100	91.59	108.74	96.24	101.83	92.96	98.00	97.45	95.95	97.71

The food grains in Table 3 are the sum of rice, wheat, other cereals, and pulses, and the average of Row 2, grains available per day to an Indian for cooking, comes out to be 446 grams. How much rice and *dal* (from pulse) and how many *roti* (from wheat) can one cook out of 446 grams? This is not enough for one meal a day, let alone three meals. Also, when an average of index-row in Table 3 is calculated and converted into an equivalent of base year 2000, it results in 445.53 grams per day. This ten-year data suggests that daily food grains availability has decreased (from 454.40 to 445.53) by 0.887 grams per day each year. When extrapolated for 1 billion people, each day 887 metric tons or each year 3,23,755 metric tonnes of less food grains is available for cooking and eating! The above results lead one to think that declining grain availability per day on a declining stock of farmlands could be one reason why we do not have enough food and why millions of Indians go hungry or remain malnourished. According to World Bank, the 'land rush' is not likely to slow down. This in future would pose challenges to global as well as Indian food security scenario, which is in a precarious situation.

Rural Livelihood Issues

Rural livelihood of people affected by land acquisition for a developmental project is a matter of great concern. According to human rights activist Medha Patkar who has been at the forefront of the Narmada Bachao Andolan (NBA), internal displacement is not a natural calamity but a political calamity (Patkar, 1998). Many poor people have faced multiple displacements. They are often displaced from their villages due to projects such as dams or Special Economic Zones (SEZ). With no land and no livelihood, they head to cities where they live in *jhugghis* that are considered illegal and subsequently demolished. Possibly as much as 50 million acres (about 6% of all the land in the country) of privately owned land, common property resources (like forests) which are not privately owned have been acquired or converted to non-agricultural use after independence (Chakravorthy, 2012).

A sociologist based at the World Bank Cernea (1995), who has researched development induced displacement and resettlement for two decades, points out that being forcibly ousted from one's land and habitat carries with it the risk of becoming poorer than before displacement. Those displaced are supposed to receive compensation of their lost assets and effective assistance to re-establish themselves; yet this does not happen for a large portion of oustees (Biradar, 2005).

In a case study of Upper Krishna Project (UKP) in Karnataka, Biradar (2005) revealed that as many as 201 villages and a major town in North Karnataka have submerged due to implementation UKP. The project has displaced four lakh people. In one of the rehabilitation centres of the UKP it was found that only about 17 per cent of the farmers could purchase replacement land, the proportion of unskilled labourers rose from 23 per cent in pre-displacement period to 53 per cent in post-displacement phase. The project was found to have affected the school-going children (28%). Around 44 per cent of the people expressed that their quality of life has been negatively affected, 18 per cent of the families have been nucleated and 84 per cent of the people have withdrawn themselves from participating in the community affairs. As much as 90 per cent of the compensation money was found to have been spent for unproductive purposes. The reasons for this scenario are several. Important reasons among those are lack of proper counselling, rudimentary rehabilitation plans, experimental resettlement methods, secretive revenue records, outdated government Acts, non-existence of civil society organizations and rampant corruption in administration have rendered the Project Affected Peoples (PAP) helpless. Now, all the sources of help have dried up and the PAPs are in search of other source of money to borrow, which will again push them into a debt trap. Studies across the countries have revealed that the project authorities have failed to restore the earlier standard of living of the displaced communities. Further, it can result in growth of landless labour population leading to greater unrest in the rural areas of developing countries (Swaminathan, 2013). Based on the findings, it can safely be said that the economic gains would not compensate for the loss in livelihood and cultural base of a community. Therefore, any resettlement package has to value these issues beyond the economic compensation framework.

Conclusion and Suggestions

Before land rush takes heavy toll of food security, social equality and the economy in general, appropriate measures are called for to halt illegal and forced land acquisitions in developing countries and India in particular. A prudent advice would be to keep acquisition of cultivable land for non-agriculture purposes to the minimum. Within the context of 'land grabbing', information on the agro-ecological potentials of current cultivated and additional potentially available land is a critical need for establishing the fair rental/sale value of land. Sound land evaluation methods, combined with participatory land use planning, are key to the principle of sustainable and mutually beneficial land resources development.

Another suggestion would be about conducting a base line survey of the common property resources, comprehensive survey of land resources, creation of durable structures of boundaries and bringing awareness of environmental impact of haphazard economic development. As land resources are non-renewable, it is necessary to adopt a positive approach to sustainable management of these finite resources. Effective land management policies are required to address these issues in addition to other concerns such as small size and fragmented holdings, tenancy, ceiling limits, acquisition and diversion of productive land, land records and inventories, climate change and land use change.

The proposed Land Acquisition, Rehabilitation and Resettlement Bill, should address inadequacies of the Land Acquisition Act of 1894, which served the colonial purposes and has been exploited by land grabbers. There is scope for refinement in the Bill to ensure a humane, participatory, informed consultative and transparent process for land acquisition. Since economic gains would not compensate for the loss in livelihood and cultural base of a community in case of rehabilitation, any resettlement package as provided in the LARR has to value these issues beyond the economic compensation framework.

References

Anonymous (2012). *India: A Reference Annual*, Ministry of Information and Broadcasting, Government of India, New Delhi.

——. (2013a). http://wikis.lib.ncsu.edu/index.php/bae_578_2010_shrinking_agricultural_lands.

——. (2013b). http://www.thehindubusinessline.com.

Balasubramanian, V. (2011). *Chairman's Report on Task Force for Recovery of Public Land and its Protection: Greed and Connivance*, Government of Karnataka, Bangalore.

Biradar, S.B. (2005). 'The Effects of Involuntary Displacement and Rehabilitation on Human Resources Development', Unpublished PhD Thesis submitted to Karnataka University, Dharwad.

Cernea, Michael (1995). 'Social Integration and Population Displacement: The Contribution of Social Sciences', *International Social Science Journal*, XLIII(I): 91–112.

Chakravorthy, S. (2012). *The Price of Land Acquisition, Conflict and Consequence*, Oxford University Press, New Delhi.

Fischer, G., E. Hizsnyik, S. Prieler and D. Wiberg (2013). 'Scarcity and Abundance of Land Resources: Competing Uses and the Shrinking Land Resource Base', SOLAW Background Thematic Report TR02, http://www.fao.org/fileadmin /templates /solaw/files/thematic_reports/tr_02_light.pdf

Gandhi, V.P. (2011). 'Agricultural Land in India Diminishing', http://www.patnadaily.com/index.php/vasant-g-gandhi/6036-agricultural-land-in-india-diminishing.html.

Ghatak, Maitreesh and Parikshit Ghosh (2011). 'The Land Acquisition Bill: A Critique and a Proposal', *Economic and Political Weekly*, 46(41): 65–72.

http://slusi.dacnet.nic.in.

Kannan, Elumalai and Sujata Sundaram (2011). 'Analysis of Trends in India's Agricultural Growth', Working Papers, Institute for Scio-Economic Change, Bangalore.

Kushwaha, Niru (2008). 'Agriculture in India: Land Use and Sustainability', *International Journal of Rural Studies*, 5(1).

Myers, N. (1998). 'The Next Green Revolution: Its Environmental Underpinnings', *Current Science*, 76(4): 507–13, http://www.ias.ac.in/currsci/feb25/articles16.htm

Patkar, Medha (1998). *Dams and Displacements: A New Framework for Decision Making*, Earthscan, London.

Nadakarni, M.V. and S.A. Pasha (1991). 'Developing Uncultivated Lands: Some Issues from Karnataka Experience', *Indian Journal of Agricultural Economics*, 46(4): 543–54.

Robinson, E.J.Z. (2008). 'India's Disappearing Common Lands: Fuzzy Boundaries, Encroachment and Evolving Property Rights', *Land Economics*, 84(3): 409–22.

Singh, Sukhpal (2012). 'Landing in Trouble: Changing Role of Land in Rural Livelihoods in India'.

Swaminathan, M.S. (2013). http://agrariancrisis.in/2011/09/14/land-rush-and-sustainable-food-security.

Uitto, J.I. and Akiko Ono (eds) (1996). *Population, Land Management, and Environmental Change*, United Nations University, Tokyo, http://www.unu.edu/unupress/unupbooks/uu03pe/uu03pe00.htm#contents

3

Population Growth and Environmental Degradation

A Sustainability Approach

M. Balasubramanian

Twenty-five years have passed since the Brundtland Commission first brought the concept of sustainable development to international limelight. Among other initiatives, they persuaded countries to sign the Convention on Biological Diversity and the United Nations Framework Convention on Climate Change, and set in motion the process of developing a framework to combat desertification. Around that time, many forests, particularly in tropical zones, were being destroyed at a faster rate than they could regrow; 1,30,000 sq. km of forests have been destroyed per year during the last 15 years. Nearly 2 billion people cope daily with the problem of finding enough water and most of the world's scientists agree that greenhouse gases – notably carbon dioxide from the burning of fossil fuels – are contributing to climate change like global warming, melting of glaciers and rising sea level. Fish are caught faster than they can restock; 15 per cent of ocean stocks are generating wastes, such as CO_2, faster than the biosphere's ability to dispose of them. As a result, the capacity of natural ecosystems to provide the necessary life support for humankind is likely to diminish in the coming decade (Galli et al., 2012). The ecosystem is affected in the course of several essential human pursuits like urbanization, population growth, economic growth, etc. Average per capita consumption of ecosystem goods and services has increased in the last four decades. As the world economy grows, humans extract and harvest increasing amounts of natural resources from the ecosystem and mines – around 60,000 billion tonnes annually. If this level of exploitation of the nature is allowed to continue, by the end of this century, global ecosystem will suffer greatly and human existence on this planet would become precarious. Overconsumption of natural resources is a major threat to the sustainability of world's environmental systems. The question, therefore, is how a developing country like India with rapidly increasing population can reach ecological sustainability? This paper, therefore, attempts an estimation of ecological footprint and biocapacity in India by taking the ecological footprint work and methodology papers for National Footprints Accounts as the starting point, in addition to articulating the challenges to ecological sustainability in the Indian context.

Ecological Footprints and Biocapacity

Environmental changes such as deforestation, collapsing fisheries and carbon dioxide accumulation in the atmosphere indicate that human demand is in excess of the regenerative and absorptive capacity of the biosphere. Several studies have found that with increasing demands upon natural systems due to the rapidly developing global economy and the need to attain better standard of living, the earth's thresholds are being exceeded and that, because of this, the biosphere's future ability to provide for humanity's needs is at risk (Haberl, 2006; Moore et al., 2012). Barnosky et al. (2012) argue that a planetary-scale critical transition is approaching as a result of the myriad human pressures, and that tools are needed to detect early warning signs and to forecast the consequences of such pressures on ecosystems. It needs to be mentioned here that Mathis Wackernagel, cofounder of Global Footprint Network and pioneer of ecological footprint research along with his doctoral thesis supervisor recently received the Blue Planet Prizes awarded annually by the Asahi Glass foundation to individuals or organizations that make outstanding achievements in scientific research and its application in helping to solve global environmental problems. The prize is considered as one of the most prestigious ones in the field of environmental conservation. It will not be out of place to quote what Helen Clark, administrator of the United Nations Development Programme and former Prime Minister of New Zealand, who recently said to Wackernagel:

> The Ecological Footprint has become a powerful and important mechanism for quantifying and communicating clearly the extent to which human demands on nature have begun to exceed the planet's regeneration rate. This concept has already inspired important new thinking around sustainable development. Your work provides a practical and powerful tool for the public and private sectors when planning for sustainable economies and human advancement. The sustainability gaps reported by the Ecological Footprint analysis have serious implications for global development, and are therefore, of particular relevance to UNDP's mission and work.

Ecological Footprint analysis is such a tool, that measures human appropriation of ecosystem products and services in terms of the amount bioproductive land and sea area needed to supply these products and services. Ecological Footprint Accounting (Wackernagel et al., 1999a, 1999b, 2002) is one of the most comprehensive ecological economic indicators for measuring the fundamental conditions for sustainability. Every human activity uses biologically productive land and/or fishing grounds. The demand for six main types of bioproductive areas, each providing different resources and ecosystem services, is considered (i) cropland for the provision of plant-based food and fibre products; (ii) grazing land and cropland for the provision of animal based food and other animal products; (iii) fishing grounds (both marine and inland) for the provision of fish-based food products; (iv) forest areas for the provision of timber and other forest products; (v) carbon uptake land for the absorption of anthropogenic carbon dioxide emissions; and (vi) built-up area representing productivity lost due to the occupation of physical space for shelter and other infrastructure. By comparing demand for and supply of bioproductive areas, the method simply documents the extent to which the human society stays within or exceeds the regenerative capacity of the planet. Ecological footprint shows a consistent trend of overconsumption (Figure 1) and according to 2010 data the footprint has exceeded the earth's biocapacity. Besides different population and footprint evolution patterns, High, Middle and Low Income countries had different footprint compositions as reported in Table 1. Here, I argue that human demand on the biosphere depends largely on demand for cropland and carbon uptake land (carbon footprint), as reported in Figure 2.

Table 1

World Ecological Footprint and Biocapacity, 2008 (global hectare in person)

	World	*High Income Country*	*Middle Income*	*Low Income*
Population in million	6739.6	1037	4394.1	1297.5
Cropland	0.59	1.03	0.53	0.47
Grazing land	0.21	0.31	0.17	0.12
Forestland	0.26	0.58	0.19	0.23
Fishing ground	0.1	0.19	0.1	0.06
Carbon	1.47	3.38	0.85	0.18
Built-up land	0.06	0.11	0.07	0.07
Ecological Footprint	2.7	5.6	1.92	1.14
Cropland	0.57	0.98	0.49	0.46
Grazing land	0.32	0.28	0.21	0.21
Forestland	0.76	1.17	0.78	0.31
Fishing ground	0.16	0.51	0.16	0.09
Built-up land	0.06	0.11	0.07	0.07
Biocapacity	1.78	3.05	1.72	1.14
Ecological deficit	–0.92	–2.55	–0.2	0

Source: World Wildlife Fund (2012).

High income countries had large carbon footprint components that grew from nearly 31 per cent in 1965 to 63 per cent in 2005. Conversely, demand for cropland decreased from about 37 per cent of the overall footprint in 1965 to 18 per cent in 2005. High income countries have registered large increase in resource consumption in average per capita footprint with smaller increases in population, say, moving from 3.62 to 6.39 gha, compared to middle income countries where it moved from 1.84 gha to 2.20 gha and low income countries where it moved from 1.24 gha to 1.01 gha (Galli et al., 2012).

Figure 1

Global Ecological Footprint, Biocapacity, per capita 1961–2008

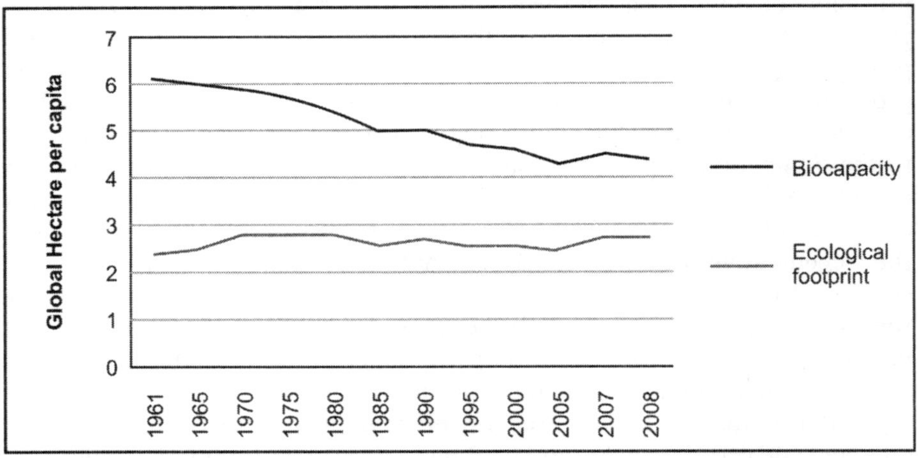

Source: World Wildlife Fund (2012).

Figure 2

Global per capita Ecological Footprint, by Component, 1961–2008

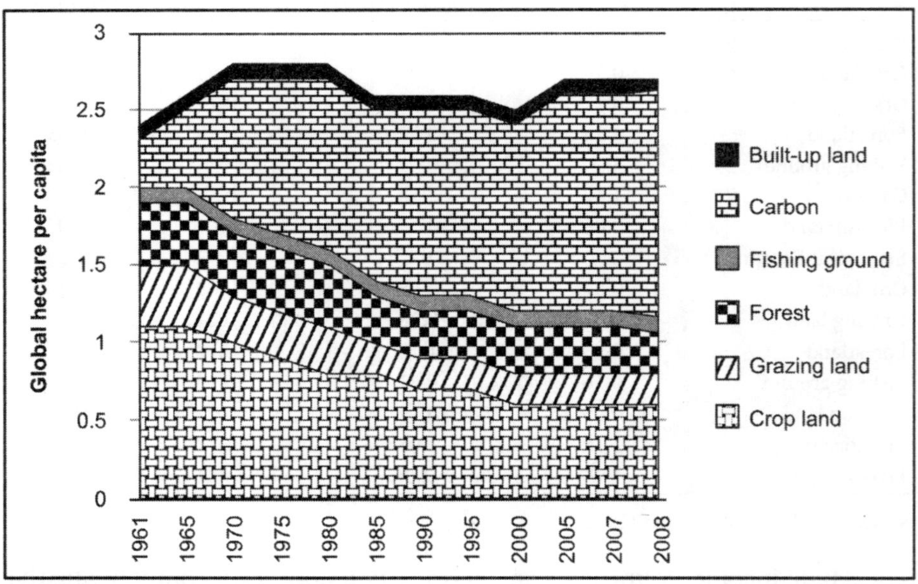

Source: World Wildlife Fund (2012).

An individual's ecological footprint varies significantly depending on a number of factors, including his country of residence, the quantity of goods and services he consumes, and different countries, therefore, have different footprints (see Figure 3). Some countries with high biocapacity do not have a large national footprint. As resources are becoming more constrained, competition is growing; the disparity between resource-rich and

Figure 3

Ecological Footprint per Person by Country, 2008

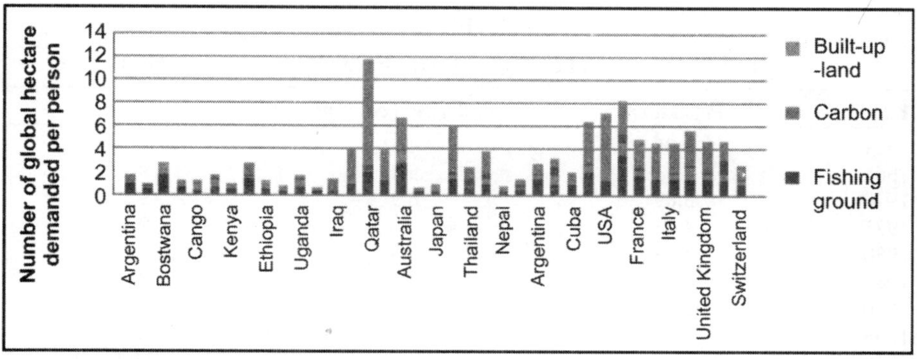

Source: World Wildlife Fund (2012).

resource-poor nations is high likely to have strong geopolitical implication in the future (see Figure 4) (World Wildlife Fund, 2012).

A growing population naturally exerts pressure to increase land occupation, especially when this population is striving towards higher living standards. The Worldwatch Institute's *State of the World* 2010 report has just been released, and takes square aim at what's at the root of the planet's current environmental woes, be it climate change or biodiversity loss or natural resources overconsumption. Population growth is a key driver of local and global environmental change. Growing numbers lead to increase in the consumption of natural resources and in land use, posing additional environmental pressures. Global population, presently 7 billion people, is expected to peak at 9 billion by 2050. The sheer increase in population means that more of the earth's resources will need to be consumed to support this growth. The growing number of consumers is a strong driver behind the increasing global footprint. The human population is forecast to grow to 7.8–9.5 billion people by 2100, and corresponding increase in ecological footprint the same year would be 12 global hectares per person

Figure 4

Biocapacity per Person by Country, 2008

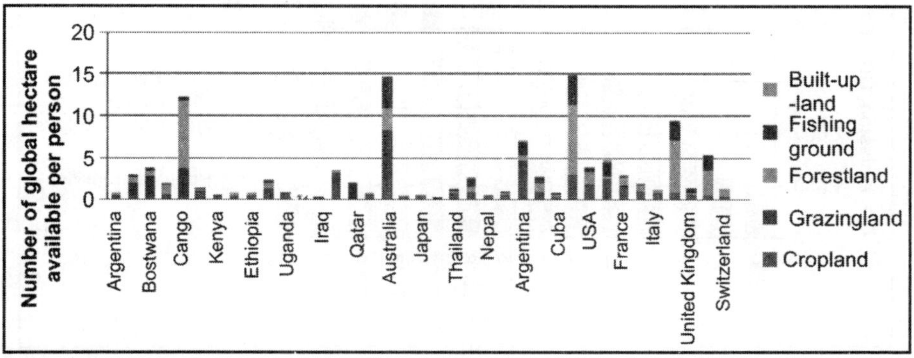

Source: World Wildlife Fund (2012).

(Table 2). Figure 5 clearly shows the increasing trend of population, GDP and CO_2 emission.

Table 2

Population Growth and Ecological Footprint (global hectare in person)

Year	*Population*	*Ecological Footprint*	*Biocapacity*
1961	3.08	4.5	9
1965	3.33	5.4	9.2
1970	3.69	6.9	9.5
1975	4.07	8	9.7
1980	4.43	9.3	9.9
1985	4.83	10.1	10.4
1990	5.26	11.5	10.7
1995	5.67	12.1	10.8
2000	6.07	13.2	11.1
2003	6.3	14.1	11.2
2025	7.8	16	12
2050	8.9	16	13
2075	9.3	14	14
2100	9.5	12	14

Source: World Wildlife Fund (2012).

The rapid economic development of Brazil, Russia, India, China and South Africa, the so-called BRICS group merits special attention when looking at the ecological footprint and the pressure on biocapacity. High population growth in the BRICS group along with increasing average per capita consumption of goods and services is contributing to an economic transformation. As a result, the BRICS economies are expanding more rapidly than the developed or high-income countries. The challenge, however, is to ensure the sustainability of both environment and the development process. As the BRICS nations become wealthier and the average

Figure 5

Population Growth, GDP, CO_2 Emission

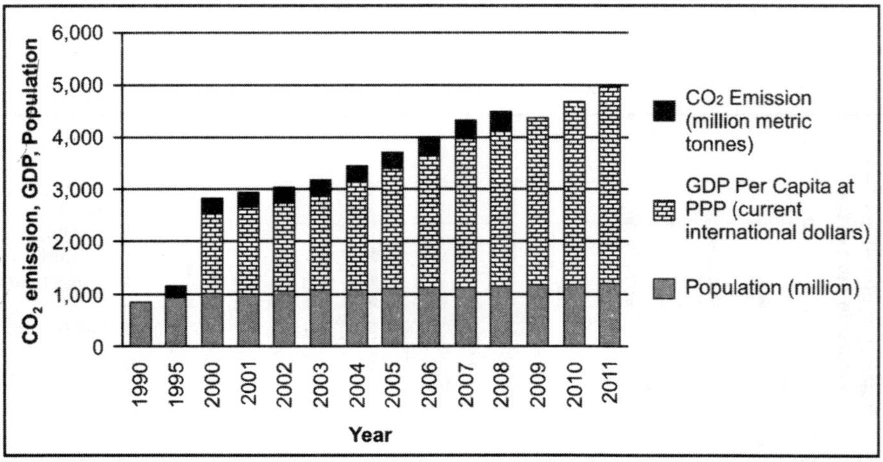

Source: World Wildlife Fund (2012).

ecological footprint increases, their consumption patterns would increasingly mirror the consumption pattern of high income countries. For instance, South Africa and China are moving toward a more equal split between each of the consumption categories' indicative income. As can be seen from Table 3, environmental impact in China is disproportionate to the accruals from economic development. These trends demonstrate the central role China will play in forthcoming economic and environmental change as well as in the sustainability debate. China and India will be of fundamental importance for future global sustainability (Galli et al., 2012).

Table 3

Brazil, Russia, India, Indonesia, China and South Africa Ecological Footprint and Biocapacity 2008 (global hectare in person)

	Brazil	*Russia*	*India*	*Indonesia*	*China*	*South Africa*
Population in million	191.5	143.2	1190.9	235	1358.8	49.3
Cropland	0.8	1.05	0.37	0.44	0.52	0.42
Grazing land	0.95	0.2	0	0.04	0.03	0.19
Forestland	0.55	0.47	0.12	0.16	0.14	0.31
Fishing ground	0.05	0.09	0.02	0.2	0.1	0.08
Carbon	0.48	2.55	0.31	0.23	1.15	1.57
Buildup land	0.1	0.04	0.05	0.07	0.09	0.03
Ecological Footprint	2.93	4.4	0.87	1.13	2.13	2.59
Cropland	1.09	0.94	0.38	0.47	0.38	0.32
Grazing land	1.03	0.34	0	0.06	0.11	0.62
Forestland	7.25	4.22	0.02	0.32	0.22	0.02
Fishing ground	0.16	1.08	0.03	0.41	0.07	0.22
Built-up land	0.1	0.04	0.05	0.07	0.09	0.03
Biocapacity	9.63	6.62	0.48	1.32	0.87	1.21
Ecological deficit	6.7	2.22	-0.39	0.19	-1.26	-1.38

Source: World Wildlife Fund (2012).

Methodology and Data Sources

The ecological footprint measures appropriated biocapacity across five distinct land use types and contrasts this with six demand categories. The reason for this discrepancy is that two demand categories, forest products and carbon sequestration, compete for the same biocapacity category, i.e. forest land. Average bioproductivity differs across various land use types, as well as across countries for any given land use type. For comparability across land use types and countries, Ecological Footprint and biocapacity are usually expressed in units of world-average bioprovinductive area, referred to as global hectares (gha). Global hectares provide more information than simply weight – which does not capture the extent of land and sea area used – or physical area which does not capture how much ecological production is associated with that land. Two important types of coefficients, the yield factors (YF) and the equivalent factor (EQF), allow results to be expressed in terms of a standardized cross-country comparable unit of measure (Monfreda et al., 2004; Galli et al., 2007).

The calculation in the National Footprint Accounts is based on data sets from UN agencies or affiliated organizations such as the Food and Agricultural Organization of United Nations (FASTAT, 2011), the UN Statistics Division (UN Commodity Trade Statistics Database – UN COMTRADE, 2011), the International Energy Agency (IEA, 2011) and Global Footprint Network (2012). Other data sources include studies in peer-reviewed journals and thematic collections.

The ecological footprint is mainly the flow indicator; however, it is measured in terms of the bioproductive land areas needed to generate such flows, and results are expressed in the unit of global hectares – gha (Monfreda et al., 2004; Galli et al., 2007). Each individual flow can be translated into the corresponding appropriation of bioproductive land area through a multi-step process, described in Eq (1):

EF = P X YF X EQU — 1

Y_N

Where P is the amount of product harvested or CO_2 emitted, Y_N is the national average yield for the product P (or its carbon uptake capacity in cases where P is carbon dioxide) and YF and EQU are the yield and equivalence factors, respectively, for the land use type in question.

Total availability of biocapacity in each Nation is calculated as the sum of the biocapacity supplied by each land use type. For any land use type, biocapacity (BC) is calculated in Eq (2):

BC – A X YF X EQF — 2

Where A is the area available for a given land use type and YF and EQF are the yield and equivalence factors, respectively.

Components of ecological footprint:

Cropland footprint: Calculated from the area used to produce food and fibre for human consumption, feed for livestock, oil crops and rubber.

Grazingland footprint: Calculated from the area used to raise livestock for meat, dairy, hide and wool products.

Fishing ground footprint: Calculated from the estimated primary production required to support the fish and seafood caught.

Forest footprint: Calculated from the amount of lumber, pulp, timber products and fuel wood consumed by a country each year.

Carbon footprint: calculated as the amount of forest land required for absorbing CO_2 emissions from burning fossil fuels, land use change and chemical processes, other than the portion absorbed by oceans.

Built-up land footprint: Calculated from the area of land covered by human infrastructure, including transportation, housing, industrial structures, and reservoirs for hydropower.

Figure 2 is the most commonly used reporting format. Normalizing factors, refereed as the yield factor and equivalence factor, are used to scale the contribution of each single land use type so that values can be added up into an aggregate number. Aggregating results into a single value has the advantage of monitoring the combined demand of anthropogenic activities against nature's overall regenerative capacity.

Figure 6

National Footprint Account (NFA) Accounting Framework

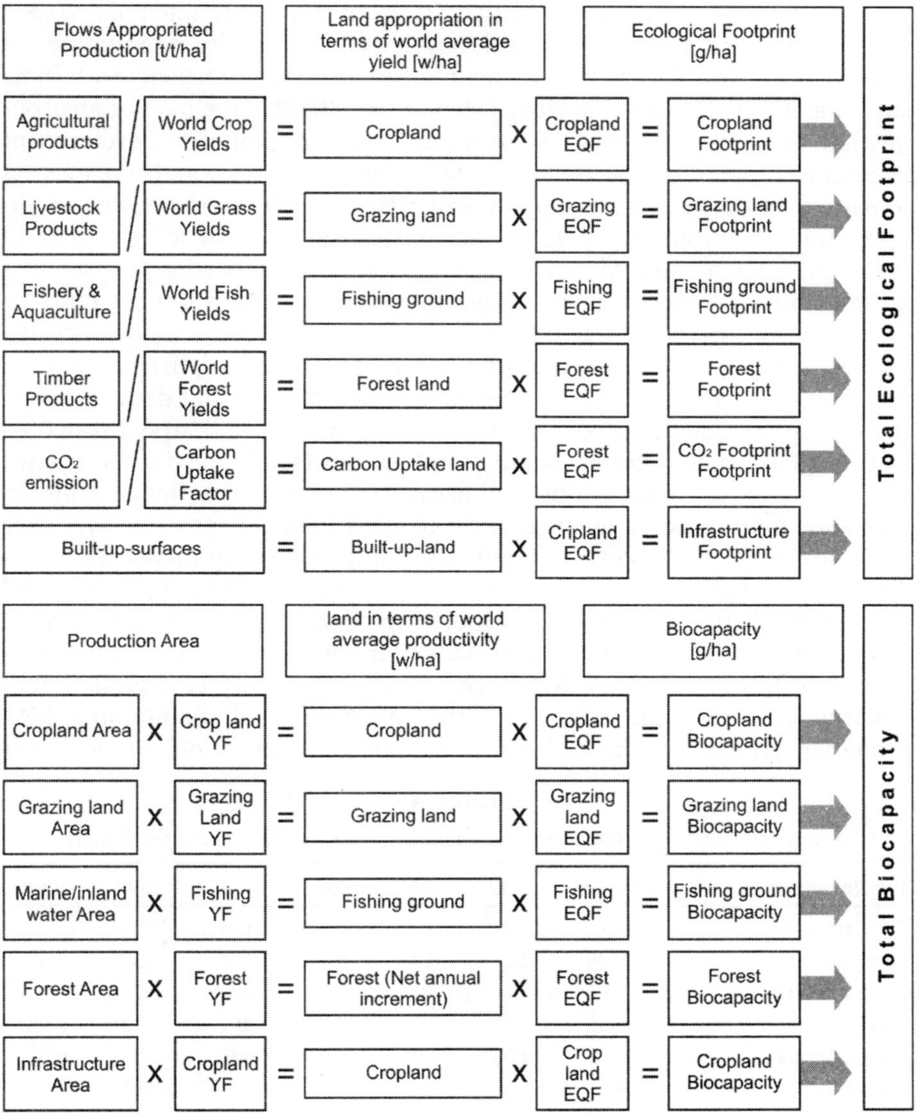

India's Ecological Footprint

As mentioned earlier in this article, India will be of fundamental importance for future global sustainability. But given the present level of economic growth and environmental pressure, how could the goal of ecological sustainability be reached? For example, economic expansion is also often accompanied by rising demands on the already scarce and often degraded natural resources (soil, fossil fuels, water and forest) and the increasing pollution footprint will negatively impact human health and growth prospects. In India's case, a remarkable growth record has been clouded by a degrading environment and growing scarcity of natural resources.

Mirroring the size and diversity of its economy, environmental risks are wide ranging and are driven by both poverty and prosperity. Environmental sustainability could become the next major economic challenge as India surges along its growth trajectory (Mani et al., 2012). Free market environmentalism is fraught with the contradictions of capitalist development leading to economic growth at the cost of land dispossession, loss of access to natural resources, and fouling human relationship with the environment. The capitalist property rights in the ownership and use of the natural resources (Naidu and Manolakos, 2010) is another barrier to attaining sustainability. Moreover, unequal distribution of natural resources tends to create more environmental pressure. For example, there was noticeable decline in India's ecological footprint compared to industrialized nations in per capita terms (from 1.06 to 0.87 gha) in the last one-half decade, but in the same period, national per capita biocapacity decreased sharply (from 0.74 to 0.48 gha), mainly due to population increase (see Table 4). As of now, there is no clear study about ecological footprint in the Indian context; therefore more studies are necessary to gain insights into the dynamics ecological foot print. Ecological deficit in India is creating market opportunities with significant potential rewards for market leaders (Naidu and Manolakos, 2010). The challenges sought to be met by India's 12th Plan are formidable in that while ensuring faster, more inclusive and sustainable growth, it has simultaneously to strive to arrest the pace of degradation of environment with due respect to the imperatives of maintaining high economic growth, in the context of galloping urbanization, unmet basic

Table 4

Ecological Footprint in India (population in million and global hectare per person)

Year/Indicators	*1996*	*1999*	*2001*	*2003*	*2005*	*2007*	*2008*
Population (Million)	949.9	999.2	1033.4	1065.5	1103.4	1134	1190.9
Cropland	0.46	0.28	0.34	0.34	0.4	0.39	0.37
Grazing land	0.05	0	0	0	0.01	0	0
Forestland	0.12	0.11	0.01	0.08	0.1	0.12	0.12
Fishing ground	0.01	0.03	0.05	0.04	0.01	0.02	0.02
Carbon	0.31		0.3	0.26	0.33	0.33	0.31
Built-up land	0.01	0.06	0.04	0.04	0.04	0.05	0.05
Total Ecological footprint	1.06	0.77	0.8	0.8	0.9	0.91	0.87
Cropland	2.64	0.28	0.29	0.29	0.31	0.4	0.38
Grazing land	4.25	0	0	0	0.1	0	0
Forestland	2.3	0.31	0.02	0.02	0.02	0.02	0.02
Fishing ground		0.04	0.03	0.03	0.04	0.03	0.03
Built-up land						0.05	0.05
Biocapacity	0.74	0.68	0.4	0.4	0.4	0.51	0.48
Ecological deficit	-0.32	0.09	-0.4	-0.4	-0.5	-0.4	-0.39

Source: World Wildlife Fund (2012).

needs and lifestyle changes. Population growth and economic development are contributing to several serious environmental problems in India. These include pressure on land, land/soil degradation, forests, habitat destruction and loss of biodiversity, changing consumption patterns, rising demand for energy, air pollution, global warming and climate change and water scarcity and water pollution. India's growing CO_2 emission is the result of both increasing population and GDP growth. Each nation's carbon footprint is arrived at by estimating its national consumption in biophysical terms, using agricultural or biological yield figures to translate the consumption into areas of biological production. India's food consumption which consists of wheat, rice/paddy, coconut, sugarcane, pulses, oil seeds, tea and coffee (Table 5) is calculated using the estimate from Food and Agriculture Organization (2012). The critical question is how can India ensure both continued economic growth and a globally replicable quality of life for its citizens?

Challenges to Sustainability

Adam Smith inquired in 1776 as to how human populations can produce greater standard of living from fixed set of inputs through a division of labour coupled with trade in the outputs of that labour guided only by the 'invisible hand' of individual's collective free decisions based on their own self-interests to buy or sell and for how much. In the mid-1800s John Stuart Mill and Robert Thomas Malthus debated whether the growth of such a system of production and reallocation could be sustained as populations grew, but the fixed base of natural capital needed to sustain them remained constant. In the 1930s and 40s, John Hicks formalized a concept later called Hicksian income that described the level at which an individual, a household, or a whole economy could retain the capital intact so as to be able to keep on consuming at the level indefinitely. Today's notion of sustainability as popularized by the Brundtland Commission in 1987 is the ability 'to meet the needs of the present generation without compromising the ability of the future generations to meet their own needs' where, the concept is both tangible and inductive. One of the key aspects of Sustainable development is that it makes us consider the problems of inter-generational and intra-generational equity.

At present, ecological footprint merely shows that current human development is unsustainable as we only have one earth (Ward and Dubos, 1972). We also need to consider which trajectories are equitable, economically and ecologically desirable and achievable. We can also foresee an ecosystem collapse. Environmental changes such as deforestation, collapsing fisheries, and carbon dioxide accumulation in the atmosphere indicate that human demand is likely to exceed the regenerative and absorptive capacity of the biosphere. As the demands upon natural systems rapidly increase due to the swelling global economy and the need to attain better standards of living, several studies suggest that many of the earth's thresholds are being exceeded, and that because of this, the biosphere's future ability to provide for humanity is at risk (Borucke et al., 2013).

Table 5

Calculation of the India's Average Ecological Footprints in India

Year	Wheat		Rice and Paddy		Coconuts		Sugarcane		Pulses		Oil seeds		Tea		Coffee	
	EFP	*BC*	*EPF*	*BC*	*EPF*	*BC*	*EPF*	*BC*	*EPF*	*BC*	*EPF*	*BC*	*EPF*	*BC*	*EPF*	*BC*
1990	0.62	0.02	0.5	0.05	1.17	0.06	1.09	0.08	0.96	0.01	0.05	0.008	2	0.13	0.45	0.003
1991	0.82	0.0027	0.5	0.004	0.11	0.0005	1.11	0.006	0.85	0.009	0.047	0.0006	2.22	0.01	1.26	0.0007
1992	0.76	0.0027	0.49	0.004	1.4	0.006	1.1	0.007	0.16	0.002	0.045	0.0006	2.29	0.01	1.21	0.03
1993	0.81	0.0027	0.52	0.004	1.43	0.006	1.12	0.006	0.5	0.006	0.08	0.001	1.79	0.3	1.16	0.001
1994	0.76	0.0027	0.52	0.004	1.46	0.007	1.15	0.007	0.81	0.009	0.09	0.0006	2.22	0.01	1.96	0.001
1995	0.84	0.0027	0.51	0.004	1.21	0.006	1.21	0.007	0.89	0.01	0.05	0.0006	2.22	0.01	1.65	0.001
1996	0.81	0.0027	0.5	0.004	1.19	0.006	1.08	0.006	0.64	0.008	0.04	0.00048	1.96	0.01	1.69	0.001
1997	0.78	0.003	0.51	0.004	0.96	0.005	1.03	0.006	0.8	0.009	0.04	0.00048	2.03	0.01	1.52	0.001
1998	0.73	0.0027	0.59	0.005)	1.03	0.005	1.1	0.007	0.53	0.007	0.05	0.0005	0.13	0.01	1.26	0.001
1999	0.69	0.0027	0.53	0.004	1.02	0.005	1.24	0.007	0.06	0.008	0.04	0.00042	1.88	0.01	1.32	0.001
2000	0.78	0.0027	0.5	0.004	0.86	0.004	1.12	0.007	0.65	0.008	0.03	0.0003	1.61	0.01	1.35	0.001
2001	0.74	0.0027	0.54	0.004	0.96	0.004	1.09	0.006	0.81	0.009	0.03	0.0003	1.49	0.009	1.75	0.001
2002	0.81	0.003	0.38	0.008	0.8	0.004	1.03	0.005	0.03	0.0004	0.018	0.0001	1.46	0.009	1.14	0.001
2003	0.73	0.0027	0.52	0.004	0.76	0.004	0.89	0.004	0.28	0.002	0.03	0.0003	1.44	0.009	1.15	0.0009
2004	0.72	0.0027	0.5	0.004	0.68	0.003	0.69	0.004	0.39	0.004	0.016	0.0001	1.47	0.009	1.07	0.001
2005	0.74	0.0027	0.52	0.004	0.68	0.003	0.82	0.005	0.28	0.003	0.016	0.0001	1.41	0.008	1.13	0.0009
2006	0.71	0.0027	0.52	0.004	0.96	0.005	0.83	0.0005	0.37	0.004	0.015	0.0001	1.47	0.009	0.92	0.0009
2007	0.69	0.0027	0.55	0.004	1	0.005	0.07	0.005	0.35	0.003	0.016	0.0001	1.46	0.008	0.92	0.0008
2008	0.71	0.0027	0.51	0.004	1	0.005	0.08	0.004	0.27	0.003	0.016	0.0001	1.4	0.008	0.82	0.0008
2009	0.72	0.0027	0.5	0.003	1.037	0.005	0.76	0.004	0.27	0.003	0.01	0.00009	1.37	0.007	0.8	0.0008
2010	0.68	0.0027	0.52	0.004	1.08	0.005	0.87	0.004	0.26	0.003	0.01	0.00009	1.28	0.007	0.87	0.0009

Source: Food and Agriculture Organization (2012).

As concern grows about the magnitude of human pressure on the biosphere, the global community is increasingly engaged in discussions about the meaning and importance of achieving global sustainability. Capitalist exploitation is the greatest challenge to future sustainability. Capitalist mode of production and consumption is giving rise to more concern about ecological sustainability. From historical and classical Marxist perspectives, the crucial point emerges that the appropriation of nature by capitalism was a *sine qua non* to the historical expansion of the system, that this appropriation inevitably leads to the degradation of the environment, and hence to ecological and economic crisis. The implication of this ecological maxim is obvious: to be sustainable, humanity must live within nature's carrying capacity. Ecological economists would say that for achieving (strong) sustainability, humanity must maintain the planet's natural capital stocks (Daly and Cobb, 1989). Sustainability has now become a universal policy goal, at least in official rhetoric.

India has experienced high rates of population growth in the post-reform era and has plans for continued high rates of economic activity in the next couple of decades. High and sustained growth in economic activity is seen as a necessity to address poverty and the government is simultaneously making efforts to put in place policies and programmes that channelize the benefits of growth to those that need it most, thereby bringing in inclusive development. Ecological footprint shows the effect inhabitants of particular region like India have on the environment they live in and on natural resources. India can remain competitive, even in this resource-constrained world. It all comes down to decisions. The ecological footprint can support and inform India's policy issues from a number of angles:

- To what extent is natural capital relevant for economic success?
- What potential risks could national biocapacity deficit impose?
- What will 2030 look like if we fail to address the 'resource limitation issue' now?
- What immediate actions can decision-makers take to ensure a viable future for their country?
- How is it in India's self-interest to make resource management a priority?

Conclusion and Recommendation

Ecological footprint accounting is one of the environmental protection indicators, that is important while estimating the sustainable development of a country. Ecological footprint accounting can assist policymakers in taking action to minimize their countries' demands on ecological assets and to build and strengthen their biocapacity reserves. Such actions not only benefit all on the planet, but are also vital to the self-interest and well-being of the nation. Environmental inequality measurement has been widely discussed in recent years because of its important implications in terms of universal ethics and environmental policy. Such literature, however, has focused mainly on narrower environmental indicators such as CO_2 emissions and hardly at all on more multifaceted indicators such Ecological Footprint. Additionally, the methods applied to measure inequalities are always correctly adjusted to suit an ecological economics framework.

Discussions of environmental sustainability must be grounded in sound assessments of the current state of human demand for ecosystem goods and services and the overall regenerative capacity of natural ecosystems. Urgently, we need a new research and policy paradigm to emerge from this proposition. *First,* Policy circles will need increasingly more robust and detailed resource accounting tools, such as ecological footprint accounts, to analyse and aggregate human pressure on ecosystems. The serious application of these tools will require investments in the order of those currently devoted to calculating other widely used social and economic indicators. *Second,* the lack of strong correlation between land degradation and HDI suggests that the results of Moran et al. (2008) are not robust enough to meet different specification of sustainability. So, ecologists should find ways to continue to increase the earth's biocapacity without putting further pressure on biodiversity. Energy as well as agriculture and food systems will play a particularly important role, making or marring biocapacity. That is, more developed nations are not necessarily associated with greater land degradation. The final result of correlation matrix is the relation between soil erosion and crop yields (Fiala, 2008). Continuously, increasing ecological pressure will almost certainly make management of demand and supply of biological capacity one of the central concerns of this century. *Third,* economists particularly are needed to estimate how much financial resources are used by biologically productive area (ecological footprint) and how much more is needed for current and future ecological supply (biocapacity). Research is also needed to identify how much capital investment would be required to redirect the global economy to a sustainable pathway. Identifying strategies for achieving these goals in the most efficient and cost-benefit manner will also be a better contribution. Only a few have examined current and future impacts on the life support system such as long-term environmental damage in ISEW (Daly and Cobb, 1989; Moffatt and Wilson, 1994). Ecological economics models enable the exploration of expenditure pattern of ecological footprint and biocapacity. Moreover, national environmental economic accounting builds on a consistent framework that is generated annually by official sources of data.

Fourth, science and technology and innovation will play an ever more important role in helping humanity to address the most important global challenge of the twenty-first century – finding ways for the global community to achieve high-quality lives on our one planet, earth. *Fifth,* behavioural framework is important for inculcating social values in determining consumption behaviour of natural resources. Behavioural framework denotes the different socio-political and psychological levels of factors influencing consumption behaviour, and illustrates how initiatives aimed at reducing consumption levels will vary in their impact depending on the level at which they effect change. As the measurement of environmental, social, economic and behavioural aspects of well-being becomes more widely recognized, passive indicators that signify these elements are being developed and tested in a variety of setting.

Ecological footprint accounts allow governments to track a city or region's demand on natural capital, and to compare this demand with the amount of natural capital actually available. Such accounts also give governmental agencies the ability to answer more specific questions about the sharing of these demands within their economy. In other words, it gives them a reliable account about their resource metabolism (Wackernagel et al., 2006). The need for sustainability arose from the recognition that the profligate, extravagant and inequitable nature of current patterns of development, when projected into the not-too-distant feature, leads to biophysical impossibilities. The transition to environmentally sustainable ways is urgent because the deterioration of global life-support systems – which compose the environment – imposes a time limit. We do not have time to dream of creating more living space or more ecosystems, such as colonizing the moon or building cities beneath the ocean. We must save the remnants of the only environment we have and allow time for and invest in the regeneration of what we have already damaged, and allow it to 'grow' into sustainability. Such efforts clearly require collaboration and consensus among ecologists, economists, technologist and behavioural scientists in order to develop effective and fail-safe solutions to the problem of resource overconsumption and environmental damage.

References

Barnosky, A.D. et al. (2012). 'Approaching a State Shift in Earth's Biosphere', *Nature*, 486: 52–58.

Borucke, Michael et al. (2013). 'Accounting for Demand and Supply of the Biosphere's Regenerative Capacity: The National Footprint Accounts' Underlying Methodology and Framework', *Ecological Indicators*, 24: 518–33.

Daly, Herman E. and John B. Cobb (1989). *For the Common Good: Redirecting the Economy toward Community, the Environment and a Sustainable Future*, Beacon Press, Boston, MA.

Fiala, Nathan (2008). 'Measuring Sustainability: Why Ecological Footprint is Bad Economics and Bad Environmental Science', *Ecological Economics*, 67(4): 519–25.

Galli, A. (2007). 'Assessing the Role of the Ecological Footprint as Sustainability Indicator', PhD Thesis, Department of Chemical and Biosystems Sciences, University of Siena, Italy.

Galli, A. et al. (2012). 'Assessing the Global Environmental Consequences of Economic Growth through the Ecological Footprint: A Focus on China and India', *Ecological Indicators*, 17: 99–107.

Haberl, H. (2006). 'The Global Socioeconomic Energetic Metabolism as a Sustainability Problem', *Energy*, 31: 87–99.

Mani, Mutuukumara et al. (2012). 'An Analysis of Physical and Monetary Losses of Environmental Health and Natural Resources in India', *Policy Research Working Paper*, 6219, World Bank.

Millennium Ecosystem Assessment (2005). *Ecosystems and Human Well-Being: Health Synthesis*, Institute of Public Health and the Environment, Netherlands.

Moffatt, I. and M.D. Wilson (1994). 'An Index of Sustainable Economic Welfare for Scotland, 1980–1991', *International Journal of Sustainable Development and World Ecology*, 1: 264–91.

Monfreda, C., M. Wackernagel and D. Deumling (2004). 'Establishing National Natural Capital Accounts Based on Detailed Ecological Footprint and Biological Capacity Assessments', *Land Use Policy*, 21: 231–46.

Moore, D. et al. (2012). 'Projecting Future Human Demand on the Earth's Regenerative Capacity', *Ecological Indicators*, 16: 3–10.

Moran, Daniel D. et al. (2008). 'Measuring Sustainable Development: Nation by Nation', *Ecological Economics*, 64(3): 470–74.

Naidu, Sirisha and Panayiotes T. Manolakos (2010). 'Primary Accumulation, Capitalist Nature and Sustainability', *Economic and Political Weekly*, XLV(29).

Wackernagel, M., L. Onistor, P. Bello, A.C. Linares, L. Falfan, J.M. Garcia, G.A.I. Suarez and E.M.G. Suarez (1999a). 'National Natural Capital Accounting with the Ecological Footprint Concept', *Ecological Economics*, 29(3): 375–90.

Wackernagel, M., L. Lewan and C.B. Hansson (1999b). 'Evaluating the Use of Natural Capital with the Ecological Footprint', *Ambio*, 28: 604–612.

Wackernagel, M., N.B. Schulz, D. Deumling, A.C. Linares, M. Jenkins, V. Kapos, C. Monfreda, J. Loh, N. Myers, R. Norgaard and J. Randers (2002). 'Tracking the Ecological Overshoot of the Human Economy', *Proceedings of the National Academy of Science*, 99: 9266–71.

Wackernagel, M., Justin Kitzes, Dan Moran, Steven Goldfinger and Mary Thomas (2006). 'The Ecological Footprint of Cities and Regions: Comparing Resource Availability with Resource Demand', *Environment and Urbanization*, 18(1): 103–12.

Ward, B. and R. Dubos (1972). *Only One Earth*, Penguin, Harmondsworth.

World Wildlife Fund (2012). *Living Planet Report 2012: Biodiversity, Biocapacity and Better Choices*, WWF International, Switzerland.

4

The Linkages of Population, Poverty and Environmental Vulnerability

A Study in the Drought-prone Region of Madhugiri Taluk of Tumkur District

B.H. Doddahanumaiah

Environmental degradation through air pollution, water pollution, land degradation and deforestation are the pressing concerns in the context of sustainable environment. In the last few decades, environmentalists and affected people have effectively cited environmental degradation and associated challenges to protect and conserve the distinct and rare species of the biomass of our earth. Migration is a vital process in modern society and it is an age-old strategy. In general, the phenomenon of migration is seen as an outcome of both pull and push factors. The processes of migration have become vital for change and development of all types of societies, i.e. Tribal, Rural and Urban. Internal migration is an evidence of chronic social and economic breakdown, which is now regarded as a major instrument for the redistribution of resources from richer to poorer localities and a prime means of raising the income of the poor.

There is a long history of study and debate about the interactions between population growth and the environment. According to the British thinker Malthus, for example, a growing population exerts pressure on agricultural land, causing environmental degradation and forcing the cultivation of land of poorer and poorer quality. This environmental degradation ultimately reduces agricultural yields and food availability, causes famines and diseases and death, thereby reducing the rate of population growth. Population growth, because it can take place increased pressure on the assimilative capacity of the environment, is also seen as a major cause of air and water pollution through solid-waste generation. As theorized by Malthus, it leads to a state of low-level equilibrium, where population enjoys low levels of both income and environmental quality. Malthus suggested positive and preventative forced control of human population, along with abolition of poor laws.

The underlying cause of environmental decay is overpopulation. The land reserve that is available on earth is finite. However, the demands are ever-increasing due to increasing population. There is only so much that can actually be extracted from the earth. This has led to widespread use of chemicals and other toxins to produce more food to feed the ever-increasing number of people. This has further caused depletion of the earth's resources and residual regenerative capacity. The widespread use of chemical fertilizers have disturbed the biological balance of earth and in the process destroyed the microorganisms so vital for environmental regeneration.

Poverty and Migration

It is generally accepted that environmental degradation, rapid growth of population and stagnant productivity are the causes for the quick spread of acute poverty in many Asian countries (Duraiappah, 1996). However, thanks to the rapid economic growth taking place around the world, particularly since the last quarters of 20th century, the world has witnessed a considerable reduction in the incidence of poverty. In this scenario, studying the nexus between population growth, poverty and environmental degradation in the context of a developing country like India, would be more appropriate for unravelling the actual causes and finding remedies for global warming and climate change. It is known that most of the India's poor live in rural areas and are engaged in agriculture. It is gratifying that government intervention through various schemes and programmes implemented under five-year plans to eradicate poverty and provide employment have been generally successful. Over the years anti-poverty employment generation schemes and programmes have brought down poverty and rural unemployment substantially. However, traditionally, the problem of poverty and unemployment was rampant in rural India and conditions in urban India were a shade better, but surprisingly, after the onset of economic liberalization and globalization, there has been an alarming increase in urban poverty in India.

However, poverty in Karnataka continues to be the highest among the southern states. Rural poverty in Karnataka has declined by 30.5 percentage during 1993–94 to 2009–10, which is much higher than the decline at the all-India level (14.2%). As a corollary, the number of rural poor in the State has also declined over the period. The decline in number of poor in Karnataka between 1993–94 and 2005–10 was higher than the national average of 14.2 per cent. District level poverty estimates indicate that there is higher concentration of poverty in the district under study than in the other parts of the state.

Migration in India is not a new phenomenon and historical accounts show that people have moved in search of work, in response to environmental shocks and stresses, to escape religious persecution and political conflict. However, improved communications, transport networks and new economic opportunities have created unprecedented levels of mobility; often conflicts over natural resources also has caused migration. But as we discuss in following sections, the increase in mobility is not fully captured in larger surveys, often leading to erroneous conclusions about mobility levels in India. Traditional rural-urban migration exists in India as villagers seek to improve opportunities and lifestyles. In 2001, about 59 million people migrated in rural-urban patterns of which 54 per cent were females. Caste and tribe systems complicate these population movements.

Environmental degradation such as the concern of environmental quality has become the utmost issue in the present scenario of increasing urbanization, industrialization under the globalization era. Rapid growth in the number of motor vehicles and the consequent higher emissions, water pollution due to the discharge of effluents without conforming to the environmental norms and standards, etc. have become threats to human health and well-being. However, population is both a major asset for a development and similarly a major source of environmental degradation, particularly in the developing countries of the world. Population growth affects the environment primarily by overusing natural resources and generating wastes. It causes environmental stress and loss of biodiversity by polluting air and water, and exerting increased pressure on agriculture land. Over the years, urban population has been increasing rapidly and necessitating expansion of urban areas, which invariably entails diversion of huge agricultural land for construction of infrastructure, such as roads, railway line and for residential purposes. This has promoted the smaller cities to bigger cities, and bigger ones to merge as metro cities and metros to transform into mega cities. Population pressure naturally leads to overexploitation of natural resources like land, air and water. It is in the light of the above discussion that this study attempts to understand the link between population, poverty and environmental degradation.

Here, 'drought' is defined as the delicate balance between water supply and demand. Whenever human demands for water exceed the natural availability of water, the result is drought. Drought can be caused by too little precipitation (rain and snow) over an extended period, as most people assume, but drought can also be caused by increased demand for the available supply of usable water even during periods of average or above average precipitation. If some of the available water sources become contaminated either temporarily or permanently, that decreases the supply of usable water, makes the balance between water supply and demand even more precarious, and increases the likelihood of drought. The associated issues include rejuvenation of degraded traditional surface water bodies, enhancing the availability of water through water harvesting measures, and recharge of groundwater resources. More important is the judicious and economic use of both ground and surface water for agricultural, industrial and domestic purposes. Karnataka is subjected to repetitive droughts. The National Irrigation Commission has identified 12 districts and 88 taluks in the state as chronically drought affected. The mean annual rainfall in the state is 1,355 millimetres with more than 73 per cent of it being received from the

South-West monsoon. In the period between 1970–2003, deficit rainfall was recorded on 22 occasions and the highest deficit of 55 per cent was observed in 1983. Annual rainfall variations across agro-climatic zones in the state are too wide, ranging from 585 millimetres in the northern dry zone to 3,893 millimetres in the coastal zone.

Study Area

Tumkur District is one of the 30 administrative districts of Karnataka state, located in the north-west of Bengaluru at a distance of about 70 km. The district is bounded by Mandya District in the south; Chitradurga and Hassan districts in the west; Chikkamangalore in the north-east and Ananthapura District of Andhra Pradesh state in the south-east direction. The total geographical area of Tumkur District is 10,596 sq km. As per 2001 census, the district has a total population of 2.5 million, comprising 1.3 million of male and 1.2 million of female population. Over 80 per cent of the district's population is categorized as rural. Total literacy rate of the district according to 2001 census is 82 per cent, in which urban literacy is higher (86%) than the rural literacy (84%). For more information, see Table 1. The major occupations of the district are agriculture, horticulture and animal husbandry, which constitute almost 80 per cent of the total workforce.

Table 1

Population Aspects of Tumkur District (2001)

	Male	*Female*	*Total*
Total Population	13,13,801	12,70,910	25,84,711
Rural Population	10,52,113	10,25,396	20,77,509
Urban population	2,61,688	2,45,514	5,07,202
Literacy	(82.56)	(64.65)	(74.32)
Rural literacy	(84.02)	(62.03)	(73.04)
Urban literacy	(86.09)	(76.03)	(82.03)
Main Workers	(55.00)	(25.08)	(40.06)
Marginal Workers	(05.07)	(17.08)	(11.07)

Source: District at a Glance, Tumkur 2001.

Note: Percentage in Parenthesis.

The District being a part of the southern Maidan region (plain) of the State is generally open tracts with undulating hills except in the south of Kunigal Taluk, where the land is wooded and hilly. The other parts are undulating plains, intercepted with cluster of all and well-grown trees. The open part of the district lies generally above sea level; but Pavagada and Sira are at a considerably lower level than the rest. The eastern part of the District is covered by narrow range of granite hills. Their average width is about 20 miles and run north to south in the District. The western parts of the District consist mostly of long ranges of hills running approximately in a south east direction.

Madhugiri is the Taluk headquarters of Tumkur District in the state of Karnataka. The taluk is bounded on the east and the north by Ananthapura district of Andhra Pradesh; on the west by Sira taluk, on the south by Koratagere taluk, and on the south and east by Gowribidanur of Kolar district. The taluk extends over an area of 1,118.4 sq kms, and recorded an annual rainfall of 847.2 mm in 2005–2007. The taluk has no perennial streams but a number of streams originate in the hill ranges which are seasonal in nature. One such stream is the Jayamangali River which forms the main source of water for tank irrigation. The taluk is frequently affected by droughts. More than half the population in the town is engaged in services, but majority of the rural population depends on agriculture. The town is also known as Maddagiri and is located around 43 km in the north of Tumkur town, and 107 km north-west of Bengaluru city. Surrounding greenery of Madhugiri is the main attraction in the taluk. The place has old temples of Venkataramanaswami and Malleshwara, built by the Vijayanagara feudatories in the Dravidian style. Geographically, the taluk is located between 13°40'N, 77°13'E and 13.66° N, 77.21°E. It has an average elevation of 787 metres (2,582 feet).

Table 2

Population Aspects of Madhugiri Taluk of Tumkur District

Population Aspects	*Male (% age)*	*Female (% age)*	*Total*
Total Population	1,35,320 (50.89)	1,30,564 (49.10)	2,65,884
Rural Population	1,21,770 (50.82)	1,17,810 (49.17)	2,39580
Urban population	13,550 (51.50)	12,754 (48.48)	26,304
Literacy	(72.07)	(49.04)	(61.02)
Rural literacy	(71.02)	(46.07)	(59.02)
Urban literacy	(85.05)	(73.04)	(79.07)
Main Workers	(59.09)	(46.04)	(47.06)
Marginal Workers	(09.07)	(25.03)	(14.08)

Source: Census of India, 2001, District Population Booklet Series No. 30, Karnataka.

Note: Percentage in Parenthesis.

The major crops grown in Madhugiri are groundnut, ragi along with mango, mulberry for sericulture, coconut and Kakada (flower). It is also known for pomegranate fruit ('daalimbe' in Kannada). The important industries are oil mills, rice mills and saw mills and registered small scale units. Drinking water is available in almost all inhabited villages of the taluk. Agriculture, horticulture and sericulture are the predominant economic activities in the taluk. They are not however well developed to full potential due to the shortage of water. Agriculture provides only seasonal employment and the economic returns from the land are low. Non-agricultural economic activities are also poorly developed. The natural resource base of the taluk has steadily declined. Traditionally-used surface storage tanks, an important source of water for all purposes, have been silted up and many are defunct. Poor and erratic rainfall coupled with poor water management practice has resulted in a steady depletion of groundwater resources. In recent decades, the decrease in biomass availability, both fuel wood and green manure from forests has had a negative impact on the livelihood.

Objectives of the Study

The major objectives of the study are following:

- To understand the linkages of population, poverty and environmental vulnerability in the study area.
- To examine the socio-economic condition of the sample households and its impact on environmental degradation in the study area.
- To study the household structure and living conditions of the sample households to trace the positive impact on environmental vulnerability in the study area.

Data and Methodology

Data for the study have been obtained from both primary and secondary sources. This is a modest study and limits its focus on the examination of the issues and questions of population, household structure and living environment. These issues have been dealt with, with a view to address policy issues in order to increase awareness among decision makers, professionals and academics about the urgency to conserve natural resources for sustainable development and healthy growth of the society. Accordingly, this study seeks to capture the dimensions of overall population migration and environmental degradation across Tumkur district in general, and Madhugiri taluk in particular. Available secondary demographic data have been used for the study. Primary data have been collected from few selected villages in Madhugiri taluk (see Table 3).

Sample size and composition of the villages were finalized after referring to census data as well as other official records. Keeping this in mind, a total of 200 households in Kodegenahalli, Bijavara, Medigeshi and Ittakadibanahalli (I.D. Halli) were chosen for investigation. Data on various issues such as household structure, family size, occupation, family background, environmental condition, sanitation facilities, etc. have been collected for the study. The respondents were selected on the basis of purposive random sampling method. The empirical findings of the study have been supplemented by secondary data. They were sourced out from libraries by reviewing existing theoretical and empirical studies on the topic, official documents, newspaper and periodicals. Internet sources were also browsed and downloaded wherever it was necessary.

Table 3

Sample Villages and their Population of Madhugiri Taluk

Villages	*Households*	*Male (% age)*	*Female (% age)*	*Total*
Kodegenahalli	1,451	3,800 (50.83)	3,575 (47.82)	7,375
Bijavara	384	1,450 (53.21)	1,275 (46.78)	2,725
Medigeshi	745	1,872 (52.21)	1,713 (47.78)	3,585
I.D. Halli	888	3,450 (60.26)	2,275 (39.73)	5,725

Source: District Statistical Office at a Glance, Tumkur, 2011.

Household Structure, Living Arrangements and Environmental Vulnerability

Before going into a detail analysis of household structure in terms of family structure living arrangements, sanitation, etc. it is necessary to present the village profile of sample villages in Madhugiri Taluk. The village of Kodigenaghalli is the headquarter of one of the hoblies of Madhugiri taluk, located at the south-east part of the taluk, abutting Hindupur of Andhra Pradesh. This village has 1,451 households with a total population of 6,966, consisting of 3,500 males and 3,466 females, the sex ratio being 990. The total literacy rate is 69.4 per cent and work participation rate of male and female was 58.6 and 30.8 per cent respectively.

The village of Bijavara is located nearby Madhugiri town at a distance of about 5 kms. This village has about 589 households with a population of 1,771 persons which comprises 901 males and 870 females. There were 966 females per every 1,000 males. Total literacy rate is 67.4 per cent and work participation rate is 62.9 for males and 31.3 per cent for females. Medigeshi village is located in the northern part of the taluk which has a total number of households of 630. The total population of Medigeshi has about 630 households with a population of 2,685 persons comprising 1,372 males and 1,313 females. The sex ratio of the village is 957. The total literacy rate is about 73 per cent and work participation rate is 57.7 for males and 49.9 per cent for females. The village I.D. Halli is located close to the border to Andhra Pradesh; it has 888 households with a total population of 4,110 persons, consisting of 2,131 males and 1,979 females. Sex ratio of this village is 929, total literacy rate 63.2 per cent and work participation rate is 60.4 per cent for males and 48 per cent for females (2001).

Table 4

Population Composition of Selected Villages in Madhugiri Taluk of Tumkur District

Villages	*Male*	*Female*	*Total*
Kodegenahalli	54	20	74
Bijavara	25	10	35
Medigeshi	29	12	41
I.D. Halli	35	15	50
Total	143	57	200

Source: Fieldwork conducted during the month of May/June 2013.

As can be seen from Table 4, the proportion of males is higher than the female respondents in all the selected villages, and among the selected households about 143 were male-headed and 57 female-headed. It can also be seen in Table 5 that the majority of respondents, 127 (63.50%) are in the age group 26–30 years, about 45 (22.50%) persons in the age group of 21–25 years, another 15 (07.50%) persons in the age group of 31–35 years and the remaining 13 (6.50%) in the age between 36–40 years. Similarly Table 5 also reveals the household structure of the respondents. Regarding the type of dwelling units, the majority 80 (41.50%) of respondents live in sheet-roofed houses, about 65 (32.75%) in tile-roofed houses, about 50 (25.50%) in mud houses and only 0.25 per cent (5) live in huts.

Table 5

Age Composition and Household Structure

Age Composition	*No. of Persons*	*Percentage*
21–25 years	45	22.50
26–30 years	127	63.50
31–35 years	15	07.50
36–40 years	13	06.50
Total	200	100
Type of House	No. of Houses	Percentage
Hut	05	0.25
Mud	50	25.50
Sheets	80	41.50
Tiles	65	32.75
Total	200	100.00

Source: Fieldwork has been conducted during the month of May/June 2013.

Household Characteristics, Occupation and Environmental Degradation

Table 6 presents a detailed picture of household types, occupation of respondents, settlement pattern, drainage system, sanitation facility and source of cooking-fuel of the selected households in the villages. Out of 200 households in the selected villages, majority of the respondents (70%) are residing in nuclear families, followed by joint families (10%), about 12 per cent live separate (mostly unmarried men) houses and the remaining 8 per cent households are in single families. However, as per our field observation in the selected villages, there is acute decline in land utilization, due to recurring failure of monsoon and consequently government has already declared these villages as drought-affected. Almost 50 per cent of the respondents are agriculture labourers, 29.50 per cent are cultivators and the remaining 25.50 per cent of respondents are involved in other occupations. The main reason for the decline in cultivator households in these villages is out-migration to the nearby city of Bengaluru. Temporary migration by marginal farmers and landless people in search of work is common during the summer season. Some of the well-to-do farmers also live in nearby towns because they offer better educational facilities and employment opportunities. Table 6 also shows that an overwhelming majority (40%) of the respondents have migrated from these villages to nearby cities for their livelihood. Out of 200 the respondent-households, about 30 per cent were permanent residents and 17.50 per cent were immigrants.

Further, as is evident from Table 6, over 60 per cent of the households in these villages do not have proper drainage system and some villages particularly are totally devoid of drainage; apparently, the Gram Panchayat has failed in properly maintaining the drainage system. Five per cent of the population of Kodegena Halli and I.D. Halli villages has access to toilets as compared to one per cent in the other villages. Kodigenahalli village has the largest number of toilets, thanks to the government housing programme for the rural poor, sponsored by UNICEF.

Table 6

Household Characteristics, Occupation and Sanitation Facilities in the Selected Villages of Madhugiri Taluk

I Family Type		
Type	*Number*	*Percentage*
Nuclear	140	70.00
Joint	20	10.00
Independent (unmarried)	24	12.00
Single parent	16	08.00
Total	200	100.00
II Occupation of the Respondents		
Nature of occupation	*Number*	*Percentage*
Cultivators	59	29.50
Agri.labourers	90	45.00
Other workers	51	25.50
Total	200	100.00
III Settlement Pattern		
Nature	*Number*	*Percentage*
Permanent settled	60	30.00
Migrated	80	40.00
Immigrants	35	17.50
Seasonal	25	12.50
Total	200	100.00
IV Drainage system		
Nature	*Number*	*Percentage*
Open system	120	60.00
Closed system	80	40.00
Total	200	100.00
V Sanitation Facility		
Nature	*Number*	*Percentage*
Toilet attached	120	60.00
Outside toilet	80	40.00
Total	200	100.00
VI Source of Cooking		
Nature	*Number*	*Percentage*
Fuelwood	60	30.00
Firewood	80	40.00
Gas connection	35	17.50
Other	25	12.50
Total	200	100.00

Source: Fieldwork has been conducted during the month of May/June 2013.

At present this Gram Panchayat has a fair percentage of new houses with toilets, while prior to 1993, there were very few houses with toilets. In the remaining villages of Bijavara and Medegeshi, people still use open fields for toilet.

Lately, the Gram Panchayat has made it compulsory for residents to build toilet facilities through government subsidies. Even though as per the field observation more than 60 per cent of the respondents of the total do not have sanitation facilities due to the shortage of water and improper drainage system in the respective villages. And all of them are forced to use open fields as toilets (40%).

Open defecation causes the spread of disease through the faecal contamination of food by houseflies, especially during the rainy season, and this habit is therefore a serious health concern. The open defecation is most often in the habitat area surrounding the houses. The stagnant water lying in drains in almost all the villages is responsible for the spread of malaria since these waters are the breeding ground for mosquitoes and flies. Faecal contamination of groundwater is also not uncommon.

In recent decades, the decrease in biomass availability, both fuel and firewood has had a negative impact on the livelihood of many rural communities. The type of fuel used for domestic purposes has shifted from firewood to the coconut fronds and leaves obtained from coconut plantations. In this regard the above table reveals that about 40 per cent of the households are dependent on firewood for cooking and 30 per cent of households use fuel sold in fair-price depots (kerosene) under Public Distribution System as cooking fuel. Income earning households or salaried people have gas connection (17.50%) and remaining 12.50 per cent households use other alternatives like electricity, biomass, etc.

Population Growth and Environment

Population growth rate during the recent decade of 1991–2001in the above villages has declined by almost 50 per cent, which is attributed to the out-migration and adoption of better family planning methods in the preceding decades. Although, permanent migration from a few villages has taken place during the present decade also, it has greatly slowed down over time. The migration of the well-to-do for better educational facilities for their children is quite high. Educated young people also migrate to towns in search of jobs. Temporary migration for employment in small industries like oil mill, rice mill and garment factories, etc. in adjoining districts is an annual occurrence during the summer months. A constant improvement is seen in the quality of life, which includes enhanced longevity, improved literacy rates, better roads, better access to transportation and increased earning power. Population growth has led to a general increase in the consumption of most natural resources. The increase in the use of timber for house construction and firewood for domestic energy has resulted in high deforestation rates. Deforestation has had negative environmental impacts including reduced water availability and low crop productivity. The improvement in the earning power for a few has been at the cost of the majority of the population and the environment.

The major uses of water are for domestic purposes, drinking water for animals and irrigation. For the large part of the year, borewells are the only source of water for these uses (drinking water comes from the hand pumps fitted on bore wells). Domestic water use has increased only marginally. Poor sanitation practices result in the spread of waterborne diseases such as cholera, typhoid, and diarrhea during the summer season. Malaria is common during the summer season due to the proliferation of mosquitoes. Even though no major epidemics have occurred, a labour shortage exists during the agricultural season due to migration.

The Linkage of Poverty and Environmental Degradation

It is generally accepted that environmental degradation, rapid growth of population and stagnant productivity are the causes for the quick spread of acute poverty in many Asian countries (Duraiappah, 1996). However, poverty is said to be both the cause and effect of environmental degradation because poorer people who cannot buy their subsistence needs, are forced to use common property resources such as forest for food and fuel, pastures for fodder and ponds and rivers for water. Hence, this directly contributes to environmental degradation through overexploitation of natural resources. It is now well accepted that poverty, population and the environment are interconnected, and various frameworks have been proposed to illustrate the linkages.

Population pressures can lead to resource degradation and poverty, while, simultaneously, one subset of the local population experiences increasing affluence. In this region, population growth has contributed to deforestation and expansion of rainfed agriculture on to hillsides where erosion rates are highest. The issue is a matter of access to resources, and in this case the critical resource is water. Water is pumped from privately owned borewells to irrigate commercial crops like groundnut. Even though fertility rates have decreased in the study area, due to the young age structure of the population, population is still growing at 1.4 per cent per annum, contributing to ever greater pressures on resources. Four central agencies of government – planning, finance, health and environment – have to take the leadership in multi-structural planning to curb environmental pollution by providing basic amenities in these villages. Policies and programmes need to be focused on the drought-prone regions of Karnataka for pointed attention. Different departments such as health, environment, agriculture, education, industry and the department of labour should take note of these findings and work together horizontally to bring about meaningful change. The public sector needs to work in coordination with international, national and local NGOs, the private sector and experts from various fields in order to develop multi-sectoral Population Poverty Environment solutions.

Summary and Conclusions

This modest study does not have any pretentions of having used any new methodology or proposed weighty remedial measures. However, the following suggestions to retrieve the situation would help administrators and policy makers: Government should first evolve a clear vision about population, migration and environmental degradation in drought-prone areas and set up a firm technology mission to formulate remedial measures. Special measures should be taken to eliminate discrimination, eradicate illiteracy, create environmental awareness and improve the sanitation facilities. By way of creating job opportunities in agriculture and allied activities, concentrated efforts should be made to ensure that benefits of training and various programmes reach them in proportion to their numbers. Developing a support structure and linkage with our regional and national processes will be needed to address some of the more severe environmental issues. Based on the findings of the study, we make the following recommendations to the respective authorities.

- Watershed management should be adopted in villages to conserve water.
- Promote dry land agriculture into horticulture.
- Increase recycling of organic wastes.
- Use of sustainable agricultural practices.
- Bring about improvements in farm implements of small farmers.
- Introduction of biomass-based enterprises for small and marginal farmers.

Overuse of natural resources has directly resulted in degradation of environment. Therefore, appropriate measures should be taken by the respective authorities to provide basic facilities in the drought-prone region like Madhugiri taluk in order to curb environmental vulnerability. Another suggestion of the study is that, apart from the community participation and promoting increasing public awareness on environment, the stakeholders need be given incentives for better resource management practices. A combination of awareness creation and incentives only can ensure healthy growth of villages and ensure a sustainable environment.

References

Dewaram, A. Nagdeve (2005). *Population Growth and Environmental Degradation in India*, IIPS, Mumbai.

District at a Glance (2001, 2011). District Statistical Office, Tumkur.

Duraiappah, Anantha (1996). 'Poverty and Environmental Degradation: A Literature Review and Analysis', CREED Working Paper Series, Institute of Environment and Development, London.

Harte, John (2007). 'Human Population as Dynamic Factors in Environmental Degradation', *Population and Environment: A Journal of Interdisciplinary Studies*, 28(4–5): 223–36.

International Institute for Population Sciences (2000). National Family Health Survey (NFHS-2) India, Ministry of Health and Family Welfare, Government of India, New Delhi.

Karnataka at a Glance, Directorate of Economics and Statistics, Government of Karnataka 2011–2012.

Kumar, Pawan (2001). 'Environmental Degradation in Rural Areas: Problems and Suggestions', *Yojana*, 45.

Lakshmana, C.M. (2008). *Effect of Population Growth on Environmental Degradation*, ISEC, Bangalore.

——. (2012). *Population Growth, Natural Resource Degradation and Environmental Pollution in India: Social and Economic Change Monographs*, ISEC, Bangalore.

SECTION II

Development versus Environment

5

Linkages of Environment and Sustainable Development Pattern in Nagaland

Vyasan R.

In India, the idea of growth/development is synonymous with population increase. The reasons for equating development with an increase in population are numerous. Increase in population is perceived as harmful to the environment in these small hill communities practising jhum cultivation, as an increase in population pushes the society and environment into a vicious cycle of environmental degradation. It is feared that if this vicious cycle is allowed to continue, it would prevent the society from adopting a more sustainable form of agricultural practice. However, this paper is divided into nine sections and is organized as below:

Development and its Linkages with Environment

The first two sections briefly look at the jhum system of cultivation that is prevalent in Nagaland and explain briefly the methods of jhumming followed. The next section looks at how population growth is equated with development. The evidence of an interlinkage is presented in the next section, by referring to the census figures of Nagaland. The evidence presented is contrasted with the existing theories and regularities examined in the literature. The analysis is based on the theory put forward by Boserup among others. The schema is presented briefly and a suggested explanation for the variation from the schema is attempted. The section titled environment trap looks at how population growth impacts on environment and development. A way out of the impasse is suggested in the concluding section.

Jhum and the Agricultural Model

The practice of slash and burn cultivation, also known as jhum cultivation, has caused environmental damage in the north-eastern parts of the country.

The benefits of jhum cultivation are far outweighed by its negative impacts on the environment including depletion of forest cover that occurs as a result of this practice. One main benefit of jhum cultivation is that it promotes agricultural diversity. This is because farmers who practise slash and burn agriculture also retain a variety of trees along with the main crops they sow, in contrast to the modern systems of agriculture which are mono-cropping based. The presence of a large variety of trees promotes biodiversity of the particular region. In areas where there is no pressure of population on land, the benefits of slash and burn cultivation justify this method. However, in areas and societies where the pressure of population on land is substantial as in Nagaland (see Sections 4 and 5 below), the negative impacts of slash and burn cultivation like depletion of forests, threat of wildfires, etc. outweighs the benefits of slash and burn cultivation.

In traditional societies the people had a fair knowledge of the local topography. This helped them in deciding where to cultivate and the best method of cultivation. However, when the society got modernized, this traditional knowledge failed to percolate down to the new generation, many of whom emigrated in search of education and other facilities. The transmission of this local knowledge has therefore been stymied. This lack of knowledge of the local climes and agricultural practices adversely affect the productivity of their lands.

Slash and Burn Cultivation in Nagaland

Jhum cultivation is practiced widely in Nagaland. In areas where traditional jhum cultivation is practised, the land is parceled out to different families by the village. The family then takes turns annually to cultivate different patches of the land that has been parceled out to them. Forest is cleared and the trees are burnt. Burning of the forest takes place between the months of February and April. The exact date/time of burning depends on the location of the village and its inclination towards the sun, the kind of crops the farmers wish to grow, etc. Forests in sunnier patches are burnt later and crops therein harvested earlier. Once the forest is burnt down, land is prepared. Seeds are sown in the cleared forest land. To ensure that the seeds are not washed away, small bamboo sticks/wood are placed all along the slope. The crops that are grown include rice, maize, some vegetables like beans, etc.

After harvesting the crop, the forest is allowed to grow back and the next year/season a different area is chosen for cultivation. A jhum cycle is the number of years before which the same patch of land is cultivated. This interval used to be anywhere between 9–11 years in the recent past, the logic being that the cultivated patch of land gets enough time to recoup fertility before cultivation occurs again. The length of the cycle is important because shorter the cycle, less is the time the land gets to regain fertility and hence reduced productivity in the future. Hence, the intervening period is extremely crucial for regaining the fertility of the land. The use of fertilizers in these areas is negligible or non-existent.

Slash and burn cultivation as has been traditionally practised in these areas has an innate tendency to keep the people in a state of low level equilibrium or relative poverty. The prime reason is the static nature of land availability combined with population expansion. In earlier times, there were virgin patches of land that were available for agricultural use by group of enterprising people. This avenue is no more available. Small hilly communities have seen population expansion resulting in increased pressure on land.

Population Expansion and Development

In these sparsely populated areas, increase in family size is encouraged indirectly by the policies of the state for several reasons. For one, certain developmental grants are linked to the number of households in a village. Developmental grants are decentralized and the funds reach the village functionaries directly. In such a system there is an inherent push towards the setting up of new villages. The setting up of new villages is encouraged by the perverse logic of decentralized development, which convinces the villagers about the need to have control over the developmental process and the funds associated with this. In big and old villages, people who wield power and have decision-making capability now dominate this scene. In tradition bound societies there is little scope for the newly educated to penetrate these circles of power. There is a demand for and a move towards setting up more and more new villages, though there is a minimum population criteria prescribed for recognizing such settlements as new villages. The activities of the government hence indirectly support population expansion (see Figure 1).

Figure 1

Population of Nagaland

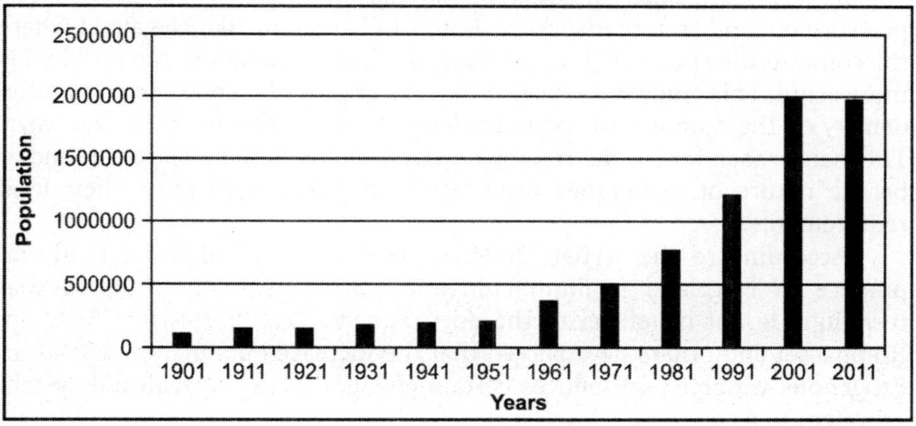

Population Pressure on Land

The pressure of population leads to two things: In such societies, land is traditionally distributed among different families/clans. Barring an occasional redistribution that may happen due to some unforeseen contingency, the traditional division of the available land remains unabated. Hence, any increase in family size in the village as a whole or in particular families results in the reduction of the fallow period for the land. Since the extent of traditionally held land is static and there is no increase in the landholding for the community as a whole, the effect is that the new villages will have less and less land for engaging in shifting cultivation.

On the one hand the developmental state creates incentives increase in population, on the other, the economic compulsions of the increased number cause great pressure on land. The increasing pressure of population on land is evidenced by the high levels of density of population in the state (see Figure 2 below).

Figure 2

Density of Population in Nagaland

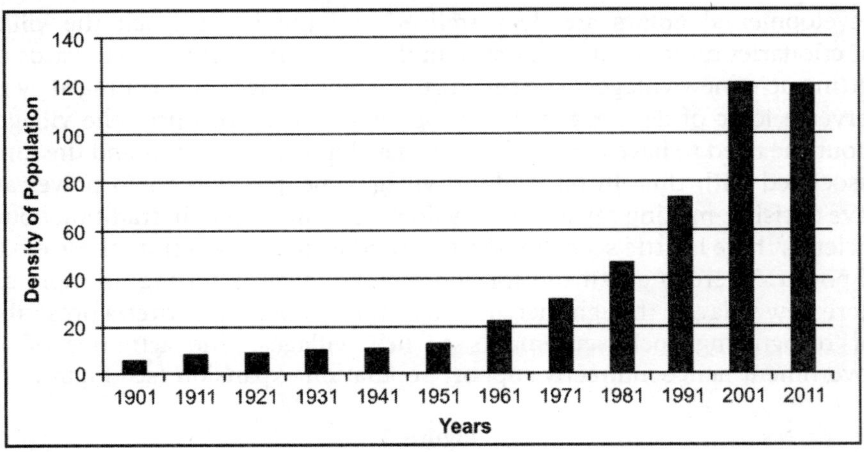

In any state such increase in population density puts tremendous pressure on land and its resources. But in hilly regions like Nagaland where the communities practise jhum or slash and burn cultivation, the problem is more acute. This study has revealed that the impact of increase in population density on the economy of communities is disproportionate in several ways. The main reason for the distressing impact of population increase is found to be the nature of techniques used by the population to grow their food requirements.

According to the NHDR 2004, over 90 per cent of the agricultural practice in Nagaland is jhum cultivation. It is generally accepted that technique is not beneficial to the environment. Economists like Boserup, Roumasset and others have shown that the increased population acts as an exogenous variable and induces certain changes in the agricultural system prevalent in a country.

Boserup and Density of Population

Boserup's frequency of cropping scheme predicts that given the levels of density of population in these regions, the people should be practising annual cropping with few months of fallow. Boserup argues that an increase in density of population should result in change in the nature of cultivation. Agriculture in Nagaland is still in the bush fallow stage where the fallow period ranges from 8–10 years. See Table 1 below for the entire sequence as mentioned in Boserup.

Writers like Roumasset (2007) have attempted to understand this sequence. The reasons that have been examined by them range from induced technical change to population induced increases in productivity. The authors who subscribe to the induced technical change theory generally use the elasticity of substitution between land and labour to examine the changes that take place in agricultural systems. Another group looks at how the marginal products and the average products change as a result of the increased population to explain the changes in the agricultural practice.

Table 1

Description of Cropping System

System	*Description of Cropping System*	*Frequency of Cropping*	*Persons per sq km*
Hunting and gathering	Wild plants, roots, fruits and nuts are gathered	0%	0–2
Forest fallow (w/pastoralism)	One or two crops followed by 15–25 years' fallow	0–10%	1–4
Bush fallow (w/pastoralism)	Two or more crops followed by 8–10 years' fallow	10–40%	4–64
Short fallow (w/domestic animals)	One or two crops followed by one or two years' fallow	40–80%	16–64
Annual cropping (w/intensive animal husbandry)	One crop each year with only a few months' fallow	80–100%	64–256
Multi-cropping	Two or more crops in the same fields each year without any fallow	200–300%	= 256

The persisting domination of jhum cultivation in Nagaland suggests that the economy is still stuck in the bush fallow period but the density of population suggests that the economy should be ideally in the Annual cropping stage.

The pressure of population on land imposes a productivity trap on the farmers. Under jhum cultivation, frequency of cultivation and rate of return are inversely related; higher the frequency in cultivating a patch of land, higher would be the decline in the rate of returns from farming. When farmers are faced with progressive diminution of returns from their land they will have no option but to revert back to the previous state of financially sound and productive agricultural practices.

Comparison of Average Product of Labour under Different Techniques

The agricultural practices followed in the hilly regions are still extensive in nature. The 'Jhum cultivation curve' in Figure 3 illustrates the position. The level of population in these parts though not high in absolute terms, is nevertheless high by the standards of the resources available here. If the population is at point C as in Figure 3, then it is economically profitable to shift from extensive techniques of cultivation like jhum to intensive forms of cultivation (depicted as terrace cultivation curve in Figure 3), or even shift to commercial crops, when population increase reaches this point at which yields from intensive and extensive techniques of agriculture are likely to be equal. If population is greater than C, the yields arising out of the intensive technique will be higher than the yields arising out of the extensive technique. It is, therefore, economically profitable for the farmers to shift from an extensive technique to an intensive technique in agriculture.

Figure 3

Jhum Cultivation Curve

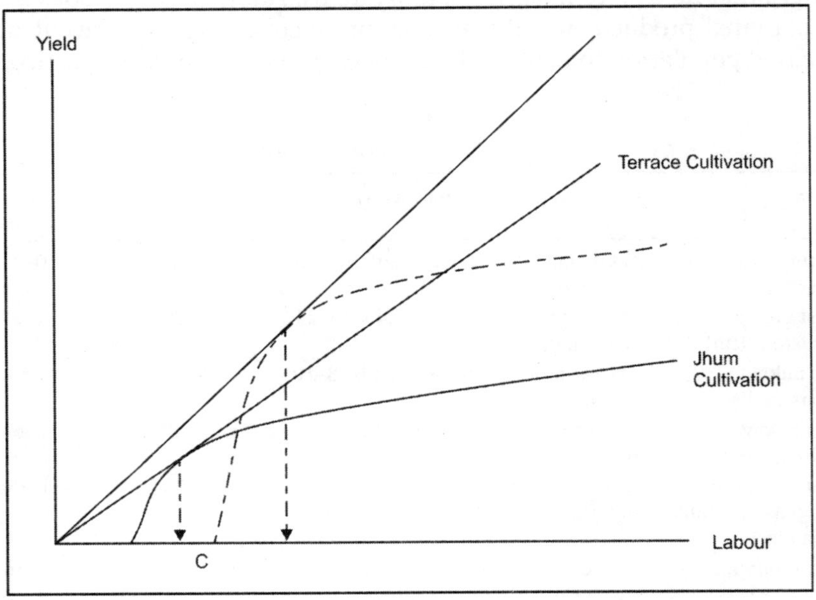

The existing agricultural practices are extensive in nature. As mentioned above, majority of the farmers use slash and burn techniques to cultivate their land. The Boserupian sequence mentions that at levels of the density of population in Nagaland and other north-eastern states, intensive form of cultivation with annual cropping has to be followed. However, majority of the farmers still practise jhum cultivation and the failure of farmers to shift away from inefficient agricultural practices has also led to severe environmental consequences in the hills. The reason for this hysteresis is primarily the lack of investable surplus in these societies. Shifting from extensive to intensive farm techniques like terrace farming, or shifting to commercial crops like rubber, orange, etc. require substantial investment of funds, and for want of investable funds, farmers continue to practise the traditional forms of agriculture like jhum cultivation.

Slash and burn cultivation has certain positive features; unlike the modern agricultural practices like monocropping, this method is environment-friendly and promotes biodiversity in the lands under plough. However, without external stimuli, the farmers are more likely to continue the slash and burn method or stick to the 'jhum curve' than to shift to innovative methods of cultivation, i.e. move to the outer curve as in Figure 3.

Environment Trap

The inability of the farmers to shift away from the less profitable form of agricultural practice to a more profitable form of agricultural can be attributed to certain dynamics akin to the poverty trap. Without external stimuli, these societies are more likely to follow their traditional practices of agriculture. Undoubtedly, it is lack of investable resources that prevent these families from adopting innovative agricultural practices. The working of this trap is explained with the help of a diagram (Figure 4 below).

In Figure 4, OE is the state of environment curve. OM is the 45° curve. These societies are in the concave part (OC) of the state of the environment curve OE below. On the x-axis is the state of the environment at time t_0. This approximates to the present state of environment of the area. On the y-axis is the future state of environment represented by t_1. This time represents the future. The state of environment in the future is impacted by the activities taken up in the present period and hence largely dependent on it. We examine how the state of the environment is impacted by the agricultural activity, in this specific instance, the slash and burn method of agriculture.

Since the agricultural techniques currently in use are extensive in nature, we assume that any increase in productivity and therefore income, will depend on the land that is brought under cultivation. More the area that is brought under cultivation more would be the agriculture produce. Similarly, lesser the fallow period, lower would be the yields from any given patch of land, as the soil does not have enough time to recuperate its fertility. Since cultivation is predominantly of a jhum variety, the state of the environment/availability of forest cover, etc. would be directly correlated to the produce of the agricultural activity. In an effort to keep up with the total product in the previous period, the farmers tend to increase the area brought under jhum cultivation. The population pressure reduces the jhum cycle Similarly, the curve, OE in Figure 4 doubles up as both the productivity curve as well as the state of the environment curve for the areas. If we assume that the present state of the environment is on the abscissa, then the farther you go from the origin the better the state of the environment.

Figure 4

Environment Trap

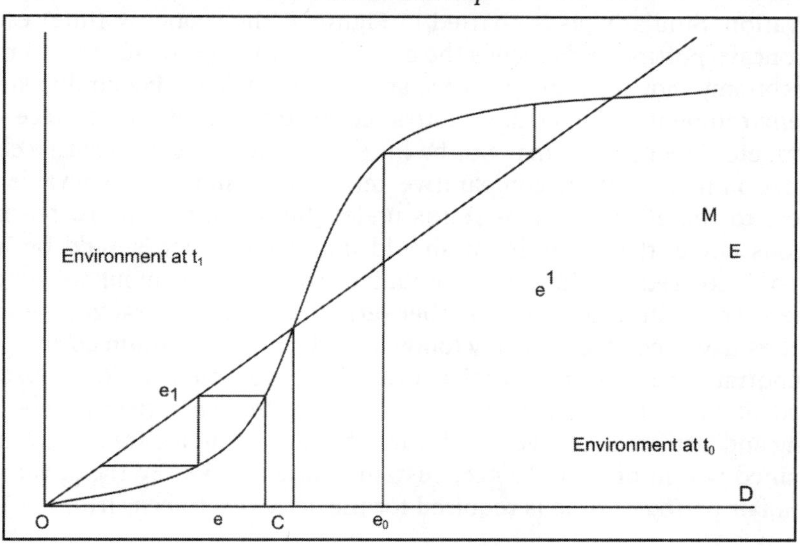

A similar analysis is possible if we think of agricultural product at time t_0 being on the x-axis of the above curve. In case of the latter, the readings from the curve can be thought of as incomes of the population.

The longer the periods of fallow, higher would be the benefits to the health of environment as also productivity. This would mean that the economy will be more towards the right as shown in the above figure. Similarly, a longer period of fallow has a beneficial effect on productivity as is evident from the product curve in the figure above. The natural fertility of the soil needs time to replenish itself. If the fallow period is short then the fertility of the soil would be low as the soil does not get enough time to replenish itself. In the traditional agricultural regime where there is no application of fertilizer, etc. low fertility of land leads to low productivity. Given the current state of the environment (product) the farmers are to the left of C in Figure 4. This means that at any point to the left of C, say e_0, the environment curve represents a future state of environment (product) e_1 which is to the left of e_0 and hence there is a comparative degradation of the environment. Hence, the agricultural model that is being followed in these parts is therefore harmful to the environment as also to the income of the farmers. It is harmful to the environment because forests are not given enough time to replenish it. This vicious cycle of impoverishment is set in motion because of the inability of farmers to shift to a different form of agriculture that is more efficient. In Figure 3, the more efficient form of production is represented by the terrace cultivation curve.

Alternative

It is however probable that because of a change in agricultural techniques either induced by increased investment or otherwise, the society as a whole shifts outward terrace cultivation method as represented by shift of terrace cultivation curve in Figure 3. This increases the productivity of labour and also has a beneficial impact on environment. The beneficial impact on the environment is vis-a-vis the earlier form of production, i.e. mainly jhum cultivation. Similarly, as is charted in Figure 4, the economy (line) escapes the concave portion and reaches the convex portion of the OE curve. From e_o the economy moves up in a positive spiral and reaches a favourable state as the environment is beneficially impacted by techniques like terrace cultivation, etc. The benefits may not be in terms of an absolute positive change in environment. But in comparative terms, this state is favourable with respect to the environmental status under jhum cultivation. To reach this virtuous circle, the government should intervene, which should be in the form of increased subsidies for alternative crops or investment subsidies for farmers who shift to terrace and other settled agricultural practices. As these societies have been traditionally following the practice of jhum cultivation, it is important that the intervention from the government is for a sustained period of time. The hold of traditional agricultural practices maybe quite strong and farmers may revert to jhum if the said subsidies are not given for a sustained period of time. Hence, sustained intervention by the government over a fair period of time is required for the activities to bear fruit.

The effect of urbanization and the migration to urban pockets in the state have also increased the jhum cycles in certain parts of the state. Urbanization may be beneficial to the environment to the extent that dependence of the population on the environmentally harmful practice of jhum comes down, thereby reducing the severity of the environment trap examined in the paper. However, urbanization brings with it a host of other environmental concerns which need to be addressed and understood in a separate paper.

References

Banerjee, A.V., Roland Benabou and Dilip Mookherjee (2007). *Understanding Poverty (Indian Edition)*, Oxford University Press, New Delhi.

Basu, K. and Annemie Maertens (2012). *The New Oxford Companion to Economics in India*, Oxford University Press, New Delhi.

Department of Planning and Co-ordination (2004). *Nagaland Human Development Report*, Government of Nagaland, Kohima.

Ray, D. (2007). *Development Economics*, Oxford University Press, New Delhi.

Roumasset, J. (2007). 'Population and Agricultural Development', in D.N. Blume et al. (eds), *The New Palgrave Dictionary of Economics*, Palgrave Macmillan, New York.

6

Development versus Environment

A Case of Industrialization (Bauxite Mining) in Koraput Region of Odisha

M. Gopinath Reddy

Industrialization is perceived as an inseparable part of economic development. Industrialization has the potential to help achieve a variety of social objectives such as employment, poverty eradication, gender equality, labour standards and greater access to education and health care. At the same time, industrial processes can have negative environmental impacts such as climate change, loss of natural resources, air and water pollution and extinction of species (European Commission, 2006). Activities like manufacturing, processing, transportation and consumption not only deplete the stock of natural resources but also add stress to the environmental system by accumulating the stock of wastes. However, public concern about the environmental problems emanating from the industrialization process has swelled significantly in recent times. The present paper looks at the ill-effects of industrialization in the state of Odisha. In this case, it is Bauxite Mining in Koraput region and its socio-economic and environmental effects that are analysed. The paper also looks at the shrinking land base of the local communities, which is their prime source of livelihood, due to bauxite mining in the region.

Context

Odisha is endowed with a variety of mineral resources and occupies an important position in India's mineral map. Among all the minerals, bauxite is prominent, and the state accounts for 51 per cent of Indian bauxite reserve, followed by Andhra Pradesh (21%).

Debate on the Positive and Negative Impacts of Mining

The conventional view on mining considers mineral reserves that can be mined profitably as part of a country's stock of natural capital, along with agricultural land, forests and other natural resources (Davis and Tilton, 2005). It was widely assumed that countries that possess rich mineral

Figure 1

Bauxite Reserves in India

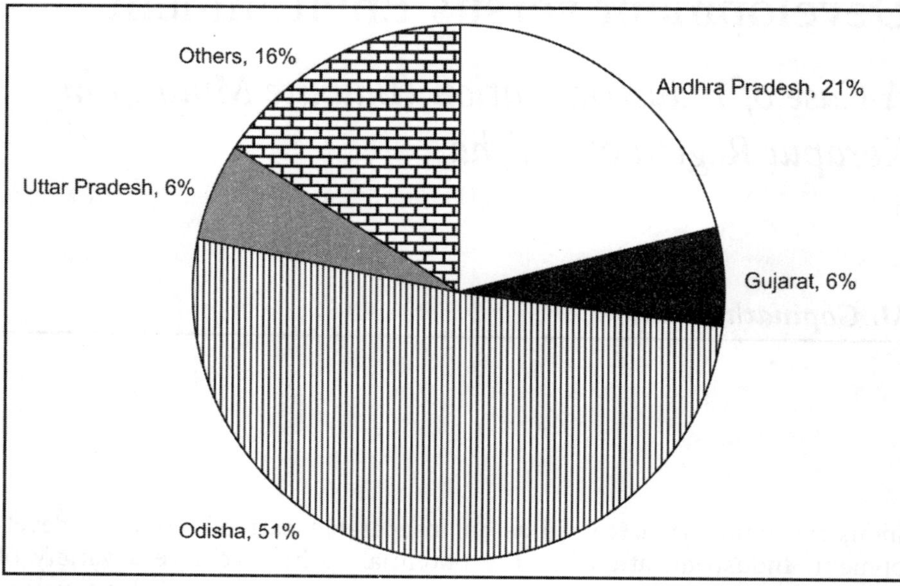

deposits are fortunate. However, over the last few decades, a more negative view of mining has emerged that questions the positive relationship between mineral extraction and economic development (Davis and Tilton, 2005). Mining profoundly impacts local communities in the form of jobs, migrant workers, land, water, air and noise, loss of wildlife habitat, increased tax revenue, etc.

Krishnaswamy et al. (2006) compared historic data with recent data and found out that mining and associated activities in Kudremukh National Park are the greatest sources of sediment entering the Bhadra River, which now carries considerably more sediment than before the mining activity started, damaging the river ecosystem and disrupting downstream water resources. Sinha, Bhattacharya and Banerjee (2007) studied the problem of local level sustainability of iron ore mining in eastern India. They tested the sustainability of iron ore mining in this region using household survey data. According to them, substitution of depleting natural capital with other forms of capital can promote long-term sustainability of the local economy. This necessitates certain policy interventions to induce mine operators to reinvest some part of their profit in the natural capital of the region.

Khatua and Stanley (2006) studied the lifestyle and livelihoods of affected communities, land use patterns, impact on natural resources and climate change in the context of mining. They focused on NALCO (National Aluminium Company) and its relationship with resource exploitation. However, the study is based only on secondary data. Patra and Murthy (year n.d.) came up with a fact-finding report on NALCO, which shows that the local tribal communities are complaining about air and dust pollution, noise emissions, unpleasant odour and discharge of untreated effluents. Stanley

(1996) explained how displacement in the NALCO area changed the occupational pattern of the local people and led to the division of society into social groups based on class, caste, tribe and sex. According to the study, mining added to the process of marginalization. Women's economic status deteriorated as they were forced to stay at home and were no longer considered as an economic asset.

The objectives of the study are:

1. To assess the socio-economic and environmental impacts and challenges of bauxite mining.
2. To analyse the policies adopted by NALCO to mitigate the effects.

The Methodology, Study Area and Sample Selection

This study has used both secondary and primary data. Secondary data are collected from the Indian Bureau of Mines, Economic Survey of Odisha, Statistical Abstract of Odisha, the websites of the Ministry of Environment and Forests, the Ministry of Tribal Affairs, Government of India, Odisha Mining Corporation, etc. To assess the positive and negative impacts of mining, Social Impact Assessment (SIA), also called Social Impact Analysis has been used in addition to the sustainable rural livelihoods framework. SIA refers to the processes and procedures for understanding and managing the social consequences of development activities. This include people's way of life, their culture, community, political and institutional systems, environment, health and well-being, personal and property rights, along with their fears and aspirations.

To study the micro impact of mining in general and bauxite mining in Odisha in particular, primary data has been collected. This study concentrates on Koraput District of Odisha because this district produces more than 98 per cent of the bauxite in Odisha. Bauxite mines in the Panchpatmali Hills of Koraput District have been considered for the study because this is the largest single bauxite deposit in the world.

NALCO was established in 1981 with the aim of producing aluminium from the vast bauxite deposits available in Koraput District of Odisha. It has three mining and extraction facilities in Odisha (Stanley, 1996):

1. Bauxite mines in the Panchpatmali Hills of Koraput District with deposits of 112.8 MT;
2. Alumina refinery complex in Damanjodi, Koraput District, 11 km from the mines. It has an installed capacity of eight lakh tonnes of alumina annually;
3. Smelter plant at Anugul District; 4.25 lakh tonnes are transported here. The plant has a captive power plant with a capacity of 55.5 MW as against its actual need of 32 MW.

Our study concentrates on the first two areas. It also includes villages near the Ash and Red Mud Pond (ARMP) areas. NALCO has divided the surrounding areas into two zones: core zones (area within a radius of 5 km either from the plant or the refinery) and buffer zones (area within a radius of 6 to 15 km either from the plant or the refinery). This has been decided by

NALCO in view of the severity of pollution effects. Villages have been selected from each zone for the study. There are 12 villages from three blocks surrounded by the refinery and nearly 40 villages from four Gram Panchayats surrounded by the mines. The criteria for selection of villages are: significant tribal population, pollution, crop loss, low compensation, health hazards, etc. There are about five to six villages under each area and the villages were selected using the above criteria besides taking the views of people's representatives. Amalabadi village was selected purposively as people from 13 displaced villages were resettled here (see Table 1 and Table 2).

Table 1

Sample Villages

Area	*Zone*	*Village*	*Total No. of Households*	*No. of Sample Households*
Mining Area	Core Zone	Kapsiput	142	38
	Buffer Zone	Kardiguda	79	21
		Putraghati	201	53
Refinery Area	Core Zone	Amalabadi	607	175
		Ambogam	133	36
	Buffer Zone	Mujanga	259	67
		Marichamal	77	21
Ash and Red Mud Ponds	Core Zone	Goudaguda	73	24
		Khoraguda	34	8
		Champapodar	84	10
	Buffer Zone	Charangaguda	72	23
Total			1761	476

Findings and Discussion: The following narration depicts the key finds and discussion of the consequences of the mining in the region on local ecology.

Table 2

Displacement Scenario of NALCO

Affected Villages	26	
Affected Families	Tribal	254 (42.55)
	Dalit	56 (9.38)
	Others	287 (48.07)
	Total	597 (100)
Land Acquired (acres)	Mines	427.30 (4.25)
	Township	2638.96 (26.24)
	Plant	6992.50 (69.52)
Total		10058.76 (100)

Source: Stanley (1996).

Note: Percentage in Parenthesis.

Stanley (1996) also examined the compensation package given by NALCO. Out of the displaced families, 74 per cent were rehabilitated and 59 per cent received jobs in compensation. Compensation per acre of land was ₹ 2,000 and compensation per tree was ₹ 100. However, there was no compensation for the Common Property Resources (CPRs) (see Table 3).

Table 3

Compensation Scenario of NALCO

Families Displaced	597
Families Rehabilitated	441 (73.87)
Jobs Received	352 (58.96)
Compensation per one acre of land (₹)	2000
Compensation per Tree	100
Compensation for CPRs	No

Source: Stanley (1996).

Note: Percentage in Parenthesis.

Demographic Details

A demographic picture of the affected villages is given below in the mining core zone, Kapsiput is our sample village. It has 142 households, out of which 141 households belong to the Scheduled Tribes category. In the mining buffer zone, Kardiguda and Putraghati are two sample villages. Kardiguda has 79 households and all belong to the Scheduled Tribes category. Putraghati has 201 households with mixed population (see Table 4).

Table 4

Demographic Features of Affected Villages

Study Zone	*Village*	*Panchayat*	*Block*	*Household Category*				
				SC	*ST*	*OBC*	*OC*	*Total*
Mining Core	Kapsiput	Bhifaarguda	Lakhimpur	1	141	0	0	142
Mining Buffer	Kardiguda	Littiguda	Koraput	0	79	0	0	79
	Putraghati			26	95	79	1	201
Refinery Core	Amalabadi	Matalput	Koraput	68	267	144	128	607
	Ambogam	Littiguda		2	131	0	0	133
Refinery Buffer	Mujanga	Mujanga	Dasamanthapur	143	93	0	23	259
	Marchimal	Matalput	Koraput	21	0	15	41	77
ARMP Core	Goudaguda	Charangul	Semiliguda	0	0	0	73	73
	Khoraguda	Podampur	Koraput	4	2	14	13	33
	Champapodar	Mujanga	Dasamanthapur	11	1	9	64	85
ARMP Buffer	Charangaguda	Podampur	Koraput	30	42	0	0	72

Source: Field Survey (2011).

In the refinery core zone, Amalabadi has 607 households. This is a rehabilitation colony consisting of 11 displaced hamlets of the refinery. It also has a mixed population. The second village in the refinery core zone, Ambogam, consists of 133 households, mostly tribal. This village is almost located in the refinery premises (1.2 km); this village was supposed to be displaced, but NALCO delayed the process and later on gave up the idea. These villagers are the victims of all immediate environmental impacts. In the refinery buffer zone, Mujanga Village has 259 households, dominated by Scheduled Castes and Scheduled Tribes. Marchimal is another village in this area having 77 households with a mixed population but no tribals.

In the ARMP core zone, Goudaguda is a village with 73 households. All the households belong to the Gouda caste, whose main occupation is livestock rearing. Both Khoraguda and Champapodar are displaced villages in this area. They are now resettled in one place but they still maintain different identities. Khoraguda has 33 households with a mixed population and Champapodar has 85 households, dominated by other castes. In the ARMP buffer zone, Charangaguda is a village with 72 households, dominated by Scheduled Castes and Scheduled Tribes population. Most of them have lost land because of the railway track constructed by NALCO. The next section shows the displacement scenario of the affected villagers.

Displacement and Compensation Scenario

In the mining core zone, 51 per cent of the households lost their agricultural land, and none of the households received any compensation for this. These villagers were practising *podu* on the top of the hills and on hill slopes. After getting permission to mine the area, NALCO evicted these villagers and disallowed them from cultivating those patches of land. As these displaced households do not have patta for their agricultural lands, they did not receive any compensation for that. In the mining buffer zone, 49 per cent of the households lost their agricultural land to the rehabilitation colony, conveyor belt and another road, which connects the mining area to the refinery site. Almost all the households here received compensation; only two households did not receive compensation because of unclear documentation. The compensation package was ₹ 1,000 to 1,500 per acre for dry land and ₹ 2,500 to 5,000 per acre for wet land (Table 5).

Table 5

Displacement and Compensation Scenario

Study Zone	*Total HHs*	*Affected HHs*	*Assets Lost*		*Compensation Received*	
			Land	*House*	*Land*	*House*
Mining Core	142	72 (50.70)	72	0	0	NA
Mining Buffer	280	138 (49.29)	138	0	136	NA
Refinery Core	740	383 (51.76)	141	361	129	344
Refinery Buffer	336	34 (10.12)	34	0	28	NA
ARMP Core	191	128 (67.02)	86	103	85	103
ARMP Buffer	72	38 (52.78)	38	0	36	NA

Source: Field Survey (2011).

Note: Percentage in Parenthesis

In the refinery core zone, 52 per cent of the households were affected by the refinery. Out of the affected households, 37 per cent (141 households) lost their agricultural land, and of these, 129 households received compensation, while it is still pending for others. The compensation package is the same. On the other hand, 94 per cent of the affected households (361 households) lost their home and homestead area; of these 344 households received compensation ranging from ₹ 500 to 5,000 depending on the type of home – hut, semi-pucca, pucca, etc. These households were also settled in the rehabilitation colony and provided with one job (per house) in NALCO.

On the other hand, in the refinery buffer zone only 10 per cent of the total households got affected. They lost their agricultural land to the refinery, and a part of the red mud pond. Out of the 34 households, 28 received compensation, while it is pending for the others.

In the ARMP core zone, 67 per cent of the households were affected; of these, 67 per cent of households lost their agricultural land. All the households received compensation excepting one. Further, in this area, 80 per cent of the households lost their home and homestead area. The compensation package is the same here.

In the ARMP buffer zone, 53 per cent of the households were affected; of these, 38 households lost their agricultural land and 36 were compensated. The next section compares the main occupation of the households in the pre- and post-displacement scenario.

As a part of the compensation package, NALCO provided job to those households that lost their home and homestead area. Therefore, it is interesting to study how the household's main occupation changed in the post-displacement scenario. It is to be noted here that we have only compared the main occupation of the households in the pre- and post-displacement scenario, irrespective of whether or not the household's head was the same person (see Table 6).

In the mining core zone, the main occupation of all households was farming during the pre-displacement period. However, in the post-displacement period, 36 per cent are engaged in NALCO as contract/wage employees – they are not permanent employees of the company. NALCO has assigned the contract works to contractors, who in turn recruit the contract/wage labour. Therefore, there is no job security for these people, and they receive weekly payment. The work in the company has been divided into four categories: high skilled works, skilled works, semi-skilled works, and unskilled works. According to the work category, the wage rates are: high skilled worker – ₹ 330 per day; skilled worker – ₹ 280 per day; semi-skilled worker – ₹ 220 per day; and unskilled worker – ₹ 190 per day. In the mining buffer zone, farming was the main occupation (82%) during the pre-displacement period followed by wage labour. However, this per cent came down in the post-displacement period and now NALCO contract/wage labour is the main occupation.

Table 6

Main Occupation of the Households: Pre- and Post-Displacement

Main Occupation	*Mining Core Zone*		*Mining Buffer Zone*		*Refinery Core Zone*		*Refinery Buffer Zone*		*ARMP Core Zone*		*ARMP Buffer Zone*	
	Pre	*Post*	*Pre*	*Post*	*Pre*	*Post*	*Pre*	*Post*	*Pre*	*Post*	*Pre*	*Post*
Farmers	118 (100)	75 (63.6)	193 (81.8)	78 (33.1)	665 (94.5)	71 (10.1)	165 (54.8)	100 (33.2)	164 (85.9)	16 (8.4)	38 (52.8)	1 (1.4)
Wage Labourers	0		43 (18.2)		27 (3.8)	207 (29.4)	132 (43.9)	172 (57.1)	22 (11.5)	90 (47.1)	34 (47.2)	65 (90.3)
Others	0			9 (3.8)	12 (1.7)	33 (4.7)	4 (1.3)	19 (6.3)	5 (2.6)	7 (3.7)	0	3 (4.2)
NALCO Contract/Wage Employee	NA	43 (36.4)		149 (63.1)	NA	98 (13.8)	NA	10 (3.3)	NA	9 (4.7)	NA	3 (4.2)
NALCO Permanent Employees					NA	295 (41.9)	NA		NA	69 (36.1)	NA	
Total	118 (100)	118 (100)	236 (100)	236 (100)	704 (100)	704 (100)	301 (100)	301 (100)	191 (100)	191 (100)	72 (100)	72 (100)

Source: Field Survey (2011).

In the refinery core zone, farming was the main occupation during the pre-displacement period (94.5%). However, in the post-displacement period, majority of the people are permanent employees of NALCO – this job was the compensation package for the many households that lost their homestead area in this zone. This is followed by wage labour and NALCO contract work. In the refinery buffer zone, during the pre-displacement period both farming and wage labour were the major occupations. However, post-displacement, wage labour has outweighed farming. Since the extent of displacement was very less here, number of workers employed in NALCO as contract/wage employed is very less (only 3.3%).

Similarly, in the ARMP core zone also, farming was the main occupation during the pre-displacement period. In the post-displacement scenario, wage labour and employment in NALCO became the main occupations. Here also the households lost their homestead land and were provided permanent employment in NALCO. In the ARMP buffer zone, the main occupation was farming and wage labour. However, in the post-displacement period it was dominantly wage labour. Because of water problem and other environmental impacts, farming is no more a profitable occupation now. As the contractors are exploiting the NALCO contract employees, these people prefer to work as wage labourers rather than as contract employees.

Besides the problems listed above, there are certain environmental and ecological problems observed in the field. Dust emanating from the conveyor belt carrying bauxite ore is affecting the agricultural lands and hence their productivity. Unfortunately, there is no mechanism to compensate such losses. Natural resources such as ponds and streams were adversely damaged due to mining and the conveyor belt; hence the water sources got totally diminished.

Leakage in Septic Water Pipe Line in Goudaguda Village

During the survey, some of the following problems were identified in Goudaguda Village: Leakage in caustic soda and septic water pipeline led to septic water flows into the agricultural fields; hence soil fertility was affected and crop production decreased. The canal water is contaminated due to caustic mud and septic water. According to the village elders, due to water contamination caused by caustic mud and septic water, a few livestock died in 1995. For this, the villagers fought against NALCO and received compensation. However, the people are facing health problems such as skin ailments, TB, and other health-related issues.

Mining and its Effects on Common Property Resources (CPRs)

In tribal and hilly habitations, CPRs play an important role in the subsistence of the livelihoods of the poor and the marginalized. In particular, in these regions, unlike in the plain areas, access and availability of CPRs to the village communities in terms of basic needs, such as grazing pastures, ponds, streams, and minor forest produce (from forests) plays an important role for their livelihood. Access to these is usually free and unrestricted, since CPRs are open access resources. However, it may be observed that though various CPRs are available in the sample villages, most of them have been affected by the refinery and ARMP areas. NALCO acquired most of the CPRs such as common lands, streams and grazing land for laying roads, constructing the conveyor belt and building colonies, particularly in the refinery (core) areas. Due to the factory activities, the streams have been logged/blocked and forest access to the community is very much restricted. In some villages, the streams and canals are contaminated due to emissions from the plant (see Table 7–9).

As already mentioned, CPRs significantly enhance the livelihood of the poor in the villages. Mostly, their access is open to all sections of the society. It was observed that NALCO acquired village common land in eight out of the twelve sample villages. Unfortunately, no compensation was paid by NALCO to the village communities and the reason offered is that these were forest lands, which did not have 'pattas'. Even in case of grazing land, the same scenario was observed. The loss of these important resources has huge bearing on the livestock holding capacity of the communities

The data on various sources of drinking water for the sample households in the project area indicate that among surface water sources, streams and ponds (cent percent in the mining core zone and refinery core zone), followed by canals and streams, are the chief sources of water supply. Among the groundwater sources, well and water supply systems (90.5% in the refinery core zone; 77.3% in the refinery buffer zone; and 45% in the ARMP core zone) are the principal sources of water, followed by hand pumps (71.6% in the mining buffer zone). In terms of impact of pollution due to mining on the water sources, the data reveal that water is very polluted in some zones (cent percent in the mining core and buffer zones; 79.5% in the refinery buffer zone; and 55% in the ARMP core zone), while the rest is not polluted. Basically, wherever water is available through streams and ponds, it is polluted and if the source is through the water supply system it is not polluted.

The analysis of the households' opinions of the various effects of mining reveals that they are experiencing air and sound pollution (cent per cent in mining core and buffer zones; 88.6% and 95.5% respectively in the refinery core and buffer zones; and 75% and 96% respectively in the ARMP core and buffer zones). This is followed by other effects such as deforestation and consequent decline in wildlife population in the project area (36.8% and 14.9% respectively in the mining core and buffer zones; 23.2% and 26.1% respectively in the refinery core and buffer zones; and 72.5% and 56% respectively in the ARMP core and buffer zones). Some households in the mining area mentioned that streams have been destroyed and as a result, they are facing water shortage (63.2% in the core zone and 40.5% in the buffer zone).

Table 7

Details of the Common Property Resources (CPRs)

Area	*Zone*	*Village*	*Availability of CPRs*	*Impact on CPRs*	*Details*
Mining Area	Core	Kapsiput	Streams, forest, and common lands	Yes	Streams are logged, forest is restricted, and common land totally acquired
	Buffer	Kardiguda	Streams, forest lands, ponds, etc.	Yes	Streams destroyed, water logged
		Putraghati	Canal, streams, village forest, grazing lands, and graveyard	Yes	NALCO occupied all the common land streams and grazing lands for the roads, conveyor belt, and R&R colony
Refinery Area	Core	Amalabadi	Canal, streams, village forest, grazing lands, and graveyard	Yes	NALCO occupied all the common land streams and grazing lands for the roads, conveyor belt, and R&R colony
		Ambogam	Forest and streams	Yes	NALCO occupied all the common land, streams, and grazing lands for the roads and conveyor belt
	Buffer	Mujanga	Forest, streams, ponds, tamarind trees, and other forest products	Yes	Due to red mud pond the CPRs are disturbed
		Marichamal	Canal and forest	Yes	Canal water declined due to water logging
Ash & Red Mud Ponds	Core	Goudaguda	Canal, stream, and forest	Yes	Stream and canal are contaminated due to caustic water and septic water
		Khoraguda	Forest	Yes	Restricted
		Champapodar	Forest	Yes	Restricted
	Buffer	Charangaguda	Hill forest and stream	Yes	NALCO acquired some of the land

Source: Field Survey (2011).

Table 8

Details of the Common Property Resource (CPR) Acquisition

Area	*Zone*	*Village*	*CPR Acquired*	*Village Common Land*				
				Acquired	*Land Possessed (in acres)*	*Land Lost (in acres)*	*Amount Offered*	*Reasons for not Receiving*
Mining	Core	Kapsiput	Yes	Yes	Not Known	Not known	0	Not offered because it is forest land and there is no patta
	Buffer	Kardiguda	Yes	Yes	Not known	Not known	0	Not offered because it is forest land and there is no patta
		Putraghati	Yes	Yes	4	0	0	Reason not known, but no amount was offered
Refinery	Core	Amalabadi	Yes	Yes	0	0	0	Reason not known, but no amount was offered
		Ambogam	Yes	Yes	0	0	0	Reason not known, but no amount was offered
	Buffer	Mujanga	No	_	0	0	0	0
		Marichamal	No	_	0	0	0	0
Ash & Red Mud Pond	Core	Goudaguda	No	_	0	0	0	0
			Khoraguda	Yes	_	0	0	0
		Champa-podar	Yes	_	0	0	0	Not offered because it is forest land and there is not patta
	Buffer	Charang-aguda	Yes	_	0	0	0	0

Village Grazing Land					*Common Forest Land*				
Acquired	*Land Possessed (in acres)*	*Land Lost (in acres)*	*Amount Offered*	*Reasons for not Receiving*	*Acquired*	*Land Possessed (in acres)*	*Land Lost (in acres)*	*Amount Offered*	*Reasons for not Receiving*
Yes	Not known	Not known	0	Not offered because it is forest land and there is no patta	Yes	Not known	0	0	Not offered because it is forest land and there is no patta
Yes	Not known	Not known	0	Not offered because it is forest land and there is no patta	Yes	Not known	0	0	Not offered because it is forest land and there is no patta
Yes	3	3	0	Reason not known, but no amount was offered	Yes	300	300	0	Reason not known, but no amount was offered
Yes	Not known	Not known	0	Reason not known, but no amount was offered	Yes	Not known	Not known	0	Reason not known, but no amount was offered
Yes	Not known	Not known	0	Reason not known, but no amount was offered	Yes	Not known	Not known	0	Reason not known, but no amount was offered
0	0	0	0	0	0	0	0	0	0
0	0	0	0	0	0	0	0	0	0
0	0	0	0	0	0	0	0	0	0
Not offered because it is forest land and there is not patta	Yes	Not known	Not known	0	Not offered because it is forest land and there is not patta	Yes	Not known	Not known	0
Yes	Not known	Not known	0	Not offered because it is forest land and there is not patta	Yes	Not known	Not known	0	Not offered because it is forest land and there is not patta
0	0	0	0	0	0	0	0	0	0

Table 9

Source of Drinking Water

Area	*Zone*	*Surface*				*Ground Water*						*Impact of Pollution*		
		Canal	*Streams and Pond*	*Canal and Stream*	*Total*	*Well*	*Well and Water Supply System*	*Leakage Water from NALCO Pipeline*	*Hand Pump*	*Water Supply from Stream*	*Total*	*Not Polluted*	*Polluted*	*Total*
Mining	Core		38 (100)		38 (100)								38 (100)	38 (100)
	Buffer			22 (100)	22 (100)				53 (71.6)	21 (28.4)	74 (100)		74 (100)	74 (100)
Refinery	Core		20 (100)		20 (100)	20 (9.5)	191 (90.5)				211 (100)	175 (82.9)	36 (17.1)	211 (100)
	Buffer	14 (100)			14 (100)	20 (22.7)	67 (77.3)				88 (100)	18 (20.5)	70 (79.5)	88 (100)
Ash & Red Mud Pond	Core					22 (55.0)	18 (45.0)				40 (100)	18 (45.0)	22 (55.0)	40 (100)
	Buffer							25 (100)			25 (100)	25 (100)		25 (100)

Table 10

Households' Opinions on the Affects of Mining

Area	Zone	Opinion 1		Opinion 2		Opinion 3		Opinion 4		
		No opinion	Degrading soil fertility due to smoke and dust	No opinion	Due to leakages of red mud pond and septic water pipelines villagers are facing health problems and also crop are getting damaged	No opinion	Air and sound pollution	No opinion	Due to mining streams are destroyed and people are facing water shortage	Due to mining and deforestation wild life population has totally decreased
Mining	Core	28 (73.7)	10 (26.3)	38 (100)	0 (0.0)	0 (0.0)	38 (100)	0 (0.0)	24 (63.2)	14 (36.8)
	Buffer	51 (68.9)	23 (31.1)	74 (100)	0 (0.0)	0 (0.0)	74 (100)	33 (44.6)	30 (40.5)	11 (14.9)
Refinery	Core	173 (82.0)	38 (18.0)	211 (100)	0 (0.0)	24 (11.4)	187 (88.6)	162 (76.8)	0 (0.0)	49 (23.2)
	Buffer	70 (79.5)	18 (20.5)	88 (100)	0 (0.0)	4 (4.5)	84 (95.5)	65 (73.9)	0 (0.0)	23 (26.1)
Ash & Red Mud Pond	Core	18 (45.0)	22 (55.0)	20 (50.0)	20 (50.0)	10 (25.0)	30 (75.0)	11 (27.5)	0 (0.0)	29 (72.5)
	Buffer	14 (56.0)	11 (44.0)	25 (100)	0 (0.0)	1 (4.0)	24 (96.0)	11 (44.0)	0 (0.0)	14 (56.0)

Source: Field Survey (2011).

Conclusion

NALCO, a profit-making public sector undertaking and a Navaratna Company called 'the pride of Odisha' shall not really be characterized as such from the perspective of the affected population. It is evident that the most vulnerable sections, viz. the Scheduled Tribes and Scheduled Castes who have lost lands, houses, and other assets could not get back their livelihood status as a result of NALCO's cash compensation policy. Since land scarcity was not there in the 80s as it is felt now, NALCO should have adopted a land-for-land policy.

With the emergence of the NALCO mining industry, the occupational profile of the households has changed from predominantly farming to NALCO contract/wage employment. Even though permanent employment in NALCO gives good income in terms of assured salaries, the contract/wage employment and the income accrued from it is far from satisfactory. Further, the households have lost self-esteem in the process of displacement, as majority of them whose main occupation was farming, are now working as contract/wage labour.

In the context of NALCO, the major economic activity of the people was agriculture before mines came into being. At that time, most of the households from all the villages were having agriculture and *podu* lands – they practised traditional agriculture such as *podu* cultivation, and their secondary occupation was NTFP collection for both self-consumption and sale. Earlier, all the resources, including natural water streams, fish ponds, hillocks, grazing lands, common lands and plenty of forest products were available in this area. However, NALCO acquired the agriculture lands, *podu* lands and other forest lands; and due to mining and refinery, most of the households from the surrounding areas lost their agriculture lands and have been restricted from entering into mining and refinery areas. Due to these changes, the people switched from agriculture to non-farm activities.

In the mining area, due to the mining activity and the conveyor belt, some of the natural streams got destroyed, while some others were diverted into the mining site. Hence, people from the surrounding villages are facing water shortage. Further, due to the mining activity, the stream water is contaminated; and due to the conveyor belt, the people are also suffering from sound pollution. In the refinery and ARMP areas, the surrounding villages are affected by smoke, caustic water and fluids. As the water is contaminated, the agriculture fields' fertility is affected, and crop production has been affected. Further, pollution has also affected the livestock. Hence, NALCO has to take some more preventive measures to reduce air, sound and water pollution.

On the whole, the resettlement and rehabilitation measures by NALCO are found to be piecemeal and ad hoc. The company with its huge profit base could have done much more for these marginalized people. It was observed that the people of the nearby villages still do not have the basic necessities of life such as drinking water, schooling, medical facilities, etc. The Government of Odisha and NALCO should work in unison to improve these areas possessing a rich mineral resource.

References

Davis, Graham A. and John E. Tilton (2005). 'The Resource Curse', *Natural Resources Forum*, 29(3): 233–42.

European Commission (2006). *Environment Fact Sheet: Industrial Development*, Miami University Libraries, Oxford, Ohio.

Khatua, Sanjay and William Stanley (2006). 'Ecological Debt: A Case Study from Orissa, India', in Athena K. Peralta (ed.), *Ecological Debt: The Peoples of the South are Creditors: Cases from Ecuador, Mozambique, Brazil and India*, World Council of Churches, Trioka Press, Quezon City, Philippines.

Krishnaswamy, Jagdish, Milind Bunyan, Vishal K. Mehta, Niren Jain and K. Ullas Karanth (2006). 'Impact of Iron Ore Mining on Suspended Sediment Response in a Tropical Catchment in Kudremukh Western Ghats, India', *Forest Ecology and Management*, 224: 187–98.

Sinha, Suranjan, Rabindra N. Bhattacharya and Rajasree Banerjee (2007). 'Surface Iron Ore Mining in Eastern India and Local Level Sustainability', *Resources Policy*, 32(1-2): 57–68.

Stanley, W. (1996). 'Machkund, Upper Kolab and NALCO Projects in Koraput District, Orissa', *Economic and Political Weekly*, 31(24): 1533–38.

7

Living Environment and its Impact on Socio-Economic Vulnerability and Well-Being of the Slum Dwellers

A Case Study of Delhi

Pravin Kumar Shukla

In the 21st century, rapid urbanization is one of the most important changes taking places in the countries of Asia, Latin America and Africa. The latest Census (2011) shows that Delhi harbours 16,753,235 persons with a population density of 11,297 persons per square km the highest density ever reached after 1951. Delhi registered impressive population growth after 1911; but it declined remarkably during the decade of 2001–2011, registering 21.0 per cent. Today, cities are home to almost half of the global population, consume close to three quarters of the natural resources and generate a significant proportion of wastes and pollution. Globalization, economic restructuring and lack of employment opportunity in rural areas are causing massive rural to urban migration. Unchecked rural to urban migration overburdens urban infrastructure, amenities and resources, particularly housing. Thus, a significant proportion of the urban poor, who cannot afford formal housing, find shelter in slums and squatter settlements. Thus, unprecedented urban growth, infrastructural inadequacy, environmental degradation and slum development are the foremost issues haunting urban planners and policy makers. These issues throw numerous challenges to the environment and human health, which include encroachment of vacant lands, water bodies, crop lands and greeneries for urban infrastructure building, and consequent loss of biodiversity, inadequate provisions of potable drinking water, sanitation and drainage especially in slums.

Literature Review

Environmental psychologists have emphasized that the living environment has a direct impact on the overall psychological development of human beings. There is a strong bond and interaction, both positive and negative, between an individual and his or her immediate surroundings (Bell, Greene, Fisher and Baum et al., 2001; Seamon and Mugerauer, 1985). The housing or shelter is one of the most important basic necessities of human beings and an essential part of a person's living environment (Smith, 1973; Sinha, 1969); it is also indicative of a person's socio-economic status as well as affluence (Kulkarni, 1990). The houses are man-made structures, which are used either to live in, or work in or to store things in (Bryan, 1933). A house with the basic amenities of water, sanitation and domestic energy, ensures privacy, safety and dignity. Formal housing with all basic facilities is the right of every human being. Unfortunately, a significant portion of population resides in dilapidated houses. A major portion of them cannot even afford to buy a formal house. Economic condition forces them to live in a slum environment (Roy et al., 2007). People living in unauthorized squatter settlements, in addition to being deprived of most urban facilities, live under the constant fear of eviction. However, people living in older slums do enjoy better socio-economic status and enjoy tenure security (Kingsley and Kristof, 1971; Mahadevia, 2009). Health vulnerability is very high in these slums; the most frequent diseases reported in the slums are malaria, dysentery, cholera, jaundice and typhoid which are closely related to poor environmental condition (Desai, 1995: 186). In spite of degraded living environment and hardship, slum dwellers prefer to live in the cities and most of them consider that life in slum is tolerable and better than the rural life (Gill, 1994: 60–85). The National Commission on Urbanization has recognized the most visible forms of urban poverty as proliferation of slums, growth of the informal sector, crushing pressure on civic amenities, high cost of educational and health contingencies, underutilization of social services and growing sense of hopelessness (Government of India, 1988). The Planning Commission has recognized various types of urban vulnerabilities in the Tenth Five-Year Plan (2002-2007), these include: *housing vulnerability* (lack of access to tenure security, poor shelter, lack of access to individual services and unsanitary living condition), *economic vulnerability* (irregular or casual employment, low pay, lack of access to formal credit, safety net programmes, low ownership of productive assets, legal constraints to self employment), *social vulnerability* (low level of education, lack of access to skills, low social status, inadequate access to food security programmes, lack of access to health services and exclusion from local institution), *personal vulnerability* (proneness to violence, lack of access to justice and awareness about rights of women, children, disabled, widow and destitute). Therefore, vulnerability has many dimensions and all these three dimensions of vulnerability are closely intertwined; social and economic vulnerability leads to housing vulnerability and housing vulnerability has a direct impact on the living environment which further aggravates socio-economic conditions of the residents (see Figure 1). This process is clearly visible in the urban slums; therefore, this paper focuses on the impact of the living environment on the socio-economic condition and well-being of the slum dwellers.

Figure 1

Types of Vulnerabilities

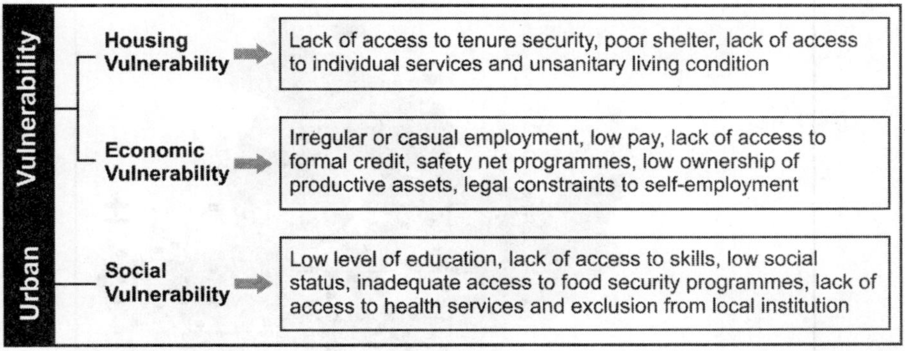

Gaps in Literature

Though many studies have been conducted on the socio-economic conditions of the slum dwellers and their housing crisis, but very few of them look at this issue in a holistic way. Therefore, in this paper an attempt has been made to see how living environment enhances socio-economic vulnerabilities of the urban poor.

Selection of the Study Area

Delhi, the national capital of India attracts many million migrants, and housing crisis is an obvious outcome of migrant influx. Thus, the city is dotted with several slums, unauthorized Jhuggi-Jhompri colonies (JJ colonies) or squatter settlements and other forms of informal housings.

The walled city records for the highest percentage of population living in slums: The Yamuna Pushta and Trans-Yamuna region contain highest number of squatter settlements while the other parts of Delhi also contain large amounts of slum dwellers living under extremely deplorable condition. In 2007, Chief Minister Sheila Dikshit had claimed that the JJ colonies in Delhi would soon be history and that the government would construct adequate low cost flats for slum dwellers and economically weaker section of the society and they would no longer be witness of forceful eviction, bulldozers in slums and uprooting of slums; that 'Slum dwellers especially those who are living in the squatters will be provided a respectful address in four-storey complex with ownership right' (*The Asian Age*, 10 June 2007). In spite of the Chief Minister's declaration of providing formal housing to the urban poor, Delhi still has a large number of people living in squatter settlements and slums. Ruhi Bhasim remarked in the *Times of India* (8 June 2007) that 'the MCD has no proper layout plan nor regularized the unauthorised colonies; it will take at least three years to get the legal tag to provide basic amenities to these JJ colonies with proper sewer and water supply. 'People living in the low income colonies of Kalyanpuri, Sunlight colony, Janata Mazdoor colony, Tigri slum, Sangam Vihar and many other do not have adequate access to sanitation, water supply, electricity and drainage' (*The Hindu*, 4 June 2007). The massive relocation of slums from the city core to

Delhi: Ward Map

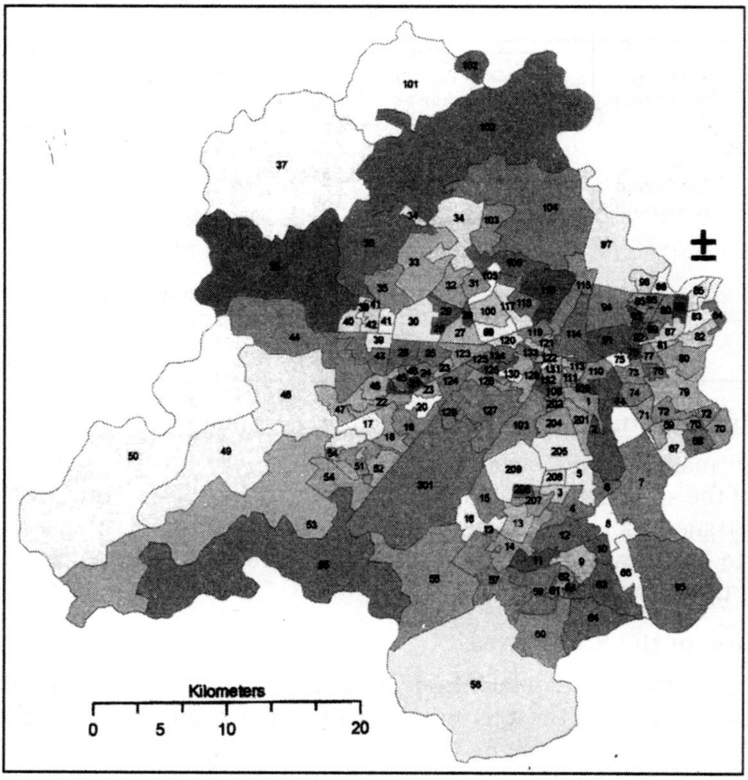

the periphery in connection with the Commonwealth Games has changed the scenario remarkably.

The objectives of this paper are the following:

1. To identify wards with highest concentration of slum households and households living in environmentally vulnerable condition.
2. To identify variations in the living environment of the slums depending on their locations
3. To identify the nature of various types of vulnerability experienced by the slum dwellers living in Delhi NCT.

Following methodology has been adopted for analysis:

1. Extraction of data on urban growth, density, areal changes from the Census 2001 and 1991; joining operations of spatial and Census data.
2. Thematic mapping using GIS technique.
3. Composite Index: With the help of Z-score method, composite index has been constructed and with the help of the average Z-score values, ward level deprivation mapping has been done. Formula used for this technique is where: μ is the mean of the population; σ is the standard deviation of the population.

The quantity z represents the distance between the raw score and the population mean in units of the standard deviation. Z is negative when the raw score is below the mean, positive when above. In statistics, a standard score indicates by how many standard deviations an observation or datum is above or below the mean. It is a dimensionless quantity derived by subtracting the population mean from an individual raw score and then dividing the difference by the population standard deviation.

Urban Growth and Regional Concentration of Slums in NCT Delhi

Delhi has a large expatriate population; according to the new Indian census conducted in 2011, the city harbours 16,753,235 people and its average population density is 11,297 persons per square km Delhi has registered impressive population growth after 1911 and reached the highest density in 2011 (see Table 1).

Table 1

Variation in Decadal Population Growth in Delhi (1901–2011)

Census Year	*Population*	*Percentage*
1901	4,05,819	–
1911	4,13,851	2
1921	4,88,452	18
1931	6,36,246	30
1941	9,17,939	44.30
1951	17,44,072	90
1961	26,58,612	52.40
1971	40,65,698	52.90
1981	62,20,406	53
1991	94,20,406	51.40
2001	1,37,82,976	46.30
2011	1,67,53,235	21.60

Source: Census of India, 2011, Provisional Population Total.

Figure 2

Demographic Transition in Delhi (1901–2011)

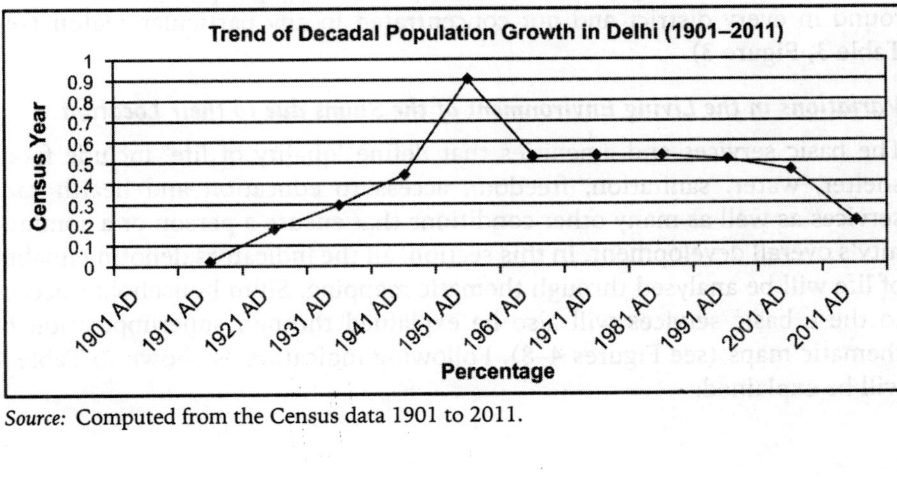

Source: Computed from the Census data 1901 to 2011.

According to Census 2011, the recent decline in population growth is mainly due to shifting of slums from the main city to the peripheral areas, especially during the Commonwealth Games. Major slum clusters were removed during the mid-2000s; these slum clusters include the widespread Yamuna Pusta, Kalakaji, Gautam Nagar clusters and many others. Maximum decadal growth takes place in south-west, north-west and north-east districts due to slum rehabilitation colonies at Narela, Bhalswa and so on (see Figure 2).

Table 2

Population Growth Rate, Percentage Slum Population and Migrant Population (1991–2001)

Municipal Corporation	*Growth Rate (%)*		*Slum Population (%)*	*UAs*	*Migrant Population (%)*
	1991	*2001*	*2001*		*2001*
Delhi	56.9	8.8	18.89	Delhi	16.4
Mumbai	20.2	20.2	52.03	Mumbai	15.1
Kolkata	6.3	4.33	32.53	Kolkata	6.2
Chennai	15.8	11.1	17.72	Chennai	6.6

Source: Census of India, 2001.

According to Table 2, Delhi contains the largest amount of migrant population among the four Indian metropolises and a significant number of them reside in slums.

Spatial distribution of slum households in Delhi exhibits a unique pattern; wards lying in the core city (Central and North Delhi) record for the highest percentage of households residing in slums. Concentration of slum households tapers off from the city core to the periphery. Moderate concentration of slum household is found along the river of Yamuna and trans-Yamuna region in the east Delhi. In the periphery, South Delhi, R.K.Puram areas have the maximum concentration of slum households in its different wards. Another unique feature is that a significant number of slum households are found throughout, from the city core to the periphery, and they are found in every district and not concentrated in any particular region (see Table 3, Figure 3).

Variations in the Living Environment of the Slums due to their Location

The basic services and amenities that define 'quality of life' include food, shelter, water, sanitation, freedom, access to education and health care services as well as many other conditions that ensure a person or a community's overall development. In this section, all the indicators denoting quality of life will be analysed through thematic mapping. Slum household's access to these basic services will also be explained through superimposition of thematic maps (see Figures 4–8). Following indicators as shown in Table 4 will be explained:

Table 3

Ward Level Concentration of Slums in Delhi (2001)

Zones	*Wards*	*District*	*Location*	*Characteristics*
Zone 1	Sadar Bazar (122), Quassabpura (112), Paharganj (108), Darya Ganj (109), Manakpura (132), Qadam Sharif (131), Bazar Sitaram	Central Delhi and North Delhi	Core city	Highest percentage of households live in slums (more than 80%)
Zone 2	Wards adjacent to zone 1 Ballimaran (111), etc.	Central Delhi and North Delhi	Core city	60 to 80 per cent of the total households live in slums
Zone 3	South Patel Nagar (126), Ramesh Nagar (124), Jama Masjid (110), Civil Lines (114), some wards of NDMC, etc.	North Delhi, Central Delhi and parts of East Delhi	Core city	More than 40 but less than 60 per cent households live in slums
Zone 4	Jahangirpur (103), Shahdara (81)R.K Puram (15), Mustafabad(98), Yamuna Vihar (95), Srinivaspuri (8),	North-West Delhi, North-East Delhi, parts of South Delhi	Periphery (Trans-Yamuna and Yamuna bank)	More than 20 to less than 40 per cent living in slums
Zone 5	Some wards of South-West Delhi, South Delhi, East Delhi	South West Delhi, South Delhi, East Delhi	Peripheral part	Less than 20 per cent households live in slums

Figure 3

Ward-wise Distribution of Households Living in Slums: Delhi (2001)

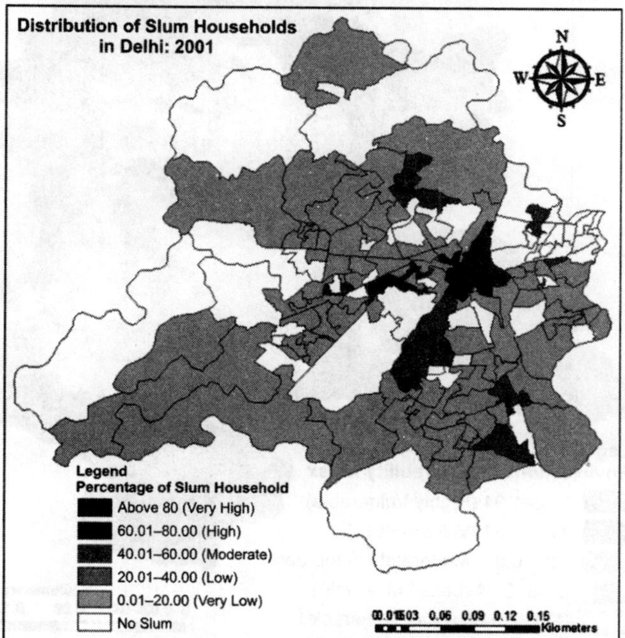

Source Census of India, 2001.

Table 4

List of Indicators for Measuring 'Environmental Vulnerability Index'

Percentage of kutcha houses	Percentage of households having access to pit latrines
Percentage of semi-pucca houses	Percentage of households having open drainage for waste water outlets
Percentage of Household with no exclusive room	Percentage of households having no drainage
Percentage of household with one room	Percentage of households not having access to none of the specified assets (television, radio, two or four wheelers, phone)
Percentage of households using firewood, crop residue and cow dung as cooking fuel	Percentage of households not having access to bank account
Percentage of households using coal, lignite, biogas, kerosene as cooking fuel	
Percentage of households not using electricity as the source of lighting	
Percentage of households having no latrine facility within houses	

Figure 4

Delhi: Environmental Vulnerability Index (2001)

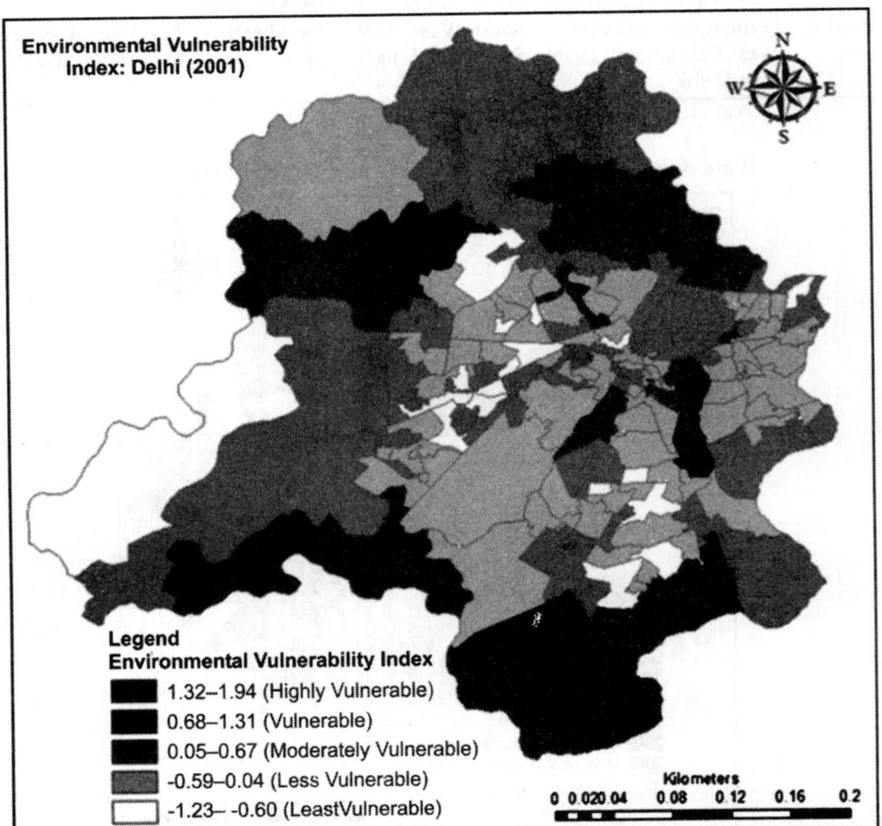

Source: Computed from Census of India, 2001.

Table 5

Spatial Distribution of Environmentally Vulnerable Wards in Delhi (2001)

Zones	*Areas*
Highly Vulnerable	Nizamudin(2), Pahladpur, Bangar(36), Sangam Vihar(64), Chattarpur (58), Harkesh Nagar (66)
Vulnerable	Mintoroad,Kanjhawala, Karawal Nagar, Jama Masjid
Moderately Vulnerable	Bijwasan, Tuglaka Bad, Seema Puri, Jaffrabad, Mustafabad, Jahangir Pur, Burari, Adarsh Nagar, Rana Pratap Bagh, Anand Parbat
Less Vulnerable	Rest Of Delhi
Least Vulnerable	Saket,Greater Kailash,Defence Colony, Rohini, Ward 208 and 206 Of NDMC Area

Source: Computed from Census of India, 2001.

Environmental vulnerability is the highest in some peripheral wards of South Delhi (Chattarpur), East Delhi (trans-Yamuna region), Sangham Vihar, Harkesh Nagar and some core regions like Nizamuddin, Minto Road, Kanjhawala, Karawal Nagar and Jama Masjid. In these regions the percentage of kutcha and semi-pucca houses are identical. The core areas have the highest percentage of authorized slums and in the peripheral areas authorized slums are less in number but the number of unauthorized ones is very high. In these regions, very few households have access to LPG or safe cooking fuel, hygienic sanitation facility, proper drainage and certain basic assets like television, radio, private vehicles and bank account. In the core region, though most of the households have access to assets and basic amenities, many of them live without any room of their own or live in one roomed dwelling units. Thus, environmental vulnerability exists both in the core and in the peripheral areas; but the nature of vulnerability differs; while the former group suffers from adequate space, the latter suffers from inadequate access to certain amenities and infrastructure.

Social and Economic Vulnerabilities Experienced by the Slum Dwellers

Slums are not only the physical manifestation of degraded living environment but also the breeding ground of social and economic backwardness. Various socio-economic indicators like literacy rate, percentage of non-workers, marginal workers, sex ratio, and percentage distribution of Scheduled Caste (SC) or deprived classes show the socio-economic profile of Delhi's slums.

Literacy rate is very low in Delhi's slums; literacy rate above 70 per cent is recorded in ward number 108 (Pahar Ganj), 107 (Bazar Sita Ram), 81 (Shahdara), 129 (Beadenpura), 121 (Sabzi Mandi), 131 (Qadam Sharif), 133 (Kishan Ganj), 120 (Shastri Nagar) (84%). Slum literacy rate is the lowest in ward numbers 39 (Kirari Suleman Nagar) and 67 (Dallopara ward). Many wards in South Delhi, South-West Delhi, New Delhi and West Delhi have registered very low literacy rate (below 40%).

Wards with very high percentage of scheduled caste population living in slums are found in the core city. In ward numbers 131-Qadam Sharif (62%), 77-Krishna Nagar (67%), 80-Viswas Nagar (60%), 76-Raghubarpura (92%),

Figure 5 and 6

Slum Literacy and Percentage of Scheduled Castes Living in Slums

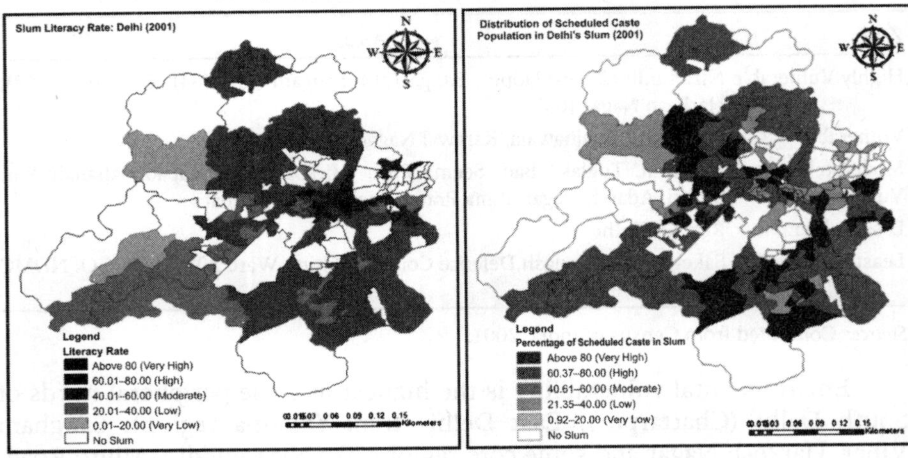

Source: Census of India, 2001.

68 (Dallu Pura), 5 (New Delhi), 42-Mangolpuri (90%), as also in some wards of Delhi Cantonment like Tigri – ward number 60, more than 60 per cent of slum dwellers are scheduled castes. Higher concentration of Scheduled Caste population residing in slums is found in Central, North-East and East Delhi districts.

Largest number of marginally employed population is found in ward number 6-Bhogal, 13 Hauz Khas (above 20%), other wards like 68 (Dallu para), 17 (Janakpuri) and 2 (Nizamuddin). Similarly, the percentage of non-workers is high in the peripheral wards. Thus, most of the slum dwellers in the peripheral part of the city are either marginally employed or unemployed.

Figure 7 and 8

Distribution of Marginal and Non-Workers Living in Slums

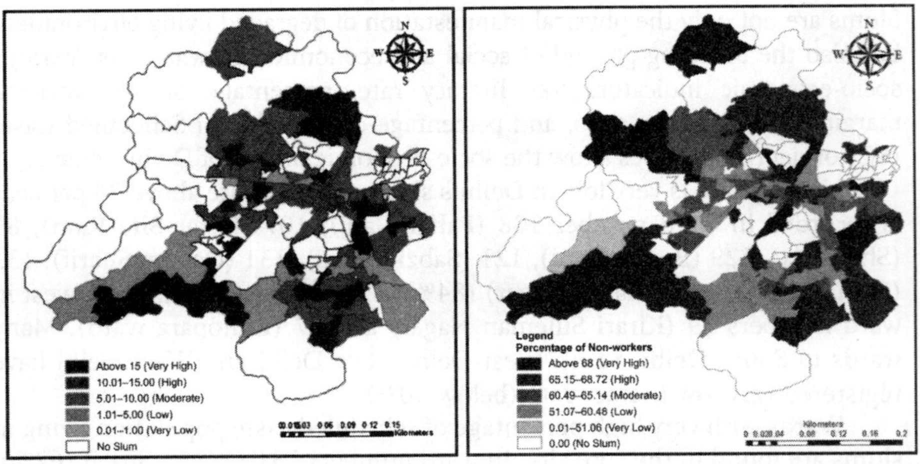

Source: Census of India, 2001.

Findings

- Areas like Chandni Chowk, Bazar Sita Ram and Sadar Bazar were teeming with slum population; but the massive relocation of the slum population from the city core to the peripheral parts in 2001 has changed the picture. The Indian Census provides data on notified slums only and not on JJ colonies or unauthorized clusters. Older and notified slums are highly concentrated in the Central Business District (CBD) area or Chandni Chowk area; whereas newer resettlement colonies, non-notified slums, canal side squatters and other types of slums are found in the peripheral parts where industrial and institutional land used to prevail. Slums are ubiquitous in Delhi, and not concentrated in few locales; even in the New Delhi area, one can find squatter settlements.
- Living environment of these slums varies remarkably depending on where they are located. Older slums located in the core city enjoy better access to basic amenities like underground closed drainage, safe sanitation, nearness of water source, electricity and safe cooking fuel; but, households here face severe space scarcity. Most of the households living here do not have any room to sleep; they live in either one room or two-room dwelling units. Their houses are mostly semi-*pucca* or *kutcha* and they use kerosene, coal, lignite, etc. as cooking fuel. Some of the vulnerable slums are located near the city core (e.g. Minto Road, Paharganj, etc.). Wards located in the periphery have poor access to sanitation, drainage, electricity, housing amenities and infrastructure; most of the households here use biomass fuel for cooking. Further, they live near open drains or without any drainage facility; most of them have either pit latrines or no latrine facility at all. They use kerosene for lighting purposes and their lifestyle is rural in nature.
- Socio-economic and demographic characteristics of people also vary remarkably between the core and the periphery. The city core has high literacy rate, low family size and high percentage of main male workers but the situation in peripheral parts is diametrically opposite. Low sex ratio is found in many wards ubiquitously distributed between core and periphery, which is a matter of great concern to demographers. Concentration of Scheduled Caste population is found in the city core as well as in the periphery, especially in East and North-East Delhi (Trans-Yamuna region) and the southern extremity.
- Thus, highly vulnerable zones are found in the extreme margins of the city; moderately vulnerable zones are found around this zone, while the remaining parts constitute the less vulnerable zone. Few posh localities like Delhi Cantonment, Greater Kailash, Defense Colony, Rohini and parts of New Delhi constitute the least vulnerable zone.

Conclusion

The demographic scenario of Delhi is unique in several respects; here most of the slums are located in the core city where land use is predominantly commercial, but the availability and accessibility of basic amenities and infrastructure in these wards are far better than the wards located in the periphery. In the core city, literacy rate is high; the percentage of marginal and non-workers is also high. Thus, these wards have better socio-economic conditions, whereas wards located in the periphery record a bizarre picture. Here, the percentage of slum population is low but there is massive deprivation in housing amenities and infrastructure facilities. Maximum concentration of Scheduled Caste population or socially deprived section of the society is found in the eastern periphery of Delhi, especially in the Trans Yamuna region. Thus, deplorable living conditions are mainly found in the peripheral wards, though the percentage of slum population is low in these areas. In the core city, most of the slums are authorized ones, but in the peripheral parts the squatter settlements are mostly unauthorized ones, and therefore Census does not provide data on these settlements. Environmental vulnerability is rated 'very high' in these peripheral wards, whereas only two areas (Minto Road and Jama Masjid) from the city core are rated as having 'high vulnerability'. 'Least' and 'less' vulnerable areas are found in NDMC wards, Rohini and wards located in proximity to these posh localities. The Delhi Government introduced lots of changes during the Commonwealth Games, especially in the form of relocation and resettlement of slums and creation of better infrastructure facilities in various parts of Delhi. However, these changes cannot be documented unless and until the new census for the city at the ward level is made available. Finally, it can be concluded on the basis of the above discussion that in Delhi environmentally vulnerable wards are mostly located in the peripheral areas, and there is an inverse relationship between existence of authorized slums and environmental vulnerability. All the posh areas are located in the NDMC zone and in Rohini. Thus, strategies for future urban planning should be focused on the creation of adequate infrastructure and provision of services in these highly vulnerable wards. This will ensure sustainable development of India's capital city which represents the heart of India.

References

Bell, P.A., T.C. Greene, J.D. Fisher and A. Baum (2001). *Environmental Psychology*, Harcourt College Publishing, San Diego, California.

Bryan, P.W. (1933). *Man's Adaptation of Nature: Studies of the Cultural Landscape*, University of London Press, London, 133.

Desai, Vandana (1995). *Community Participation and Slum Housing: A Study of Mumbai*, Sage Publications, New Delhi.

Gill, Rajesh (1994). *Slums as Urban Villages*, Rawat Publications, Jaipur.

Government of India (1988). *Urban Poverty: Report of Working Group for National Commission on Urbanisation*, Ministry of Urban Development, New Delhi.

Kingsley, Thomas and Frank Kristof (1971). 'A Housing Programme for Metropolitan Kolkata', Ford Foundation, Advisory Planning Group, Calcutta, March.

Kulkarni, K.M. (1990). *Geographical Patterns of Social Well-Being: Gujarat*, Concept Publishing Company, New Delhi, 32.

Mahadevia, Darshini (2009). 'Deprivations, Vulnerabilities and Shelter Security: Linkages in Urban India', *SPA Working Paper*, second draft.

Roy, A.U.K., M. Ahadzi and S. Saha (2007). 'Mass-Industrialized Housing to Combat Consistent Housing Shortage in Developing Countries: Towards an Appropriate System for India', World Congress on Housing, Kolkata, India.

Seamon, D. and R. Mugerauer (eds) (1985). *Dwelling, Place and Environment: Towards a Phenomenology of Person and World*, Martinus Nijhoff Publishers, Netherlands.

Sinha, V.N.P. (1969). 'Houses and House Types of the Chotanagpur Plateau', *Geographical Knowledge*, 2: 91.

Smith, D.M. (1973). *The Geography of Social Well-Being in the United States: An Introduction to Territorial Social Indicators*, McGraw-Hill, New York, 71, 85.

8

Is Tourism a Complimentary Factor in Sustainable Urban Growth or is it Degrading the Environment?

Study in Karnataka

Ananya Mitra B.

It is predicted that 21st century will be the urban century with almost 60 per cent of the world population living in urban areas by 2030, the highest ever share of population living in urban areas. This is mainly because unlike previous centuries, current and future centuries are likely to experience rapid shift in human occupations from primary to non-primary, mainly due to changing resource base and environmental conditions, and swift advances in areas like science, technology, management and development. India currently harbours the world's largest population after China. While the country's geographical area is just 2.4 per cent of the world's total, its population is over 17 per cent of the world's total. Historically, the growth of urban population in India was very slow until 1971. Though the subsequent two decades witnessed substantial increase in urban population, it was with the onset of globalization, liberalization and privatization in the 90s, that increase in urban population became alarming. Karnataka has followed this national trajectory, led in particular by the unprecedented growth of its capital city, Bengaluru. The State's urban population is expected to grow by 35 per cent in the next 20 years, i.e. to 28 million by 2026, which is much above the national average. Currently, 39 per cent of state's population resides in urban areas.

Karnataka is one of the most industrialized and urbanized states in India. The share of agriculture in the State's economy has been dwindling in recent years; the share of agriculture in GSDP halved from 36 per cent in 1993 to 18 per cent in 2005, and as a corollary, employment in agriculture shrank from 65 per cent to just 61 per cent during the same period. While the contribution of industry to GDSP has remained rather constant at approximately 27 per cent, that of the service sector increased appreciably to 54 per cent. The increasing disparity between agriculture and other sectors is likely to have a decisive impact on the economy of the state.

Objectives

- To study the role of tourism in urban growth with special reference to Karnataka.
- To investigate the trend and the process of urbanization, its visible effect on environment.
- To discuss the linkages of urban growth and its relative impact on environment in Karnataka.

Data Source

Data for the study have come from census and reports which were available with Census of India. Available data with regard to urban population have been collected and used for the analysis.

Process of Urbanization in India

Historically, the process of urbanization in India was very slow during pre-independence period; however this process has been swifter in the post-independence period. The total urban population of India in the year 1901 was 25.85 million; it increased to 44.15 million by 1940. Further, in the post-independence period, increase in urban population in terms of number has been significant; the total size increased from 62 million in 1951 to 159.46 million by 1981. Further, during the post-liberalization period, i.e. 1981–2011 the total population increased by more than twofolds (159.46 in 1981 and 377.25 million in 2011). On the other hand, the share of urban population in the total was 10 per cent in 1901 and the percentage increase of urban population in the total was not significant till 1951, but it gradually picked from 17.29 per cent in 1951 to 25.72 per cent by 1991, and further increased to 31.17 per cent by 2011(Table 1).

Table 1

Indian Urban Population, 1901–2011

Year	*No. of UA/ Towns*	*Total Population (in millions)*	*UA/town Population (in millions)*	*% Urban Population*
1901	1827	238.39	25.85	10.84
1901	1825	252.09	25.94	10.29
1921	1949	251.32	28.08	11.18
1931	2072	278.97	33.45	11.99
1941	2250	318.66	44.15	13.86
1951	2843	361.08	62.44	17.29
1961	2363	439.23	78.93	17.97
1971	2590	598.15	109.11	19.91
1981	3378	683.32	159.46	23.34
1991	3768	844.32	217.17	25.72
2001	5161	1027.01	285.35	27.78
2011	5497	1210.19	377.25	31.17

Source: Census of India of various census.

Note: The total number of UA/Towns include out-growth cities.

Even though, India is among the countries with low level of urbanization, the number of towns nevertheless increased from 2590 in 1971 to 5497 by 2011. However, the increase in the proportion of urban population in the total during the same period was 11 per cent (from 18% in 1971 to 31.17% by 2011). Strangely, about 70 per cent of urban population is concentrated in class I towns/cities only. This has resulted in big cities attaining inordinately large population size and density, leading to virtual collapse of urban services and severe degradation of environment. Thus, the onset of economic development and resultant liberalization, privatization and globalization have positively led to a steep increase in urban population in India especially in class I cities, and to some extent in class II cities.

While the land area under the urban swathe remains small, the effects of urban land dynamics have been considerable. First, the implication of location – the likelihood of urbanizing unproductive and eco-sensitive areas; second, spatial dimensions of urbanization – globally, cities classically sprawl and disturb land area twice their built up area – this correlation remains to be studied in India and third, low density urban development results in inefficient use of resources like energy in sectors like transport, infrastructure, etc.

Urbanization Trends in Karnataka

Karnataka had a total population of 19.4 million in the year 1951. By 2001, the population of Karnataka had increased to 52.85 million which increased further to 61.09 million in 2011, of which the urban population was 23.6 million or 28 per cent of the total. Karnataka ranks 7th in the degree of urbanization as can be seen from Table 2. The decadal growth of urban population in Karnataka over the last 50 years is reflected in this table. In the last 5 decades, urbanization in Karnataka recorded rapid growth except for the period of 1951–61, when the rate of growth was only 18.26 per cent. The maximum growth was recorded during 1971–81 (50.6%). However, during the subsequent two decades, the eighties and nineties, the rate of growth of urban population declined to 29.09 per cent and 28.85 per cent respectively; Table 3 presents the pattern of decadal growth of urban population in Karnataka. As can be seen from Table 3, the decadal growth of urban population during 1951–1961 was 18.26 per cent, which increased to almost 32 per cent by 2001–2011.

As can be noted from the tables mentioned, urban population in Karnataka has been growing more rapidly than the rural population; during 1991–2001, the former registered a growth rate of nearly 29 per cent in contrast to 12 per cent of the latter. Three aspects account for the growth of urbanization in the State: natural growth, migration and reclassification of cities. For the purpose of the study, towns of Karnataka have been classified into six categories on the basis of their population size. In order to understand the direction of the urbanization process, it is necessary to look into the distribution of population across different classes of towns and regions and study their growth trends.

Table 2

Percentage of Urban Population to Total Urban Population in Ranking Order by States/UTs of India (2001–2011)

India/State/ Union Territory	*Urban Population of 2011 (in Millions)*	*Percentage Share*	*Rank in 2011*	*Urban Population of 2001 (in Millions)*	*Percentage Share*	*Rank in 2001*
India	377.10	100.00	0	286.11	100.00	0
Maharashtra	50.82	13.5	1	41.10	14.36	1
Uttar Pradesh	44.47	11.8	2	34.53	12.07	2
Tamil Nadu	34.94	9.3	3	27.48	9.61	3
West Bengal	29.13	7.7	4	22.42	7.84	4
Andhra Pradesh	28.35	7.5	5	20.80	7.27	5
Gujarat	25.71	6.8	6	18.93	6.62	6
Karnataka	23.57	6.3	7	17.96	6.28	7
Madhya Pradesh	20.05	5.3	8	15.96	5.58	8
Rajasthan	17.08	4.5	9	13.21	4.62	9
NCT of Delhi	16.33	4.3	10	12.90	4.51	10

Source: http://censusmp.nic.in/censusmp/All-PDF/3Trendsinurbanization21.12.2011.pdf

Table 3

Decadal Growth of Urban Population in Karnataka

Year	*Number of Towns*	*Total Population (In Millions)*	*Urban Population (In Millions)*	*Percentage of Urban to Total Population*	*Percentage Decadal Growth Rate*
1951	285	19.4	4.4	22.95	-
1961	213	23.5	5.2	22.33	18.26
1971	227	29.2	7.1	24.31	35.23
1981	250	37.1	10.7	28.29	50.65
1991	254	44.8	13.8	30.91	29.09
2001	237	52.7	17.9	33.98	28.85
2011	347	61.09	23.62	38.7	31.95

As per 2001 Census, the number of census towns or urban settlements in Karnataka is 237. The most important feature to be illustrated noted here is that as much as 120 lakh or 66.4 per cent of the urban population of the state is concentrated in 23 class I cities. The largest number of towns (101) is in class III category accounting for 17 per cent of the urban population or 31 lakh people. The highest growth rate has been registered in class I towns (34%) followed by class III towns (4.82%) and class II (2.81%). Other classes have registered negative growth rates. However, there exists a data gap as population distribution across various classes of towns is yet to be published by the Census authorities. Therefore, a further research incorporating this elusive data needs to be done in future for more accurate results.

There is extensive disparity in the degree of urbanization across different districts of the state, as shown in Figure 1. Bangalore urban with 90.94 per cent of its population living in urban environs is the most urbanized district, and accounts for 28 per cent of the urban population of the state according to 2011 census. The second highly urbanized district is Dharwad with an urban population of 55 per cent. All the other districts have

Figure 1

Urban Population in Karnataka (District-wise) 2001

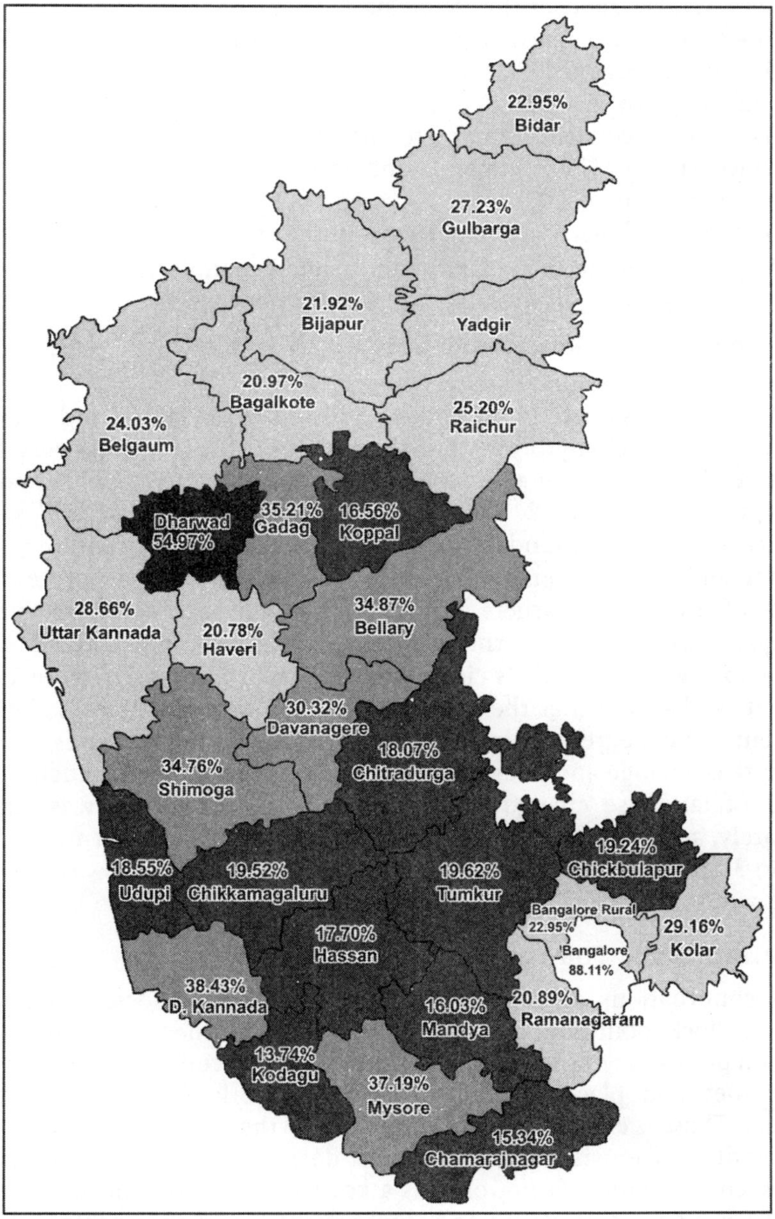

Source: Urban Development Policy (2001).

fewer than 40 per cent of the populace living in the urban core. Percentage of urbanization is below 30 in 10 districts and below 20 in 9 other districts. The least urbanized district is Kodagu (13.8%).

It is apparent that the pattern of urbanization in Karnataka is not uniform throughout the state, and there is significant variation in the spread and concentration of urbanization across different regions. A study of the regional pattern of urbanization carried out by ISEC across the four physiographic regions of the state viz., Coastal, Malnad, Southern Maidan and Northern Maidan exposes the following:

1. The highest urbanized region is Southern Maidan (81%) and lowest is the coastal region (7%); medium levels of urbanization are in Malnad and Northern Maidan.
2. By regional concentration of towns, northern maidan has the highest concentration (71 numbers), and the coastal region has the lowest number of towns (30).
3. By functional distribution of towns in the state, about:

- 14 per cent are in secondary sector, namely manufacturing,
- 28 per cent in tertiary sector,
- 31 per cent in primary sector and
- 26 per cent in multi function sectors.

The changes visible in Urban Built-up Area and Land Cover in Bangalore convincingly prove that the pace of urbanization is very fast in the State. The graphic images for land use pattern in 1992, 2001 and 2009 are captured in Figure 2. Karnataka's urban infrastructure and services constitute the basic foundation for urban settlements' economic, social, cultural and environmental dynamics. Improving them is more than a matter of investment targets and per capita access to services; these are strategic investments in the structure, functionality, liveability, and sustainability of Karnataka's cities. In the span of 8 years, i.e. from 1992 to 2000, it is observed that the extent of built-up area has increased by 30.8 per cent. The degree of increase in built-up area illustrates only the enormity of change and does not explain the pattern of this transition. The extent of land use change from non-built-up to built-up was analysed separately, according to which the percentage increase in built-up areas was around 30 per cent while the reduction in non-built-up area was 3 per cent in the same time span.

Urbanization and Tourism

Urban conurbations mirror the problems faced by the society as a whole: traffic gridlock, pollution, lawlessness and unemployment. They are not just the main places in which wealth is created and the focus of cultural and social development, but places where people live and work, shop and enjoy leisure pursuits. There is evident diversification due to the growing awareness about the potential of tourism among political decision-makers who are increasingly keen to promote it not only as a key factor in economic development but also as a source of wealth and employment. Tourism is perceived as the cornerstone of a policy of urban development that combines a competitive

Figure 2

Temporal Change in Built-up Area in Bangalore

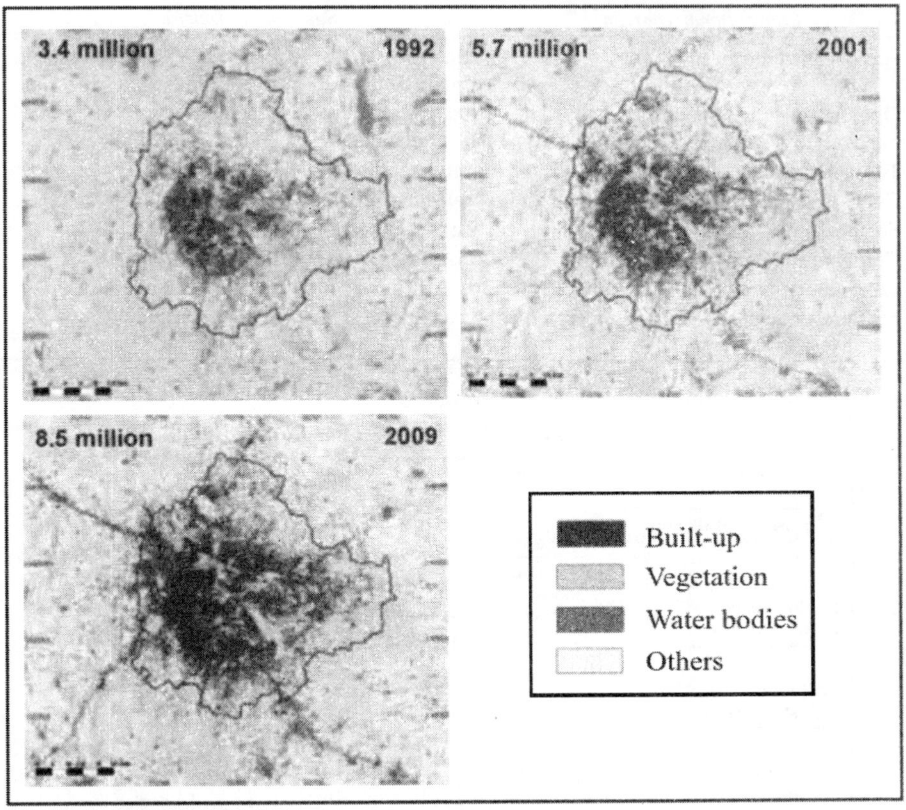

Source: IIHS Working Paper (2011).

supply chain engineered to meet visitors' expectations with a positive contribution to the development of towns and cities and the well-being of their residents. Though it is difficult to discern the distinct role of tourism in urban growth, influence of tourism can nevertheless be seen on urbanization. Increased tourist flow, development of tourism related infrastructure like hotels, highway motels, buses and taxi services have all contributed greatly in augmenting urbanization. Tourism is now considered as a complimentary factor for sustainable urban development. Popular tourist destinations attract more and more tourists every year and when tourism infrastructure like hotels, road and transport infrastructure comes up, it automatically complements.

The factors identified by the study as responsible for the development of tourism in Karnataka include industrial and economic growth, demographic factors, the rich culture, the transport network, growing educational facilities, and a generally investment friendly government in the state. All these in turn have stimulated the emergence of hundreds of tourism entrepreneurs in Karnataka. It is, therefore, clear that augmenting urbanization encouraging tourism is mutually complementary (see Table 4 and Figure 3).

Table 4

Sustainable Tourism vs Conventional Tourism

Conventional Tourism	*Sustainable Tourism*
Has one goal: profit	Planned with three goals: profit, environment, and community
Often not planned in advance: 'it just happens'	Usually planned in advance with involvement of all stakeholders
Tourist oriented	Locally oriented
Controlled by outside parties	Locally controlled, at least in part
Focus on entertainment for tourists.	Focus on educational experiences
Conservation is not a priority	Conservation of resources is a priority
Communities not a priority	Appreciation for local culture a priority
Much revenue goes to outside operators and investors	More revenue stays with local community.

Figure 3

Tourism and Urban Growth

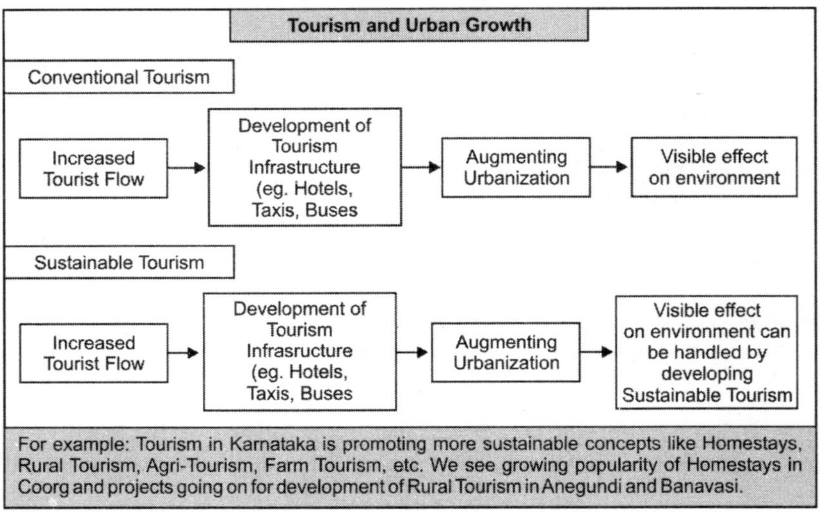

The need for development of a sustainable form of tourism:

- Tourism planning, development and operations should be in the spirit of sustainable development in being cross-sectoral and integrated, involving different government agencies, private corporations, citizens groups and individuals so as to reap extensive benefits.
- Agencies, corporations, groups and individuals should follow ethical principles which respect the culture and environment of the host area, the economy and traditional way of life, the community and traditional behaviour, leadership and political patterns.
- Due regard should be given to the protection and appropriate economic use of the natural and human environment in the host areas.
- Tourism should be undertaken with equity in mind, with the idea of access to a fair distribution of benefits and costs among tourism promoters and host peoples and their areas.

- Good information, research and communication on the nature of tourism and its effects on the human and cultural environment should be available prior to and during development. This information should be disseminated to all parties, including the local people, so that they are in a position to participate in and influence the direction of development in their area. This would reinforce the community spirit and negate the sense of alienation.
- Local people should be encouraged to undertake leadership roles in the planning and development of their regional assets with the assistance of government, financial, business and other interests.
- There should be integrated environmental, social and economic planning to link with existing uses, ways of life and environmental considerations.
- Careful monitoring should be done to allow local community to take advantage of opportunities offered by new change.

Thus, lucid and sustainable urban development is not a choice but a necessity if cities are to meet the needs of their citizens. Some of the most critical problems facing Karnataka, concern the health impacts of urban pollution generated by inadequate water, sanitation, drainage, poor waste management and air pollution. This set of problems combined with issues such as depletion of water and forest resources, progression of environmentally fragile lands, occupation of areas prone to flooding, landslides, etc. and the carbon emissions from energy use, heating, industry and transport now known as 'Climate Change Issues' all pose serious challenges to the health of the ecosystem of the urban areas and its people. To tackle these issues, an Urban Environmental Management Action Plan must be formulated. A city-specific plan would be required for large cities such as Bengaluru, Mysuru, Dharwad, etc. and a common strategy can be evolved for other towns and smaller cities in the State. Developing the tertiary sector with help of sustainable tourism industry is a way out or way forward (see Table 5 and Figure 4).

Table 5

Contribution of Tourism in Urbanization of Karnataka

The Salient Features of Karnataka's Urbanization	*Tourism Scenario in Karnataka*
Karnataka ranks high in the degree of urbanization among the major states in India after Tamil Nadu, Maharashtra and Gujarat.	Karnataka ranks 4th in Tourism Development after the states of Uttar Pradesh, Andhra Pradesh and Tamil Nadu.
The urban population has been growing faster than the rural population but the rate of growth has been declining over the last two decades.	The urban areas like Bengaluru, Mysuru and the surroundings see the highest number of tourist visit in the state. The 2nd most populous city of Dharwad is located very close to the World Heritage Site of Karnataka, Hampi, which is one of the major pillars of Karnataka Tourism.

Cont'd...

...Cont'd

There are wide regional disparities in the degree of urbanization. Example: The maximum urbanized region is Southern Maidan (81%) and least is coastal region (7%); medium levels of urbanization is in Malnad and Northern Maidan.	The southern districts of Karnataka such as Mysuru, Chickmagalur, Mandya account for more than 40 per cent of tourism inflows. 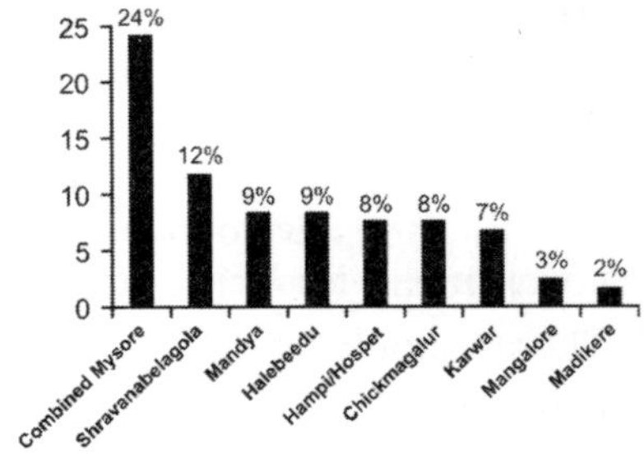
Migration is towards the higher order urban centres with 66 per cent of the urban population concentrated in 23 Class I cities.	The Class I cities like Bengaluru for instance provides the highest number of job opportunities, thus better per capita income. A superior per capita income enhances the standard of living of that local population. Thus we see that people have the excess income to invest on tourism. More job opportunities and better infrastructure facilities of the Class I cities not only ensure more investment in service sector like Tourism but also provides scope for ethnic tourism.
Bengaluru, the only metropolitan city in the State, enjoys demographic and economic dominance.	Bengaluru city as an Urban Tourist Complex with the attraction of tourists from various destinations. Bengaluru is famous for Urban Tourism, Medical Tourism, MICE (Meeting, Incentive, Conference and Exhibition) Destination as well as Shopping Tourism. Such diverse facets of tourism are not available in any other city of Karnataka.
Hubli-Dharwad and Mysuru are emerging as metropolitan cities.	As already discussed the Southern Complex and the Northern Complex of Tourism in Karnataka are most popular and visited.
By 2025, 50 per cent of Karnataka's population (40 million) is expected to live in urban areas.	The Karnataka Government is eyeing to make the state a leading tourism destination by 2016-17.

Environmental Challenges

The physical expansion and demographic growth of urban areas have exerted an adverse impact on the urban environment. The large scale conversion of agricultural land in the urban periphery for urban uses like industries, housing and infrastructure has resulted not only in loss of greenery but in creation of urban heat islands. A large number of trees and water bodies have given way to concrete structures. The increase in motor vehicular traffic in cities and industrialization has contributed to air pollution which in turn has an adverse effect on the health of the people. Cities are huge consumers of energy and resources, generating more waste than they can absorb. The increasing consumption of water is leading to depletion of water resources, particularly underground water. The enormous quantities of waste generated in cities, proliferation of slums and lack of sanitation are serious environmental hazards.

The physical extension and demographic growth of urban areas have adversely impacted the urban environment. The large-scale alteration of agricultural land in the urban fringe for urban uses like industries, housing and infrastructure has resulted not only in loss of greenery but in creation of urban heat islands. Therefore, the Department of Tourism in Karnataka is now focusing on sustainable development of tourism. New concepts like Green Hotels have received acceptance, and several such 'green projects' have come into existence in the capital city, Bengaluru. ITC Royal Gardenia and Taj Group have already undergone Green Certification, consequently are aiming for a greener and healthier city. A large number of trees and water bodies have given way to concrete structures. The mounting motor vehicular traffic in cities coupled with industrialization has added to air pollution which in turn has an adverse effect on the health of the people. Hence, tourism in Karnataka is promoting more sustainable concepts like Homestays, Rural Tourism, Agri-Tourism, Farm Tourism, etc. In some destinations like Hampi and Bannerghatta National Park, battery-operated eco-friendly cars have already been introduced by the Department of Tourism, Government of Karnataka to combat pollution.

Figure 4

An Overview of Sustainable Tourism Practice in Karnataka

Cities are huge consumers of energy and resources, generating more waste than they can absorb. The increasing consumption of water is leading to exhaustion of water resources, particularly underground water. The enormous quantities of waste generated in cities, proliferation of slums and lack of sanitation are serious environmental hazards. Rules and regulations are enforced in the core environmentally sensitive areas by declaring them as plastic free zones. Even tourists on trekking are given special instructions not to contribute to the solid waste accumulation in tourist destinations. There is also an ongoing programme to educate tourists as to how tourism can be enjoyed without degrading the natural and cultural environment and also how to preserve these tourism resources for the generations to come. Department of Tourism, Government of Karnataka in their present Tourism Policy (2009-14) has taken development of sustainable tourism as one of their key agendas. But environmental consequence of growth in tourism and as a result urbanization cannot be denied. Table 6 presents some indicators of environmental stress. Values are in a scale of minus [(-3) – worst] to plus [(+3) – best]. The bars going upwards show better than average (of all 28 states) performance and the bars going downwards show less than the average (of all 28 states). Higher number of longer upward bars is desirable and indicates good performances.

Table 6

Indicators of Environmental Problems in Karnataka

Indicator	*Score*
Population Pressure	0.47
Air Quality and Pollution	0.06
Water Quality and Availability	0.12
Land-use and Agriculture	0.18
Forest and Biodiversity	0.14
Energy Management	-0.02
Environmental Budget	-0.60
Waste Generation and Management	-0.04
Impact on Human Health and Disaster	-0.24

Source: Environmental Sustainability Index for Indian States, ESI (2010).

For any given sub-index, the upward going column is a sign of better than average (of all 28 states) performance and the columns going downwards show less than average performance (of all 28 states). The height of the upward going column indicates the degree to which a state has performed better than others in that particular sub-index. All values are in standardized scores. All are sub-indices area adjusted in such a way that higher values indicate better performance in that aspect of sustainability.

Table 6 clearly shows the environmental ill-effects of urbanization. The present study observes that as a destination attains more popularity, there is a general tendency for the area to become more urbanized. In the name of developing tourism infrastructure the destination becomes more and more urbanized and ultimately loses several time its original charm. The tourists' pressure thus often increases the population load on the city or town and invariably the volume of solid waste generated and pollution level increase with the increase in number of vehicles. It is also noticed that sometimes there appears indications of economic leakages as foreign investors flock in or foreign products are preferred over indigenous products. Pressure on the available local resources like water and electricity is also noticed. Thus, clearly tourism attracts urbanization and the same urbanization later on becomes a reason for downfall of the destination's popularity. Several examples can be found of this phenomenon in our country and even abroad such as Oceanville, USA; Ooty, Shimla and now Bengaluru to a certain extent. Tourists who had visited Bengaluru, say 20 years back and have a great memory of the city are often disappointed when they visit the city now. Thus, the current study suggests a 'sustainable tourism pattern' for real development of tourism with the motto of 'exploring not exploiting'.

Summary and Conclusions

Augmenting urbanization resulting in environment degradation is no more a fancy issue discussed in a boardroom meeting of the bureaucrats, but a stark reality today. The world is waking up and inhaling the pollution – and it is not a pretty scent. Resource depletion and plundered ecosystems have caused water shortages and madly fluctuating fuel prices. No longer just a scientific jargon, global warming and the extinction of species are issues being addressed in schools and debated in the UN. All human activity from eating and drinking to manufacturing, from entertainment to travel, is now measured against a standard of sustainability. Issues of expanding urbanization and its obvious environmental ill-effects are common concerns faced by all countries. Concern is not to decide who is the major contributor – developed or the developing countries, but to 'act' towards it. Each person from each corner of society has to participate in it. No wonder we see these days the latest advertisements of a famous mobile company where a celebrity comes and asks people to reduce paper use and start using mobile; 'Go Green campaign' started by famous TV news channels. Time has come to act, otherwise days are not far when man has to leave earth and go to 'Pandora' in search of resources.

The tourism sector has an important place in that framework, given its global economic and social value, its role in sustainable urban development and its strong relationships with environment. Environment is a key resource for tourism and the sector is highly sensitive to the impacts of environmental degradation; so the tourism sector must rapidly respond. In view of the fact that the phenomenon of tourism involves a lot of interaction with the environment, it is inevitable that we have to take care of it. The basic components of tourism which need the highest infrastructural development are – accessibility (transportation) and accommodation, which leads to booming urbanization and vice versa. Environmental degradation cannot be fought by one entity alone; it is something that needs the joining of many hands, individually and collectively.

Thus, sustainable urban development is not a choice, but a necessity if cities are to meet the needs of their citizens. In a wide spectrum, spatial distribution of urban areas and their emerging demographic trends, the infrastructure shortfall on several fronts, the challenge of ensuring the basic welfare of the poor in urban areas and the need for strengthening their governance, planning and administration can be solved by developing 'sustainable tourism'. Tourism can provide foreign investment, circulate money better, create multiplier effect, and provide better per capita income and standard of living, thus creating a sustainable urban growth.

The major components of the action plan could be the following:

1. *Conservation of Water Resources:* The objective should be to reduce the demand for fresh water. Conservation measures such as rainwater harvesting should be made mandatory.
2. *Waste-water Management:* The recycling and reuse of waste water should be encouraged in cities which generate substantial quantities of sewerage and sullage. Decentralized waste water treatment plants must be set up at appropriate places.
3. *Controlling Air Pollution:* Air quality monitoring systems must be set up to measure various pollutants like particulates of carbon dioxide, carbon monoxide, etc. Controlling air pollution depends upon factors such as density of vehicular traffic and emission from industries. The Prevention of Air Pollution Act will have to be enforced strictly.
4. *Energy Conservation:* Cities consume enormous quantities of energy. In view of the shortage of electrical power, it is imperative to promote the use of renewable energy such as solar and wind power and other energy efficiency measures. Urban design will have to take into account the efficient use of energy and promote green buildings.

Contribution of Sustainable Tourism to Environmental Conservation: An example 'GREEN ADAPTATIONS' from 'GREEN HOTELS':

1. Conserve earth's fresh water:
   - Low flow shower heads
   - Aerators in bathroom sink faucets
   - 1.6 gpm dishwashing valves,
   - Low-flow toilets
   - Low flow water fixtures
2. Conserve energy supply:
   - Compact fluorescent bulbs, which use 75 per cent less energy than incandescent bulbs
   - Ceiling fans
   - Lights out cards
   - Motion sensors for public rest rooms, meeting rooms, exercise rooms, etc.
   - Heating and cooling system controlled by computerized building management system that allows hotel rooms to be powered down when not in use and calibrated for specific occupancy expectations.
3. Eco-friendly recreational activities provided:
   - Cycling
   - Yoga
   - Cooking
   - Walking

- Fishing
- Nature trails
- Bird watching
- Golf
- Painting
- Tennis
- Horse riding
- Swimming

4. New line of environmentally safe housekeeping – need for recycling policy – (what the State should ensure):
   - Products are biodegradable
   - Sold in recycled packaging
   - Water bodies are free from chlorine, carcinogens, harmful vapours, and other toxins that could harm people or aquatic life
   - Kitchen facilities have recently set new standards to reduce their use of natural gas as well as enforce it
   - Furniture are recycled
   - Hoteliers can ask vendors to deliver products in minimal wrapping. Vendors can be asked to deliver products one day, and pick up the packaging materials the next day
   - Using guestroom towel-rack hangers
   - Sheet-changing cards
   - Tree-planting throughout the property – On each floor the open-air atrium is lined with lush plants, which help remove harmful pollutants from the air by acting as air filters
   - Desk pads and folio binders use recycled paper
   - Water purification system for all bottled water, these are sterilized and reused
   - Containers, coffee cups, straws, utensils and napkins used at the restaurants are biodegradable
   - Exclusive use of non-CFC producing refrigerants
   - 100 per cent organic cotton bedsheets, towels, bath mats, bathrobes.

References

Census of India (1990). Bangalore District Gazetteer, Government of Karnataka, Bangalore.

Government of India (2007). Planning Commission (Tourism Cell), New Delhi.

Government Order No. ITY 296 TTT 2000 4-5-2002. Department of Tourism, Government of Karnataka, Bangalore.

http://en.wikipedia.org/wiki/bangalore

http://www.greenhotels.com

http://www.touristplacesinindia.com/eco-tours/green-hotels.html

http://www.zerowaste.org

Karnataka Industrial Policy (2009–14). 2010 Notification, Department of Industries and Commerce, Government of Karnataka, Bangalore.

Karnataka Traveler (2008). Department of Tourism, Government of Karnataka, Bangalore.

Mitra, Ananya and B. Eswarappa (2010). 'Green Hotels in the Garden City of Bangalore: A Geographical Perspective', 31st IIG Meet and International Conference On: Environment, Agriculture and Food Security.

Percy, K. Singh (1996). *Fifty Years of Indian Tourism*, Kanishka Publishers & Distributors, New Delhi.

Ravi, S. and Georgina (2006). 'A Road Guide to Karnataka', TTK Healthcare Limited, Publications Division, Chennai.

Report on Indian Tourism Policy (2008). Department of Tourism, Ministry of Tourism, Government of India.

State/UT Tourism Statistics (2007). Department of Tourism, Government of India.

Urban Development Policy for Karnataka (2009).

Urban India (2011). *Evidence: A Report by Indian Institute for Human Settlement.*

SECTION III

Urban Growth and Environment

9

Land Use Change and Land Acquisition

Insight into an Enamouring Development

Animesh Roy

Change in land use has been a phenomenon ever since the beginning of human civilization. However, this phenomenon has attained momentum in recent years, particularly in developing countries. Conversion of agricultural land into non-agricultural land for various non-farm activities has emerged as a major concern across the countries in the world. Numerous empirical studies on both developed (Best and Champion, 1970; Shaklee et al., 1984; Pyle, 1985; Blewett and Lane, 1988; Drozd) and developing countries (Ding, 2007; Narain, 2009; Kumar et al., 2011; Dadhich and Hanaoka, 2011; Kumar, 2012; Bhupal, 2012; Ge, 2012; Tang et al., 2012; Hui and Bao, 2013) have confirmed the fact that cultivable land is continuously going out of agriculture and is being used for rapid urbanization. This phenomenon has generated debate and controversy and turned into a critical issue for land use planning for quite some time in developed (Shaklee et al., 1984; Plantinga and Miller, 2001; Drozd and Johnson, 2004) as well as in developing countries like India (Narain, 2009), Bangladesh (Dewan and Yamaguchi, 2009), China (Su et al., 2011) and so on, in recent years. In India, the pace of conversion of cultivable land has accelerated with expanding developmental activities after the end of colonial rule. The adoption of Nehruvian model of development in the form of industrialization, urbanization and infrastructure building by the post-independence Congress government increased the demand of land substantially among all the major states in the country. In recent years, the requirement of land for non-agricultural purposes has increased tremendously, especially after the adoption of neoliberal economic policy in 1991 and enactment of SEZ Act 2005 which have encouraged private entrepreneurs significantly. The neoliberal economy has led many states including West Bengal to compete with each other for pulling in industries and infrastructure developers by providing lucrative incentives, which in turn has led the incidence of land acquisition to be far more numerous than ever before.

West Bengal started experiencing pressure on agricultural land since independence; and it has deepened over time with increasing demand of land for non-farm activities. A phenomenal change in land use pattern has been discernible in several parts of the state in recent years, particularly in different pockets of districts (North 24 Parganas, South 24 Parganas, Nadia, Hooghly and Howrah) around Kolkata. Following the economic reforms in the Centre in 1991, the Left Front Government (LFG) of West Bengal brought about substantial reforms in industrial policy that promoted internal and foreign investments and transfer of foreign technology on an unprecedented scale (Commerce and Industries Department, Government of West Bengal, 2008: 3). The pro-peasant and pro-poor government which began its career in 1977 with a vision of social, political and economic change through successful implementation of land reforms and redistribution of surplus or unclaimed land among the landless and land-poor came to be more interested in acquiring private land since the second half of 1990s for various development projects were largely launched by private capitalists. Land acquisition drive of the LFG continued in the last half of its power regime too, and acquired or tried to acquire large tracts of land in several places in the state in order to develop business centres, dwelling units and industries. Among them, Singur and Nandigram are the two places which have drawn much attention of politicians, intellectuals and social activists. However, the place that has witnessed the largest dispossession of farmers from their agricultural land is Rajarhat in North 24 Parganas district. However, it has remained unnoticed by many because of two reasons: first, the pace of land acquisition in Rajarhat was very slow compared with the much debated Singur;[1] second, unlike Singur and Nandigram, anger of those evicted from land in Rajarhat could not be mobilized into an agitation due to lack of support from any major political party in the state (Dey, 2011). Here the government has acquired 6,933.72 acres of agricultural land, ponds and fishing embankments for developing a business centre (IT Hub) and dwelling units known as Rajarhat New Town. Conversion of acquired land into non-agricultural land has not only ruined the livelihood of the dispossessed farming households by divesting them of their primary base of economic activities but has also depleted their natural resource-base by filling up most of the water bodies (fishing ponds and irrigation sources) with infertile rubble. Moreover, the rapid real estate boom in post-acquisition phase is gobbling up cultivable land, mango orchards and tree groves for building housing complexes, etc. thereby changing the land use pattern. Hence, the instance of Rajarhat has been taken up as case study to bring the significance of these changes into light, in view of insights gained from the analysis of secondary data for 101 C.D. blocks around Kolkata in West Bengal. The aim of this paper is to capture the pattern of growth and change in land use with particular focus on area under non-agricultural use as well as cultivable land at different blocks in districts around Kolkata; to examine the pattern of change in livelihoods of farmers who lost agricultural land on acquisition and conversion into non-agricultural land in Rajarhat; to highlight the degradation and diminution of some resources as a consequence of change in land utilization consequent on acquisition.

Data and Methodology

The data for this study has been collected from both primary and secondary sources. Secondary data has been obtained from two sources (Department of Agriculture and Cooperation, Government of West Bengal and Population Census of India) for fourteen years from 1996–97 to 2009–10[2] while primary data has been collected through sample household survey carried out in four revenue villages of Rajarhat C.D. Block in West Bengal. The sample design has been chalked out on the basis of two assumptions: first, acquisition of agricultural land has substantially changed the pattern of livelihood activities of the dispossessed households; and second, the real estate boom has emerged as an immense potential factor for changing the existing pattern of land use around the project area in post-acquisition stage. Two sets of sample households have been purposively selected for this study. The first set comprises those households which have lost agricultural land due to acquisition while the second includes households that have sold cultivable land in post-acquisition phase. For first set, 150 dispossessed households from cultivable land have been randomly[3] drawn from two revenue villages (75 from each), namely Thakdari[4] and Chakpachuria[5] of Rajarhat, whereas for second set 69 households have been surveyed from Rekjoani and Kalaberia revenue villages[6] of the same block. The sample households of last set have been identified in two ways: first, on the basis of available records of registrations of land sale or agreements entered into, in post-acquisition phase at Rajarhat Land Registration Office; and second, with the help of local land brokers who maintain updates of recent transactions in the locality. The key informant for every sample is the head of household. Location coefficient (LQ) has been used to assess the level of concentration of non-agricultural land across blocks in districts around Kolkata. The formula for LQ is given below.

Location Coefficient (L) =

Where,

= area of jth category of land in ith block,

= area of all categories of land in the same block,

= area of jth category of land in the district and

= area of all categories of land in the district.

Multivariate linear regression has been applied to identify the factors affecting variation in share of area under non-agricultural land across the same set of blocks. The regression equation is:

Y = + + + + …… + +

Where,

Y = dependent variable,

X_1, X_2, X_3 … = predictor variables

= intercept,
$\hat{a}_1, \hat{a}_2, \hat{a}_3 \ldots$ = regression coefficients and
= residual error

Field Site at a Glance

Rajarhat is a C.D. Block abutting Netaji Subhas Chandra Bose International Airport (Kolkata Airport) in West Bengal. According to the Primary Census Abstract (2001), Rajarhat Block consists of a population of 1.45 lakh, predominantly (95.37%) living in rural areas. The LFG has acquired 6933.72 acres of agricultural land and fishing embankment from this block between April 1995 and March 2007 (CAG-Comptroller and Audit General of India, 2007) under the provisions of Land Acquisition Act-I, 1894 to develop a business centre (IT Hub) and housing estate in the form of a planned township under the purview of public purposes. Out of the total land so acquired, 314.01 acres (942. 03 bigha) are from sample village Thakdari and 724.32 acres (2,172.96 bigha) from sample revenue village Chackpachuria. According to one estimate, acquisition of land in Rajarhat has dispossessed about 25,000 landowners and 5,000 registered tenants from their primary source of livelihoods, entirely altering their occupational structure. Due to low lying nature of large proportion of the land acquired, before acquisition, the dispossessed farmers cultivated only aman paddy on it during rainy (*kharif*) season before acquisition. Crops were often damaged by flooding of fields in monsoon season. However, in both winter (*rabi*) and summer seasons, they were able to cultivate profitably some vegetables (like potato, onion, cauliflower, cabbage and spinach) and *boro* paddy.

Dynamics in Area under Non-agricultural and Cultivable Land: Block Level Scenario

The growth in area under non-agricultural land has been highly varied across the Blocks (Figure 1). Although none of the C.D. Blocks abutting Kolkata has witnessed high annual growth in this category of land, two blocks namely Sonarpur and Thakurpukur (for names of blocks see Figure 1A in Appendix) have registered moderate growth with a growth rate greater than three per cent per annum. Majority of the blocks have witnessed positive growth (Table 1), and the increase in land area under non-agricultural use was mainly due to conversion of valuable cultivable land (Table 1A in Appendix). Eleven blocks have experienced high growth (more than 6% per annum) in non-agricultural land, of which none is contiguous with Kolkata. Nineteen blocks have witnessed moderate growth, most of which are not adjacent to Kolkata, but well connected to it by road or rail. On the other hand, majority of C.D. Blocks have registered negative growth (Figure 2) as well as decline of share in cultivable land, over time. Notably, there has been a decline in share of net area sown in most of C.D. Blocks (Table 1B in Appendix) due to increasing demand of land for non-farm uses. All blocks abutting Kolkata have witnessed decline in cultivable land area with negative growth rates below –3.00 per cent annum.

Figure 1

Growth (%) in Area under Non-agricultural Land across Blocks around Kolkata between 1996–97 and 2008–09

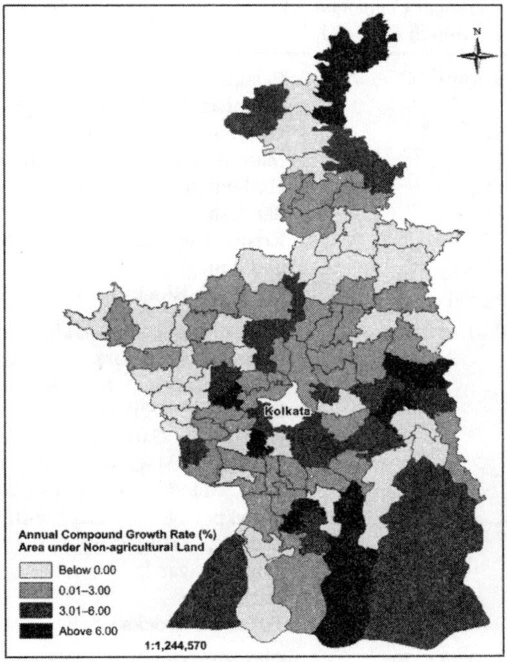

Figure 2

Growth (%) in Area under Cultivable Land across Blocks around Kolkata between 1996–97 and 2009–10

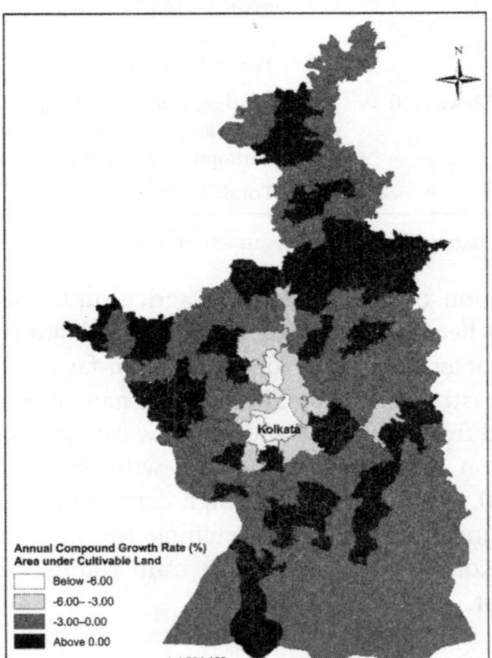

Table 1

Pattern of Growth in Area under Non-agricultural Blocks around Kolkata

Pattern of Growth	*Annual Compound Growth Rate (%)*	*Blocks*
Negative Growth	Below 0.00	Balagarh, Pandua, Haripal, Chanditotal-I, Pursura, Arambag, Khanakul-II, Goghat-II, Bagnan-I, Amta-I, Udaynarayanpur, Bhangore-II, Joynagar-II, Basanti, Maheshtala, Bishnupur-I, Budge Budge-II, Diamond Harbour-II, Kakdwip, Namkhana, Habra-I, Sandeshkhali, Swarupnagar, Bagdah, Bongaon, Krishnanagar-II, Tehatta-II, Nakasipara, Ranaghat-I and Ranaghat-II **Total: 31 Blocks**
Low Growth	0.01 to 3.00	Polba-Dadpur, Dhaniakhali, Tarakeswar, Jangiapara, Serampur-Uttarpara, Khanakul-I, Goghat-I, Bally-Jagachha, Sankrail, Domjur, Uluberia-I, Bagnan-II, Shyampur-I, Amta-II, Bhangore-I, Joynagar-I, Canning-I, Budge Budge-I, Diamond Harbour-I, Magrahat-I, Magrahat-II, Patharpratima, Falta, Mandibazar, Amdanga, Barasat-I, Barasat-II, Brrackpore-I, Barracpore-II, Deganga, Habra-II, Baduria, Hinjalganj, Sandeskhali-II, Gaighata, Krishnanagar-I, Nawadip, Santipur, Hanskhali, Haringhata **Total: 40 Blocks**
Medium Growth	3.01 to 6.00	Chinsura-Mogra, Singur, Chanditola-II, Jagatballavpur, Uluberia-II, Shyampur-II, Sonarpur, Baruipur, Canning-II, Gosaba, Thakurpukur-Metiabruz, Mathurapur-II, Sagar, Rjarhat, Haroa, Hasnabad, Chapra, Krishnaganj, Kaliganj **Total: 19 Blocks**
High Growth	Above 6.00	Panchla, Kultali, Bishnupur-II, Mathurapur-I, Kulpi, Basirhat-I, Basirhat-II, Minakhan, Karimpur-I, Karimpur-II and Tehatta-I **Total: 11 Blocks**

Source: Derived from data published by Department of Agriculture and Cooperation, GOWB.

The proportion of land under non-agricultural use at both base and current years has been higher in blocks around Kolkata (Figure 3 and 4) due to intensive use of available land for various non-farm uses such as housing, roads, parks, infrastructures, etc. Three blocks namely Singur, Basirhat-I and Minakhan moved from high, low and very low categories of non-agricultural land concentration to very high category, with location coefficient values greater than 1.50. Interestingly, very high concentration of this category of land has been linear in fashion, stretching toward north and north-east direction from Kolkata along two busy train routes: Sealdah-Barasat and Sealdah-Ranaghat.

Figure 3

Concentration of Non-agricultural Land among Different Blocks around Kolkata in 1996–97

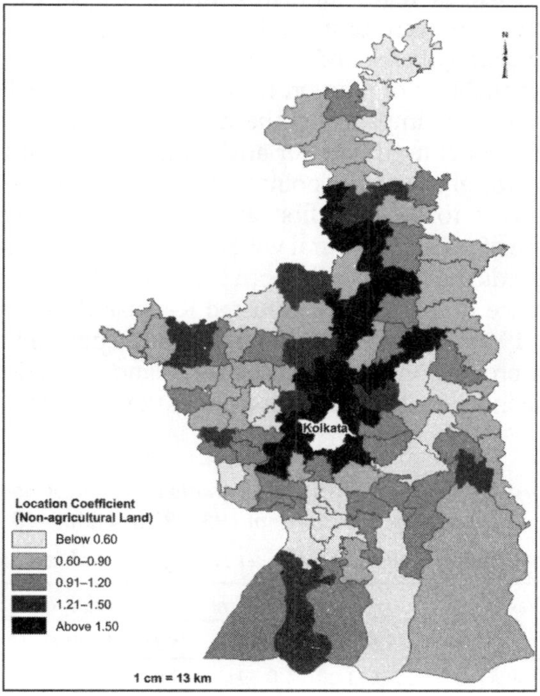

Figure 4

Concentration of Non-agricultural Land among Different Blocks around Kolkata in 2009–10

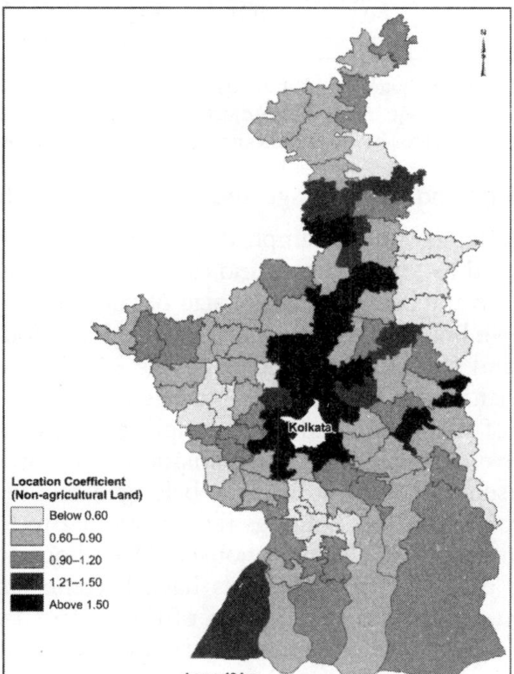

Factors Responsible for Change in Share of Non-agricultural Land

Several factors such as real estate investment, length of roads, per capita income, net output per acre of agricultural land, etc. play significant roles in altering the proportion of area under non-agricultural use (dependent variable). However, non-availability of data on these factors at block level comes in the way of estimating their impacts on the dependent variable. The multivariate linear regression model used here for analysing variation in proportion of area under non-agricultural use at two points (1996–97 and 2009–10) of time across C.D. blocks appears to be good fits[7] and sufficient to determine household density and share of non-agricultural worker in total labour force and constitute the significant predictor variables for both base and current years at one per cent level of significance (Table 2). The adjusted R-squared values of 0.63 and 0.58 successively for 1996–97 and 2009–10 imply that 63 per cent and 58 per cent of the variation in proportion of non-agricultural land to total reporting area are explained by the independent variables used in the analysis.

Table 2

Regression Analysis of Factors Affecting Variation in Share of Non-agricultural Land Across C.D. Block in 1996–97 and 2009–10

Dependent Variable: Share of Area under Non-agricultural Land to Total Area

Independent Variables	*Regression Coefficient*		*t-value*		*Standard Error*	
	1996–97	*2009–10*	*1996–97*	*2009–10*	*1996–97*	*2009–10*
Number of households per square km	0.33	0.34	5.63***	4.48***	0.095	0.231
Share (%) of non-agricultural workers to total labour force	0.19	0.30	2.02***	3.49***	0.076	0.105
Literacy	0.26	0.10	3.33**	1.58	0.110	0.008
Intercept	–28.69	–21.83	–3.09	–1.80	9.277	12.13

Note: (i) For year 1996-96, R-squared = 0.64, Adjusted R-squared = 0.63, F = 56.61 and N = 101.
(ii) For year 2009-10, R-squared = 0.59, Adjusted R-squared = 0.58, F = 43.54 and N = 101.
(iii) ***, ** and * indicate level of significance at 1, 5 and 10 per cent level respectively.

Land Acquisition, Land Use Change and Changing Livelihoods in Rajarhat

The size of landholdings among sample dispossessed households before acquisition is considered as an important indicator for the determination of their agrarian status. On the basis of a mean size of landholdings (5.85 bigha) per household, sample households have been grouped into four categories: large, medium, small and marginal households (Table 3A). The study, however has found that acquisition of agricultural land has resulted in drastic decline in agrarian status of the project affected sample households in Thakdari and Chakpachuria revenue villages. In preacquisition phase, majority (44.67%) of the sample households of these villages belonged to the category of small farming households with landholdings ranging from 2 to 5 bigha (Table 3A). There was not even a single sample household without any cultivable land, whereas 85 per cent of the households have become landless agricultural labourers in post-acquisition stage. None of the sample families reported as coming under large or medium farming household category in post-acquisition stage. The largest share (43.76%) of acquired land has come from large farming households (Table 3B). Surprisingly, an extremely meagre proportion (0.67%) of households that lost their land partially to acquisition has stuck to cultivation even in post-acquisition phase, and consider cultivation as their prime[8] source of household income (Table 4). Majority of the sample households have shown casual and waged non-farm work as their main means of livelihood in post-acquisition phase while others have shown either petty or flourishing business as their principal means of livelihood. More than four-fifths of the working population of sample households in these two villages were engaged in agriculture based livelihood activities before acquisition (Table 5). A small share of workforce was engaged in non-farm activities. However, a contrasting scenario has emerged in post-acquisition stage due to conversion of agricultural land into non-agricultural use, i.e. for developing 'Rajarhat Newtown' locally known as 'Megacity'. Majority of the workforce from dispossessed households have established their foothold in non-farm economic activities, and taken up sundry jobs like construction labourer, security guard, vegetable seller, hawker, petty shopkeeper on trolley, mason, carpenter, rickshaw and trolley puller, domestic servant, etc. (Table 5). A minor share of the workforce is engaged in supplying mortars to construction sites by forming informal cooperatives, which are locally known as 'syndicates'. A few of project affected workforce have turned into real estate brokers and are making good fortune.

Table 3A

Change in Agrarian Status of Dispossessed Households in Thakdari and Chakpachuria, Rajarhat

Status of Households	*Before Acquisition*		*After Acquisition*	
	Households	*%*	*Households*	*%*
Large (above 8 bigha)	28	18.67	–	–
Medium (5–8 bigha)	41	27.33	–	–
Small (2–5 bigha)	67	44.67	4	2.67
Marginal (below 2 bigha)	14	9.33	18	12.00
Without cultivable land	–	–	128	85.33
Total Households	150	100.00	150	100.00

Source: Household Survey, 2010.

Table 3B

Farming Household-wise Scenario of Land Acquisition

Category of Farming Households	*Before Acquisition*		*Land Acquired (Bigha)*	*Land Acquired (%)*	*After Acquisition*	
	Total Land (Bigha)	*%*			*Land Remained (Bigha)*	*%*
Large	391.27	44.55	384.32	43.76	6.95	0.79
Medium	256.63	29.22	245.52	27.95	11.11	1.26
Small	212.75	24.22	204.13	23.24	8.62	0.98
Marginal	17.68	2.01	17.22	1.96	0.46	0.05
Total	878.33	100.00	851.19	96.91	27.14	3.09

Source: Household Survey, 2010.

Note: (i) N = 150 households, (ii) Mean size of landholdings at household before acquisition = 5.85 bigha.

Table 4

Nature of Land Loss and Change in Prime Economic Activity of Dispossessed

Nature of Land Loss Among Dispossessed Households	*Change in Prime Household Activity in Post-acquisition Stage*							
	Cultivator to Agricultural Labour	*Cultivator to Casual and Waged Non-farm Worker*	*Cultivator to Business*	*Cultivator to Others (Driver, Conductor, Rickshaw Puller and Security Guard)*	*No Change in Main Occupation*	*Cultivator to Jobless*	*Cultivation was not prime activity in pre-acquisition stage*	*Total Households*
Partially lost (only part of agricultural land)	-	9	6	4	1	-	2	22 (14.67)
Completely lost (entire agricultural land)	2	49	39	29	-	3	6	128 (85.33)
Total Households	2 (1.33)	58 (38.67)	51 (34.00)	27 (18.00)	1 (0.67)	3 (2.00)	8 (5.33)	150(100.00)

Source: Household Survey, 2010.

Note: Figure in parentheses indicates percentage to total sample households.

Land Acquisition and Resource Degradation

According to West Bengal Housing Board (1999), about 68 per cent of the area to be acquired for the Rajarhat project consists of agricultural land, whereas 32 per cent (2218 acres) comprises wet land, fishing embankment and land under miscellaneous tree groves. The wetlands and fisheries were rich sources of fish for the villagers and inhabitants of Kolkata. Six sample households of Thakdari and Chakpachuria villages have claimed that they had 9 fishing bheris (fisheries) extended over an area of about 39 bighas (13 acres) where they cultured several species of fish. Dey (2011) has substantiated that more than fifty different species of rare fish were found in Rajarhat wetlands. Although the left government had promised to develop more water bodies and trees in the new townships, nothing has materialized until now. The rapid urbanization on acquired cultivable land, ponds, fishing embankments and wetland in Rajarhat has degraded the ecological conditions (Image 1) and destroyed large number of trees.

Emerging Real Estate in Rural Rajarhat and Changing Resource Base

Although the real estate business began to bloom in western countries from the 1960s, its presence became noticeable in India, particularly in metropolitan cities like Mumbai, Delhi, Kolkata and planned cities like Bengaluru, Chandigarh, etc. and their abutting rural urban fringe areas immediately after the economic liberalization in 1991. Surprisingly, within two decades since then, it has dramatically captured all the class one cities and many more class two urban centres in the country. The farmers willing to buy or sell land in fringe areas are now often monitored and controlled by the land brokers, speculators and realtors, particularly in places where various development projects are being implemented or proposed by the government or large capitalists.

Table 5

Change in Livelihoods of Working Population of Dispossessed Households in Thakdari and Chakpachuria, Rajarhat

Livelihood/Economic Activity	*Occupation before Acquisition*		*Occupation after Acquisition*	
	Count	*%*	*Count*	*%*
Cultivators	271	81.14	2	0.60
Agricultural labourers	1	0.30	3	0.90
Dairy and fishing	18	5.39	7	2.10
Non-farm workers and waged non-farm labourers	3	0.90	79	23.65
Carpenters, painters and mason	3	0.90	38	11.38
Syndicate business	-	-	29	8.68
Divers, rickshaw drivers and conductors	-	-	15	4.49

Cont'd...

...Cont'd

Business (other than syndicate)	5	1.50	61	18.26
Brokers	-	-	5	1.50
Security guards	-	-	6	1.80
Government/private company employees	24	7.19	26	7.79
Electricians and mechanics	4	1.20	5	1.50
Others	5	1.50	12	3.59
Jobless	-	-	46	13.77
Total workers	334	100.00	334	100.00

Source: Household Survey, 2010.

Note: Here those workers have been considered whose age was above 15 years but below 60 years at the time of acquisition and who were engaged in economic activities.

The rapid urbanization on acquired land in Rajarhat in the form of a planned township is dramatically changing the characteristics of adjacent rural areas. Rajarhat has now become the centre of attraction to real estate giants and speculators (Image 2). Real estate giants and speculators are willingly paying substantial premium above the actual market rates to obtain desirable parcels of land for developing as housing estates. These new and non-traditional owners of land consider their property as highly consumptive rather than productive asset (Pyle, 1985). Our field study shows that 54 per cent of the land parcels comprising 67 per cent of total land sold by the households in post-acquisition stage has been purchased by the realtors alone (Table 6A and 6B), whereas about 89 per cent of land parcels has been purchased by realtors and speculators together. No individual seems to have played any significant role in land market of Rajarhat in the post-acquisition phase. It is seen that larger land plots have mainly been purchased by real estate agents and speculators. The land value

Image 1

Filling of Fisheries in Thakdari, Rajarhat

Image 2

Blooming Real Estate Skyscrapers on Acquired Land

Figure 5
Change in Average Price of Cultivable Land after Acquisition

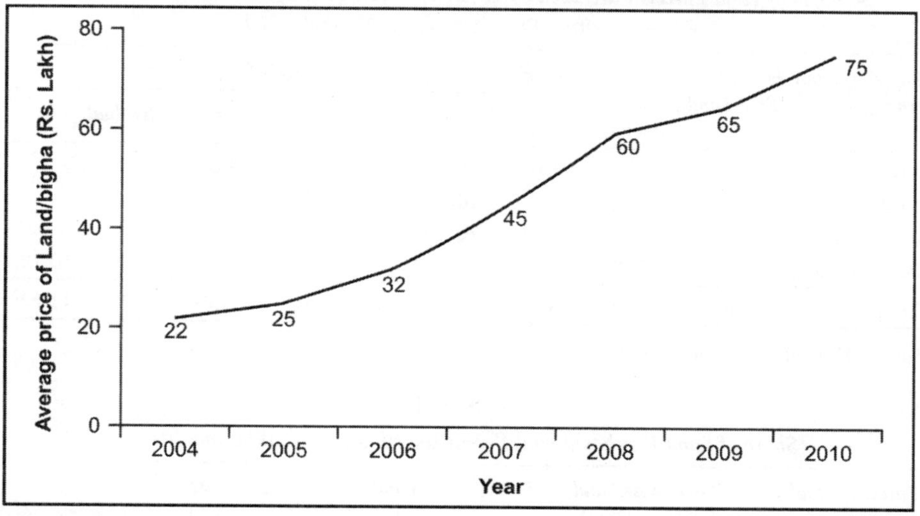

Source: Household Survey, 2010 (N = 69 households).

has gone up manifolds in post-acquisition stage. The price per bigha of cultivable land around the acquired land in Rekjuani and adjoining Kalaberia has witnessed an increase of 240 per cent in a short span of six years (Figure 5). By 2004, immediately after the completion of land acquisition in their vicinity, the average price of one bigha cultivable land had risen to ₹ 22 lakh, which rose further to ₹ 75 lakh by 2010. The interaction of agricultural land with urban land market results in accruing values to farmland owners (Chicoine, 1981). On the other hand, the compensation offered by Government (collector) to the dispossessed households was only ₹ 1.27 lakh for the same unit of land in 1998. Compensation was revised by the government in 2003 and it became ₹ 2.70 lakh which was eight times lower than the price offered by the realtors for one bigha cultivable land in 2004. The rapid rate of construction of buildings and development of infrastructures has resulted in felling a huge number of trees and destruction of flora and fauna, making the environment more fragile. The agricultural resource base is in great stress in these areas. Many partially lost farming households have stopped cultivating crops on their remaining farm land around the project, rendering such lands barren/unproductive. Most of such landowners are virtually waiting for better deals to sell off their land. The rapid emergence of real estate activities is taking away existing grazing lands, roadside ponds, mango orchards, etc. and converting them into concrete jungles. Large scale construction works for multistoried buildings, roads, drainage, etc. are causing air pollution and creating waterlogging problems during rainy season.

Table 6A

Scenario of Land Parcels Purchased by different Buyers in Rekjoani and Kalaberia in Post-acquisition Phase between 2004 and 2010

Parcel of Land (in bigha)	Households Sold Land	Land Sold (bigha)	No. of Parcels Sold	No. of Parcels Purchased by					
				Realtor	%	Speculator	%	Individual	%
Above 1.50	9	37.25	19	15	15.31	4	4.08	-	-
1.00–1.50	16	31.65	23	16	16.33	7	7.14	-	-
0.50–1.00	22	25.60	32	20	20.41	11	11.22	1	1.02
Below 0.50	22	11.25	24	2	2.04	12	12.24	10	10.20
Total	69	105.75	98	53	54.08	34	34.69	11	11.22

Source: Household Survey, 2010.

Table 6 B

Share of Land Purchased by different Buyers between 2004 and 2010

Parcel of Land (in bigha)	Parcel wise Land Sold (in bigha)	Land (in bigha) Purchased by		
		Realtor	Speculator	Individual
Above 1.50	37.25	30.50	6.75	-
1.00–1.50	31.65	22.40	9.25	–
0.50–1.00	25.60	17.00	7.95	0.65
Below 0.50	11.25	0.95	5.40	4.90
Total	105.75 (100.00)	70.85 (67.00)	29.35 (27.75)	5.55 (5.25)

Source: Household Survey, 2010.

Note: (i) N = 69 households; (ii) Figures in parentheses indicate percentage to total land sold.

Conclusion

The study substantiates that majority of the blocks in districts around Kolkata have gained in share of land area under non-agricultural use mainly at the expense of cultivable land. The worrisome phenomenon is that the share of net sown area has been declining over time across the blocks. The multivariate linear regression used for analysing variation in share of area under non-agricultural land (dependent variable) across C.D. Blocks appears to be a good fit and sufficient to determine household density and share of non-agricultural worker in total labour force, as significant predictor variables at one per cent level of significance. However, household survey at Rajarhat Block has revealed that land acquisition has drastically brought about a downward shift in the agrarian status of project dispossessed households. More than 80 per cent of them have become landless in the post-acquisition phase. The obliteration of cultivation and rapid urbanization, post acquisition and conversion of agricultural land into non-agricultural use, have not only forced a majority of those who were dependent on these dispossessed households, to seek myriad low profile non-farm livelihood activities but also has irreversibly degraded the natural resource base. The development-induced real estate boom in Rajarhat is rapidly changing the rural characteristics of the project affected villages. The lure of windfall gains and the practical difficulties of cultivation are forcing many villagers to dispose of the remaining cultivable and grazing lands and seek any available job for their sustenance. Nevertheless, the paper has identified few critical issues of concern such as declining share of net sown area, drastic increase in price of agricultural land after acquisition, resource degradation and the diversification of rural livelihoods toward non-farm low profile economic activities. All these issues need to be dealt with great attention by the government. Continuous decline in net sown area may pose uncertainty in food production, especially in a year with natural calamities and vagaries of monsoon. Sudden rise in price of agricultural land in rural areas may increase economic inequality among the farming households as the benefits of increase in land price go to those households that possess land around the project.

Notes

1. In Singur, the acquisition of 997.11 acres of land was completed within a short span of only three and half months between 20 July and 4 October 2006, whereas in Rajarhat acquisition was performed step by step over a period of twelve years between 1995 and 2007.
2. In 1996-97 the Government of West Bengal, for the first time, estimated Block-wise nine fold land utilization categories. Hence, this year has been taken as the base year for this study.
3. The sample households have been randomly drawn because of two reasons. First, the lists of land loser households were not given by the concerned offices (panchayat office, land acquisition cell or West Bengal Housing Infrastructure Development Corporation Limited). Second, not every dispossessed farmer was ready to provide necessary information about land acquisition.
4. Thakdari comes under Mahisbathan-II village panchayat in Rajarhat. Here process of land acquisition started in 1998 and ended in 2002. The collector assessed the total compensation as ₹ 6,352.50 per *cottah* irrespective of the type and quality of agricultural land in 1998 and added 5 per cent premium on it for the estimation of total compensation for same unit of land in 1999 and thereafter (1 bigha = 20 cottah; 1 acre = 3 bigha).
5. Chakpachuria comes under Patharghata village panchayat. Here acquisition process was started in 2004 and completed in 2006. The dispossessed households informed that in 2003 the compensation rate was revised and the collector gave ₹ 13,500 per *cottah* land. The premium for next year was same as in Thakdari.
6. Revenue villages Rekjuani and Kalaberia come under the jurisdiction of Rajarhat-Bishnupur-I panchayat. A tract of 1149.54 acres (3448.62 bigha) of agricultural land was acquired by the government from this panchayat.
7. Initially, four predictor variables, namely household density, population density, share of non-agricultural worker to total labour force and literacy were used in the regression models for both base and current years. However, due to higher multi-collinearity between household density and population density, the latter has been dropped from the regression model.

8. The prime economic activity of a sample household was determined by the respondent of that household at the time of field survey.

References

Best, R.H. and A.G. Champion (1970). 'Regional Conversions of Agricultural Land to Urban Use in England and Wales, 1945-67', *Transaction of the Institute of British Geographers*, 49(March): 15–32.

Bhupal, Darshan Singh (2012). 'Changing Land Use Pattern in India and its Impact on Supply of Fresh Vegetables', *Journal of Agricultural Science and Technology*, 2: 952–61.

Blewett, Robert A. and Julia I. Lane (1988). 'Development Rights and the Differential Assessment of Agricultural Land: Functional Valuation of Farmland is Ineffective for Preserving Open Space and Subsidizes Speculation', *American Journal of Economics and Sociology*, 47(2): 195–205.

Booklet retrieved from http://www.wbidc.com/images/pdf/industrial_land_use_in_west_bengal.pdf

Chicoine, David L. (1981). 'Farmland Values at the Urban Fringe: An Analysis of Sale Prices', *Land Economics*, 57(3): 353–62.

Dadhich, Pran Nath and Shinya Hanaoka (2011). 'Spatio-Temporal Urban Growth Modeling of Jaipur, India', *Journal of Urban Technology*, 18(3): 45–65.

Dewan, Ashraf M. and Yasushi Yamaguchi (2009). 'Land Use and Land Cover Change in Greater Dhaka, Bangladesh: Using Remote Sensing to Promote Sustainable Urbanisation', *Applied Geography*, 29(3): 390–401.

Dey, Pronab (2011). *Rajarhat Where the Government Turned Dacoit* (*Rajarhat-Sarkar Jakhon Luthera*), Nagarik Mancha, Kolkata.

Ding, Chengri (2007). 'Policy and Praxis of Land Acquisition in China', *Land Use Policy*, 24(3): 1–13.

Drozd, David J. and Bruce B. Johnson (2004). 'Dynamics of a Rural Land Market Experiencing Farmland Conversion to Acreages: The Case of Saunders County, Nebraska', *Land Economics*, 80(2): 294–311.

Ge, H.E. (2012). 'Farmland Acquisition System in China: Problems and Responses', *Canadian Social Science*, 8(4): 258–63.

Government of West Bengal (2008). Industrial Land Use in West Bengal, Commerce and Industries Department.

Hui, Eddie C.M. and Haijun Bao (2013). 'The Logic Behind Conflicts in Land Acquisition in Contemporary China: A Framework Based Upon Game Theory', *Land Use Policy*, 30(1): 373–80.

Kumar, Amit et al. (2011). 'Evaluating the Long Term Urban Expansion of Ranchi Urban Agglomeration: India Using Geospatial Technology', *Journal of the Indian Society of Remote Sensing*, 39(2): 213–24.

Kumar, Vinit (2012). 'SEZs Land Linked Conflicts: In Quest of Amicable Resolutions', *Indian Streams Research Journal*, 2(7): 1–15.

Narain, Vishal (2009). 'Growing City, Shrinking Hinterland: Land Acquisition, Transition and Conflict in Peri-urban Gurgaon, India', *Environment and Urbanisation*, 21(2): 501–12.

Plantinga, Andrew J. and Douglas J. Miller (2001). 'Agricultural Land Values and the Value of Rights to Future Land Development', *Land Economics*, 77(1): 56–67.

Pyle, Lizbeth A. (1985). 'The Land Market Beyond the Urban Fringe', *Geographical Review*, 75(1): 32–43.

Shaklee, Ronald V., Curtis J. Sorenson and Charles E. Bussing (1984). 'Conversion of Agricultural Land in Wyandotte County, Kansas', *Transactions of the Kansas Academy of Science*, 87(1-2): 1–11.

Su, Shiliang et al. (2011). 'Transformation of Agricultural Landscape under Rapid Urbanization: A Threat to Sustainability in Hang-Jia-Hu Region, China', *Applied Geography*, 31(2): 439–49.

Tang, Ying, Robert J. Mason and Ping Sun (2012). 'Interest Distribution in the Process of Coordination of Urban and Rural Construction Land in China', *Habitat International*, 36(3): 388–95.

West Bengal Housing Board (1999). *New Town Calcutta: Rapid Environmental Impact Assessment and Environmental Management Plan Report*, Ghosh, Bose and Associates, Kolkata.

Appendix

Figure 1A

Name of C.D. Blocks around Kolkata

Table 1A

Change in Share of Various Land Use Categories between 1996–97 and 2009–10

Blocks	*Forest*		*Area under Non-agricultural Land*		*Barren and Unculturable Land*		*Permanent Pastures and other Grazing Land*		*Area under Miscellaneous Tree Crops and Groves*		*Cultivable Land*	
	1996–97	*2009–10*	*1996–97*	*2009–10*	*1996–97*	*2009–10*	*1996–97*	*2009–10*	*1996–97*	*2009–10*	*1996–97*	*2009–10*
Balagarh	–	–	23.13	19.02	–	–	–	–	0.08	0.83	76.79	80.15
Pandua	–	–	32.81	31.73	–	–	–	–	0.30	0.32	66.88	67.94
Chinsura_Mogra	–	–	43.14	65.78	–	–	–	–	0.16	0.71	56.70	33.51
Polba_Dadpur	–	–	18.06	20.96	–	–	–	–	0.08	0.50	81.85	78.54
Dhaniakhali	–	–	15.32	19.40	0.60	0.18	–	0.18	0.46	0.89	83.61	79.35
Tarakeswar	–	–	20.07	23.52	0.43	0.18	–	–	0.79	0.13	78.72	76.17
Haripal	–	–	25.18	23.04	–	0.27	–	0.01	1.28	0.74	73.54	75.94
Singur	–	–	34.30	53.11	0.04	–	–	–	1.45	2.45	64.21	44.45
Jangiapara	–	–	19.81	22.29	–	0.01	0.10	0.17	2.98	0.59	77.10	76.95
Chanditola–I	–	–	17.85	15.26	–	–	–	–	0.02	0.16	82.13	84.58
Chanditola–II	–	–	40.61	64.21	0.01	–	–	0.13	0.37	0.87	59.00	34.79
Serampur_Uttarpara	–	–	68.72	90.92	0.12	–	–	–	0.74	0.23	30.42	8.85
Pursura	–	–	25.89	25.26	–	–	0.04	0.02	0.38	1.29	73.69	73.42
Arambag	1.74	1.74	32.57	31.05	1.69	0.02	–	0.02	0.06	0.10	63.95	67.09
Khanakul-I	–	–	19.01	24.00	0.03	0.48	–	0.13	–	0.66	80.95	74.74
Khanakul-II	–	–	25.62	23.27	–	0.32	–	–	0.04	0.13	74.33	76.28
Goghat-I	0.55	0.01	21.37	28.26	–	–	–	–	3.21	0.05	74.87	71.68
Goghat-II	0.10	–	23.29	18.85	–	–	–	–	0.01	0.05	76.60	81.09
Bally-Jagachha	–	–	81.43	98.41	–	–	–	–	–	–	18.57	1.59
Sankrail	–	–	77.04	83.09	–	0.03	–	1.41	0.61	1.44	22.35	14.03

Cont'd…

...Cont'd

Panchla	–	–	15.85	38.67	–	–	–	–	1.58	2.32	82.57	59.01
Domjur	–	–	41.37	55.28	–	–	–	–	1.89	1.45	56.74	43.27
Jagatballavpur	–	–	13.07	23.62	0.01	–	–	–	0.93	0.62	85.99	75.75
Uluberia-I	–	–	31.79	36.23	–	–	–	–	–	0.23	68.21	63.54
Uluberia-II	–	–	30.89	44.16	–	–	–	–	0.37	1.82	68.74	54.02
Bagnan-I	–	–	42.29	36.15	0.13	–	–	–	1.89	0.76	55.69	63.09
Bagnan-II	–	–	31.61	31.52	–	–	–	–	–	0.83	68.39	67.65
Shyampur-I	–	–	24.30	31.48	–	–	–	–	0.21	1.71	75.48	66.81
Shyampur-II	–	–	14.14	20.64	–	–	–	–	0.28	0.03	85.58	79.33
Amta-I	–	–	27.43	22.17	–	–	–	–	0.66	1.35	71.92	76.48
Amta-II	–	–	25.38	29.21	–	–	–	–	0.89	0.07	73.74	8.48
Udaynarayanpur	–	–	27.87	22.30	0.03	–	–	–	1.28	1.10	70.82	76.60
Bhangore-I	–	–	18.80	20.32	–	–	–	–	2.18	1.29	79.02	78.40
Bhangore-II	–	–	22.70	19.32	1.27	–	0.05	–	3.63	0.87	72.35	80.48
Sonarpur	–	–	40.45	66.67	0.67	–	–	–	2.36	0.70	56.53	32.63
Baruipur	–	–	18.24	28.48	–	–	–	–	0.85	0.10	80.91	71.42
Joynagar-I	–	–	22.25	23.55	–	–	–	–	0.20	1.35	77.55	75.11
Joynagar-II	–	–	22.13	14.95	–	–	–	–	0.01	0.01	77.86	85.03
Kultali	–	–	3.13	20.20	–	–	–	–	0.31	–	96.56	79.80
Canning-I	–	–	21.76	25.73	–	–	–	–	–	0.01	78.24	74.25
Canning-II	–	–	12.10	20.42	–	1.50	–	–	–	0.08	87.90	78.00
Basanti	–	–	24.72	22.43	–	–	–	–	–	–	75.28	77.57
Gosaba	–	–	16.89	27.16	–	–	–	–	1.02	–	82.09	72.84
Thakurpukur	–	–	69.57	100.00	1.10	–	–	–	–	–	29.33	–
Maheshtala	–	–	92.32	85.88	–	–	–	–	0.02	–	7.67	14.12

Cont'd...

...Cont'd

Bishnupur-I	–	–	22.02	21.06	–	–	–	–	2.76	–	75.22	81.93
Bishnupur-II	–	–	18.39	51.69	–	1.09	–	0.41	0.20	0.13	81.41	46.67
Budge Budge-I	–	–	48.62	52.63	–	–	–	–	1.46	4.21	49.92	43.16
Budge Budge-II	–	–	32.19	20.59	–	–	–	0.01	2.09	0.15	65.72	79.25
Diamond Harbour-I	–	–	20.41	28.89	0.87	–	–	–	0.33	0.22	78.40	70.89
Diamond Harbour-II	–	–	23.40	20.41	–	–	–	–	1.35	0.18	75.25	79.41
Magrahat-I	–	–	14.28	17.48	–	0.01	–	–	0.75	1.81	84.97	80.70
Magrahat-II	–	–	11.68	12.92	–	0.04	–	–	6.30	0.86	82.01	86.18
Mathurapur-I	–	–	2.44	10.71	–	–	–	–	0.08	0.30	97.48	88.99
Mathurapur-II	–	–	14.87	25.49	–	–	–	–	1.26	0.04	83.87	74.47
Patharpratima	–	–	22.24	30.38	1.26	–	–	–	0.56	3.52	75.94	66.10
Kakdwip	–	–	26.37	18.81	–	–	–	–	0.27	–	73.36	81.19
Namkhana	–	–	28.09	19.45	–	–	–	–	0.90	–	71.00	80.55
Sagar	–	–	20.11	37.52	0.08	–	–	–	0.02	0.32	79.79	62.16
Falta	–	–	19.52	21.57	0.44	–	–	0.01	–	0.11	80.04	78.31
Mandirbazar	–	–	12.45	16.31	–	–	–	–	–	0.02	87.55	83.67
Kulpi	–	–	5.96	28.11	–	–	–	–	–	0.01	94.04	71.88
Amdanga	–	–	18.30	20.91	–	–	–	–	0.53	0.71	81.17	78.38
Barasat-I	–	–	42.82	56.11	–	–	–	–	3.75	0.78	53.43	43.12
Barasat-II	–	–	32.77	39.11	2.75	–	–	–	–	0.16	64.48	60.73
Barrackpore-I	–	–	54.84	62.90	0.03	–	–	–	0.26	0.30	44.87	36.81
Barrackpore-II	–	–	76.90	85.83	–	–	–	–	0.60	0.14	22.50	14.02
Deganga	–	–	15.00	19.59	0.30	–	–	–	–	0.94	84.69	79.48
Habra-I	–	–	40.78	40.39	–	–	–	–	2.55	1.95	56.67	57.66
Habra-II	–	–	27.35	32.35	–	–	–	–	1.16	3.70	71.50	63.95

Cont'd...

...Cont'd

Rajarhat	–	–	40.89	64.23	–	–	–	–	2.08	0.81	57.02	34.96
Baduria	–	–	27.18	28.87	–	–	–	–	0.53	2.63	72.29	68.50
Basirhat-I	–	–	23.38	48.70	–	–	–	–	3.82	1.94	72.79	49.36
Basirhat-II	–	–	10.27	28.00	–	–	–	–	0.91	2.33	88.81	69.68
Haroa	–	–	21.16	30.55	–	–	–	–	0.27	–	78.57	69.45
Hasnabad	–	–	21.52	23.38	–	–	–	–	2.33	3.44	76.15	73.18
Hinjalganj	–	–	18.15	18.97	–	–	–	–	–	1.83	81.85	79.20
Minakhan	–	–	12.75	53.68	–	–	–	–	–	–	87.25	46.32
Sandeshkhali-I	–	–	25.05	20.80	–	–	–	–	–	–	74.95	79.20
sandeshkhali-II	–	–	38.01	38.03	–	–	–	–	–	0.68	61.99	61.29
Swarupnagar	–	–	16.03	14.44	–	–	–	–	2.19	3.84	81.78	81.71
Bagdah	–	–	17.91	17.90	–	–	–	–	3.18	0.45	78.92	81.65
Bongaon	–	–	22.30	16.19	–	–	–	–	0.70	0.47	77.00	83.34
Gaighata	–	–	16.36	17.20	–	–	–	–	0.91	0.78	82.72	82.02
Krishnanagar-I	0.12	0.12	25.01	29.26	0.23	–	–	–	0.68	0.89	73.95	69.72
Krishnanagar-II	1.25	1.25	17.31	16.25	–	0.06	–	–	0.56	0.43	80.88	82.01
Nabadwip	–	–	30.55	33.86	–	1.69	–	–	0.26	0.23	69.19	64.21
Chapra	0.70	0.70	9.04	13.85	0.33	0.04	0.01	–	0.62	0.90	89.30	84.50
Krishnaganj	–	–	17.76	28.50	0.16	–	1.28	–	1.59	0.13	79.21	71.37
Karimpur-I	–	–	5.07	24.39	0.20	–	–	–	4.72	1.49	9–	74.12
Karimpur-II	–	–	6.69	16.26	–	–	–	–	0.72	0.98	92.59	82.76
Tehatta-I	–	–	9.58	21.69	0.15	–	–	–	2.43	0.40	87.84	77.91
Tehatta-II	–	–	22.75	19.56	–	–	–	0.08	1.52	1.06	75.73	79.29
Kaliganj	–	–	12.99	19.15	0.13	–	–	–	0.20	3.37	86.69	77.47
Nakashipara	0.86	0.86	16.43	15.32	–	–	–	–	0.09	0.32	82.62	83.49

Cont'd...

...*Cont'd*

Santipur	0.70	0.70	33.96	37.88	–	–	–	–	0.18	0.30	65.16	61.12
Hanskhali	0.22	0.22	16.01	22.32	–	–	–	0.04	0.81	1.02	82.96	76.40
Ranaghat–I	0.62	0.62	40.79	30.29	–	–	–	–	0.24	0.46	58.35	68.62
Ranaghat-II	0.72	0.72	17.82	16.40	0.03	–	0.05	0.31	0.48	0.87	80.91	81.71
Chakdah	–	–	39.95	37.64	–	–	–	–	0.46	0.89	59.59	61.47
Haringhata	–	–	19.79	20.86	–	0.06	–	–	1.44	1.21	78.77	77.87

Source: Department of Agriculture and Cooperation, Government of West Bengal.

Table 1B

Changing Share of Cultivable Waste Land, Fallow Land and Net Sown Area Across C.D. Blocks

Blocks	Cultivable Waste Land		Fallow other than Current Fallow		Current Fallow		Net Area Sown	
	1996–97	2009–10	1996–97	2009–10	1996–97	2009–10	1996–97	2009–10
Balagarh	–	–	–	–	0.52	–	76.27	80.15
Pandua	0.52	0.65	0.03	–	–	–	66.33	67.29
Chinsura_Mogra	1.56	–	0.86	0.02	–	–	54.28	33.49
Polba_Dadpur	0.30	0.30	0.04	0.09	–	0.26	81.51	77.89
Dhaniakhali	0.51	2.62	–	0.73	–	1.72	83.10	74.27
Tarakeswar	1.43	0.85	0.01	–	–	–	77.28	75.32
Haripal	3.28	0.79	–	–	–	–	70.26	75.15
Singur	0.06	–	–	–	–	–	64.15	44.45
Jangiapara	2.39	2.07	–	–	–	–	74.71	74.88
Chanditola-I	–	1.13	–	0.24	–	–	82.13	83.21
Chanditola-II	0.24	0.99	–	0.03	–	–	58.76	33.77
Serampur_Uttarpara	–	0.01	–	–	–	0.11	30.42	8.73
Pursura	0.09	0.02	–	–	0.52	–	73.08	73.40
Arambag	0.14	0.04	0.49	0.38	–	–	63.32	66.67
Khanakul-I	–	0.06	–	0.33	0.45	–	80.50	74.34
Khanakul-II	0.02	–	–	0.13	–	0.35	74.32	75.79
Goghat-I	4.29	–	–	0.03	–	–	70.58	71.65
Goghat-II	2.78	1.15	–	0.02	0.19	–	73.64	79.92
Bally-Jagachha	–	–	–	–	4.36	1.43	14.21	0.16
Sankrail	–	0.05	0.03	–	1.75	4.20	20.57	9.78
Panchla	0.11	0.70	0.42	0.17	6.50	4.60	75.53	53.53

Cont'd...

...Cont'd

Domjur	–	–	0.21	–	28.33	1.84	28.20	41.43
Jagatballavpur	0.07	–	0.38	0.05	5.11	6.91	80.44	68.80
Uluberia-I	–	–	–	0.15	0.62	0.90	67.59	62.49
Uluberia-II	–	–	0.10	0.10	10.40	7.09	58.24	46.82
Bagnan-I	–	0.38	2.26	0.24	27.39	2.41	26.04	60.07
Bagnan-II	–	–	–	0.25	–	2.94	68.39	64.46
Shyampur-I	0.09	0.01	–	0.03	7.36	0.84	68.03	65.94
Shyampur-II	0.10	–	0.01	0.03	3.48	1.40	81.99	77.90
Amta-I	–	0.01	0.81	0.47	16.61	1.08	54.50	74.92
Amta-II	0.12	–	3.42	0.01	3.90	0.52	66.30	7.95
Udaynarayanpur	0.26	–	0.73	0.23	24.33	3.07	45.51	73.31
Bhangore-I	–	0.16	–	–	5.90	0.63	73.11	77.60
Bhangore-II	–	–	0.33	–	1.13	–	70.89	80.48
Sonarpur	1.19	–	–	–	3.01	0.61	52.32	32.03
Baruipur	–	–	–	–	1.02	6.03	79.89	65.39
Joynagar-I	–	–	–	–	–	–	77.55	75.11
Joynagar-II	–	–	–	–	1.52	–	76.35	85.03
Kultali	–	–	–	–	–	0.67	96.56	79.13
Canning-I	–	–	–	–	–	–	78.24	74.25
Canning-II	–	2.11	–	–	–	0.26	87.90	75.63
Basanti	–	–	–	0.16	1.35	0.27	73.94	77.14
Gosaba	–	–	–	–	0.59	0.71	81.50	72.13
Thakurpukur	0.26	–	–	–	0.07	–	29.00	–
Maheshtala	0.02	–	–	–	0.65	1.08	7.00	13.05
Bishnupur-I	–	–	–	–	1.24	8.33	73.99	71.22

Cont'd...

...Cont'd

Bishnupur-II	–	2.23	–	–	–	0.15	81.41	44.29
Budge Budge-I	–	–	–	–	0.32	0.06	49.60	43.10
Budge Budge-II	–	–	–	0.04	–	0.79	65.72	78.42
Diamond Harbour-I	2.06	–	–	–	4.17	1.78	72.16	69.11
Diamond Harbour-II	–	–	–	–	0.58	1.49	74.67	77.93
Magrahat-I	–	–	–	–	1.01	3.14	83.96	77.56
Magrahat-II	–	–	–	–	0.27	0.56	81.74	85.62
Mathurapur-I	4.77	–	–	–	0.02	0.59	92.69	88.41
Mathurapur-II	–	–	–	–	0.05	–	83.83	74.47
Patharpratima	0.55	–	0.08	0.34	1.92	–	73.39	65.76
Kakdwip	–	–	–	–	–	–	73.36	81.18
Namkhana	–	–	–	–	–	0.65	71.00	79.90
Sagar	–	–	–	–	–	1.20	79.79	60.96
Falta	0.05	–	0.11	–	–	0.47	79.89	77.84
Mandirbazar	–	–	–	–	0.23	0.03	87.31	83.64
Kulpi	–	–	4.39	–	–	0.89	89.65	70.99
Amdanga	0.03	–	–	–	2.58	0.47	78.56	77.91
Barasat-I	–	–	–	–	0.33	0.29	53.10	42.83
Barasat-II	–	–	–	–	–	–	64.48	60.73
Barrackpore-I	0.14	–	–	–	2.38	0.69	42.35	36.12
Barrackpore-II	–	–	–	–	6.17	–	16.34	14.02
Deganga	–	–	–	–	–	–	84.69	79.48
Habra-I	–	–	–	–	–	0.48	56.67	57.18
Habra-II	1.44	–	1.02	–	–	0.38	69.04	63.57
Rajarhat	–	–	–	–	2.09	7.08	54.93	27.88

Cont'd...

...Cont'd

Baduria	–	–	–	–	–	–	72.29	68.50
Basirhat-I	–	–	–	–	–	0.30	72.79	49.06
Basirhat-II	–	–	–	–	–	0.71	88.81	68.97
Haroa	–	–	–	–	–	–	78.57	69.45
Hasnabad	–	–	–	–	–	–	76.15	73.18
Hinjalganj	–	–	–	–	30.08	–	51.77	79.20
Minakhan	–	–	–	–	–	0.37	87.25	45.95
Sandeshkhali-I	–	–	–	–	12.04	–	62.91	79.20
sandeshkhali-II	–	–	–	–	–	2.55	61.99	58.74
Swarupnagar	–	–	–	–	–	–	81.78	81.71
Bagdah	–	–	–	–	–	0.37	78.92	81.28
Bongaon	0.02	–	–	–	–	0.23	76.98	83.11
Gaighata	–	–	–	–	1.09	–	81.63	82.02
Krishnanagar-I	–	–	0.22	–	4.99	1.81	68.75	67.91
Krishnanagar-II	–	0.47	–	–	6.14	1.02	74.74	80.52
Nabadwip	0.83	1.76	–	–	5.00	5.54	63.35	56.92
Chapra	0.84	0.30	0.24	–	13.47	5.90	74.75	78.30
Krishnaganj	0.30	–	0.18	–	–	1.23	78.73	70.14
Karimpur-I	0.14	0.43	0.69	–	–	–	89.18	73.69
Karimpur-II	–	0.08	–	–	12.66	3.52	79.93	79.16
Tehatta-I	–	–	–	–	11.45	3.79	76.39	74.13
Tehatta-II	–	0.86	–	–	–	0.02	75.73	78.42
Kaliganj	0.02	–	–	–	–	–	86.67	77.47
Nakashipara	–	–	–	–	3.31	–	79.31	83.49
Santipur	0.11	–	–	–	–	0.26	65.05	60.86

Cont'd...

...Cont'd

Hanskhali	–	–	–	0.29	–	–	82.96	76.11
Ranaghat-I	0.50	0.07	–	0.02	0.44	–	57.41	68.53
Ranaghat-II	–	–	–	–	–	–	80.91	81.71
Chakdah	–	0.13	–	–	0.62	–	58.97	61.33
Haringhata	1.36	1.48	0.21	0.04	0.04	0.08	77.17	76.28

Source: Department of Agriculture and Cooperation, Government of West Bengal.

10

Intra-city Variation in Urban Growth, Migration and its Impact on Standard of Living

A Case Study of Kolkata Metropolis

Anuradha Banerjee

Contemporary world is marked by unprecedented urban growth; the surplus urban population may represent a considerable volume of urban poor facing multiple deprivation and insecurity of housing as well as livelihood. In Asia, 2.2 billion people or one out of two people live in urban centres, and the continent has more than 11 mega cities each with more than 10 million people. These urban centres act as economic growth engines, cultural hubs and focal points of administrative as well as commercial activities, but the urban paradox exhibits poverty amidst wealth in every Asian city. Many of the causes of urban poverty can be traced to the complexity of resource management and lack of planning for urban growth, land use pattern and urban governance. India's urban transition is an epochal phenomenon, and its abundant creative potential needs to be harnessed to solve poverty, underemployment in rural areas and to deliver a better standard of living to all Indian citizens; but for achieving these goals India's urbanization should go hand in hand with the country's ongoing demographic transition. Thus, there is a need to address India's urban dynamics in terms of both spatial and demographic terms. Kolkata is the third largest metropolis of India (after Greater Mumbai and Delhi: Census 2011) which still shows the typical characteristics of a colonial port city with unplanned urban growth, mixed land use pattern and mushrooming slums almost everywhere within the city. Therefore, unprecedented urban growth, infrastructural inadequacy, environmental degradation and the sprawl of slum colonies are the foremost concerns of urban planners and policy makers. Maladies such as environmental degradation and the resultant threat to human health, encroachment of vacant lands, water bodies, crop lands and greeneries, unregulated construction spree, deterioration in the standard of living especially in slums and low income colonies, etc. have their roots in the 'concerns of foremost importance' cited earlier in the paragraph.

Literature Review

India's urbanization is a legacy of colonial exploitation. There are several studies that have gone into this particular topic with the help of Census data. Class I and II cities recorded rapid increase in population, i.e. by 4.5 and 4.1 respectively between 1971 and 1981. In fact, big cities are growing at a faster rate in India. Few states like Maharashtra, Tamil Nadu, Uttar Pradesh, West Bengal and Gujarat account for over 48.2 per cent of the total urban population of India. On the other hand, Himachal Pradesh and Bihar contain hardly 10 per cent of the urban population (Crook and Dyson, 1982). However, the rate of growth of urbanization is not uniform across the states that have high percentage of urban population, but show the primacy of few metro cities in the urbanization process (Desai and Sita, 1990).

Various historical factors like migration, ecological set-up, landholding system and functions of a city explain regional variation in urbanization (Dasgupta, 2000). Punjab endowed with rich agricultural resources, has no metro city, but many small towns. Agro-based industries and small industries dominate the economic scene of these towns. Punjab has recorded very low rural to urban migration. Kerala on the other hand has small cities and bigger villages, but lacks cities that meet the definition of 'metro-city', which is more in line with Sri Lankan model of urbanization. West Bengal has typical features of the developing world's urbanization. Lopsided urban growth which is largely Kolkata-centred huge population, unemployment and vast backward rural areas remain as rude reminders of past colonial exploitation. Concentration of land in few hands creates large number of landless labourers in agricultural sector and unemployment in villages. It encourages huge rural to urban migration in favour of Kolkata.

In West Bengal urbanization is predominant only in the Bhagirathi-Hooghly basin, and this became even more pronounced after Partition and in order to accommodate refugee population, many new urban centres were set up in this region. Gayeshpur, Taherpur, Fulia, etc. are notable examples of refugee settlements. Refugee migration is, therefore, one of the most important causes behind high urban growth in this region (Kar, 1962). Refugee influx and urban in-migration from rural as well as urban hinterlands have had a severe impact on the standard of living. The concept of 'standard of living' is closely related to living environment; living environment has a direct impact on the overall psychological development of human beings. There is a strong bond and interaction, both positive and negative, between an individual and his or her immediate surroundings (Bell, Greene, Fisher and Baum et al., 2001; Seamon and Mugerauer, 1985).

Housing or shelter is one of the most important basic necessities of human beings and an essential part of a person's living environment (Smith, 1973; Sinha, 1969); housing indicates a person's socio-economic status as well as affluence. According to D.T. Herbert, 'Deprivation' implies a standard of living or a quality of life below that of the majority in a particular society, to the extent that it involves hardship and inadequate access to resources.

Comparisons are made less to an average than to a threshold and all writers on the subject have emphasized the relative nature of these comparisons and standards. Therefore, standard of living is one of the crucial indicators of deprivation, but standard of living changes with time and space. Old mansions built during the 19th century cannot be treated as good ones in the twenty-first century; similarly, people living in the American ghettos live in luxury compared to the slum dwellers of India, because the general standard of living is high in the USA.

Though there are considerable literature on urban growth, migration and urban deprivation; very few of them try to correlate uneven urban growth and unprecedented migration with standard of living. This paper aims to highlight the intracity variations in urban growth and its impact on the standard of living through the following objectives:

Objectives

1 To identify intracity (ward level) variations in urban growth and density within Kolkata
2 To highlight the spatial concentration of slums, and relationship with urban growth and density
3 To reveal intracity (ward level) variations in the Standard of Living

Data and Methodology

The data for the study have come from various census sources like Census of India, 2001 Series-20, West Bengal, Final Population Totals and the distribution of Rural-Urban Population, Director of Census Operations, Kolkata, West Bengal (2001), Registrar General and Census Commissioner, Government of India. *Census 2001; H – Series (Table: H3a, H3b, H3c, H5, H9, H8, H11 and H13)* Director of Census Operations, Kolkata, West Bengal (2001). Following methodology has been adopted for analysis:

- Extraction of data on urban growth, density, areal changes from the Census 2001 and 1991; joining operations of spatial and Census data to find out the localities with haphazard urban growth and high slum population; and finally,
- Thematic mapping using GIS technique.
- Composite Index: With the help of Z-score method, composite index has been constructed and with the help of the average Z-score values ward level deprivation mapping has been done. Formula used for this technique is where: μ is the mean of the population; σ is the standard deviation of the population.

The quantity *z* represents the distance between the raw score and the population mean in units of the standard deviation. *Z* is negative when the raw score is below the mean, positive when above. In statistics, a standard score indicates by how many standard deviations an observation or datum is above or below the mean. It is a dimensionless quantity derived by subtracting the population mean from an individual raw score and then dividing the difference by the population standard deviation.

Index of Substandard Living

North-eastern wards (Tangra-Tiljala-Narkeldanga) and western peripheral wards (Garden Reach and Metiabruz) have the highest concentration of slums. These wards record more than ninety-nine per cent of their population living in slums or they can be called as 'slum wards'. Apart from these wards, few wards in the southern extremity also record acute housing deprivation, though these are not slum wards. North-eastern and southern peripheries of Kolkata are the major urban growth pockets receiving continued migration from South 24 Parganas district and Bangladesh.

Historical Background

Kolkata is the third largest metropolis of India (after Greater Mumbai and Delhi (Census 2011). Till 1911, it was the capital of British India and in 1912 the British moved the capital to Delhi. However, it continued to be the major trade centre and gateway to eastern India. Since independence, Kolkata is the capital of the State of West Bengal. The major contributory factors for the growth of the city can be listed as:

Political Changes: The chance mid-day halt by Job Charnock and the three villages of Sutanuti, Gobindopore and Kalikata form the foundations of the city. The defeat of the then Nawab of Bengal, Shiraj-Ud-Doula in 1757 exemplified British history of annexation and fortification (Fort Williams) at the strategic point of the city. With this came the opening of business offices and series of large business godowns along the river Hooghly.

Economic Transformation: Initially, Kolkata grew with small business houses which gradually became larger and larger, and a number of these houses established their administrative head offices in the city. Apart from the foreign investors, a group of landed class also transferred their surplus from agriculture to trade, commerce and industries. The administrative measures of the then colonial power played a vital role in the rapid transformation of the town economy. All these forces helped the growth of the city directly or indirectly.

Post-Independence Changes: With the influx of refugees after independence from the then East Pakistan and migrants from the neighbouring states and districts, Kolkata witnessed a substantial increase of population in and around the city, particularly in its peripheral areas. A group of municipal towns (39) came to encircle the city over time and have actually turned the erstwhile isolated town of Kolkata to a large urban agglomeration. In fact, economic as well as social factors have contributed much for the expansion of the city over a period of time. Spatial expansion may be attributed to pull forces which gradually transformed the surrounding rural settlements to new town areas and emergence of Kolkata Metropolitan Area (KMA). Pattern of growth of KMA over the years has direct bearing on the development of infrastructure, density of population and intracity variations. Thus, recent developments superimposed on a colonial port city, have burdened Kolkata with unplanned urban growth, mixed land use pattern and development of slums. Unprecedented urban growth has its impact on the standard of living intra-city (Ward Level) variations in urban growth and density in Kolkata

Figure 1

Population Growth (1991–2001) (Kolkata Municipality)

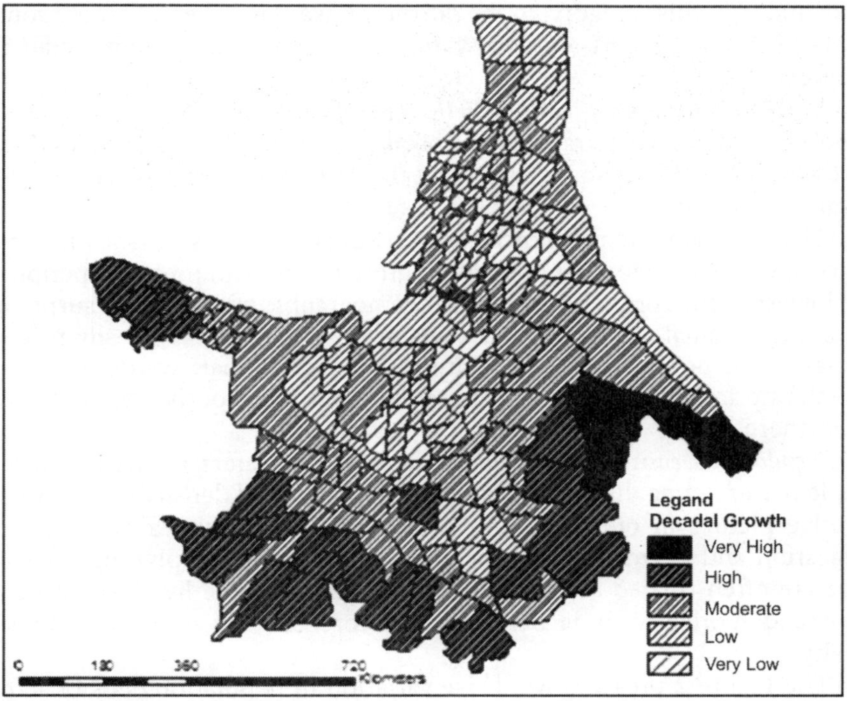

Source: Census 2001, Final Population Totals, West Bengal.

Urban Growth (1991-2001)

The growth rate of a population at time 't' is defined as the change in number per unit population at the time period (rt = dn/Ntd). The rate usually changes with time as the population increases or decreases. Figure 1 exhibits wardwise variations in urban growth (1991-2001) across Kolkata. Population growth is the highest in ward number 108. According to the decadal population growth, the entire city can be categorized into five zones viz.

1. *Very High Growth*: Very high growth rate is found in ward number 108, located in the south eastern fringe of Kolkata.

2. *Wards with High Growth Rate:* Ward number 106, 107, 109, 101, 113, 111, 114, 122, 123, 124, 125, 127, 128, 129,139, 138, 140 and 141 are areas with very high population growth. All these wards are located in the southern periphery of Kolkata. Among them, ward number 139, 138, 140 and 141 are situated near the Kolkata port, depicting extreme urban congestion.

3. *Wards with Moderate Growth Rate:* This zone includes most of the wards of Kolkata and are found equally across the city; most of the wards of

the north and Central Kolkata come under this category. Wards in the immediate vicinity of high growth wards have also recorded moderate growth rate.

4. *Wards with Low Growth Rate:* Wards with low growth rate are found in the central Kolkata. In the north, ward number 1, 2, 3, 4, 5 and 14 are included in this category; in the northeast, ward number 57, in the south, ward number 79, 78, 81 and few wards of Central Kolkata come under the category.

5. *Wards with Very Low Growth Rate:* Wards with very low growth rate are found in the central part of Kolkata (ward number 15, 28, 34, 35, 36, 47, 64, 69, etc.). This also indicates that the core area is progressively moving towards depopulation.

The demographic differences across Kolkata's wards, as shown above, clearly indicate the fact that population growth is maximum at the periphery and lowest at the core. The centrifugal demographic trend is least surprising for an old colonial city like Kolkata where the city core has already reached saturation point. But, the most interesting fact is that, wards with high growth rate are found mainly in the southern periphery of the city, and not in its northern border.

Population Density (2001): Population density refers to the number of people per unit area during a specified time. The word density conjures up a negative picture in our mind. An area with high density always denotes congestion and overcrowding. Therefore, in urban geography high density areas are often treated as deprived locales where people live in inadequate space and moreover, it is believed that core city always shows highest density.

The Figure 2 presents wardwise variation in population density across Kolkata, and five such 'density zones' have been identified.

Figure 2
Population Density in Kolkata (2001)

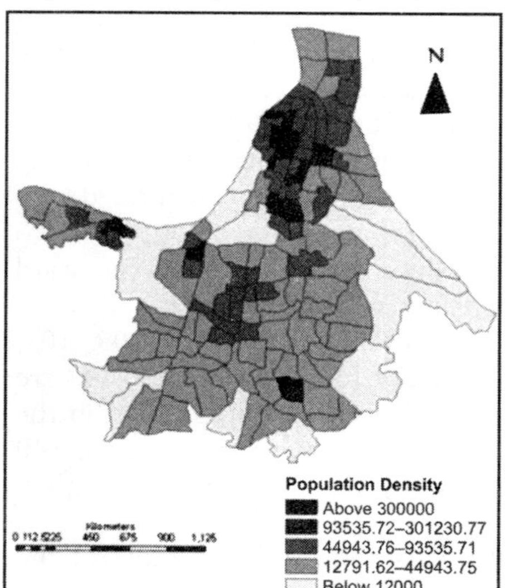

Figure 3
Household Density in Kolkata (2001)

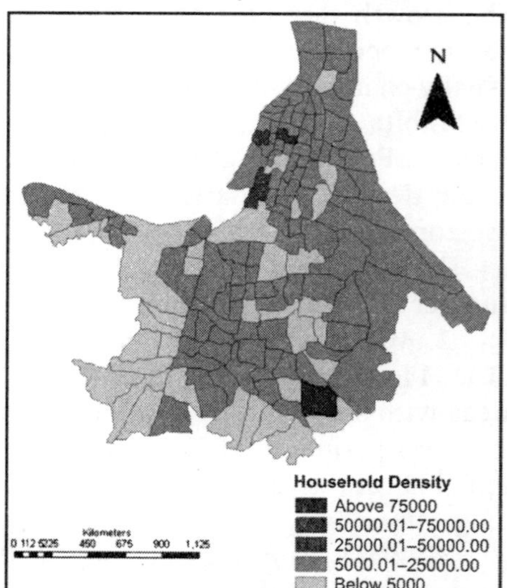

Household Density (2001)

A household is a unit composed of the group of people living in the same dwelling space, sharing meals and have at least one common plot or one income generating activity (for example, herding, business or fishing) and acknowledge the authority of a man or woman who is the head of the household. Household density refers to the number of households per unit area. Figure 3 depicts ward-wise variation in household density across Kolkata. Highest household density is recorded in ward no. 101 (Jadavpur area) and very high density is recorded in few wards of north and central Kolkata, while the rest of the city has moderate household density. Low and very low density zones are located in the south-western part of Kolkata and near the port area. It is interesting to note that, in Garden Reach-Metiabruz area, urban growth and population density are very high but household density is r.

Correlation between Density and Existence of Slum Settlements in Kolkata:

Table 1

Slum Locales of Kolkata

Main Slum Locales	*Location*
Cossipore-Chitpur-Belgachia, North Kolkata	North Kolkata (ward number 6, 3, 1, 12 and 5)
Tangra-Tiljala-Topsia, North-eastern fringe	North-eastern fringe of Kolkata, near the Eastern Metropolitan Bypass (ward number 58,57, 56, etc.)
Metiabruz-Graden Reach, West Kolkata	West Kolkata, near the port
Central and South Kolkata	Scattered slum settlements in few wards

Generally, urban geographers argue that slum and squatter settlements are found in high density areas and, therefore, congestion is one of the salient features of urban slums, but it is not totally true. The highest number of households living in slums is found in very low density areas, i.e. ward number 55, 56, 57, 58 and 59 (Tangra-Tiljala-Topsia region). It cannot be concluded that wards with high density have very negligible percentage of slum households, because high-density wards like 138, 137, 133 in Graden Reach-Metiabruz area also have very high percentage of slum households. The highest density is recorded in Jadavpur area (ward number 99) but this region has less than 20 per cent household residing in slums. Some wards with moderate density (ward number 6, 13, 14 in the north, 87 in the south and 46, 47 in the central part of Kolkata) have a high percentage of household residing in slums. It is clear, therefore, that in Kolkata slum settlements are found in very low density areas as well as in high and moderate density areas.

Figure 4 and Table 2 illustrates that Kolkata's top five wards where more than 90 per cent of the total population live in slums, are located mainly in low density areas with high urban growth, except two wards in Metiabruz area. According to Census 2001, Tangra-Tiljala and Narkeldanga

Figure 4

Correlation between Population Density and Existence of Slums in Kolkata (2001)

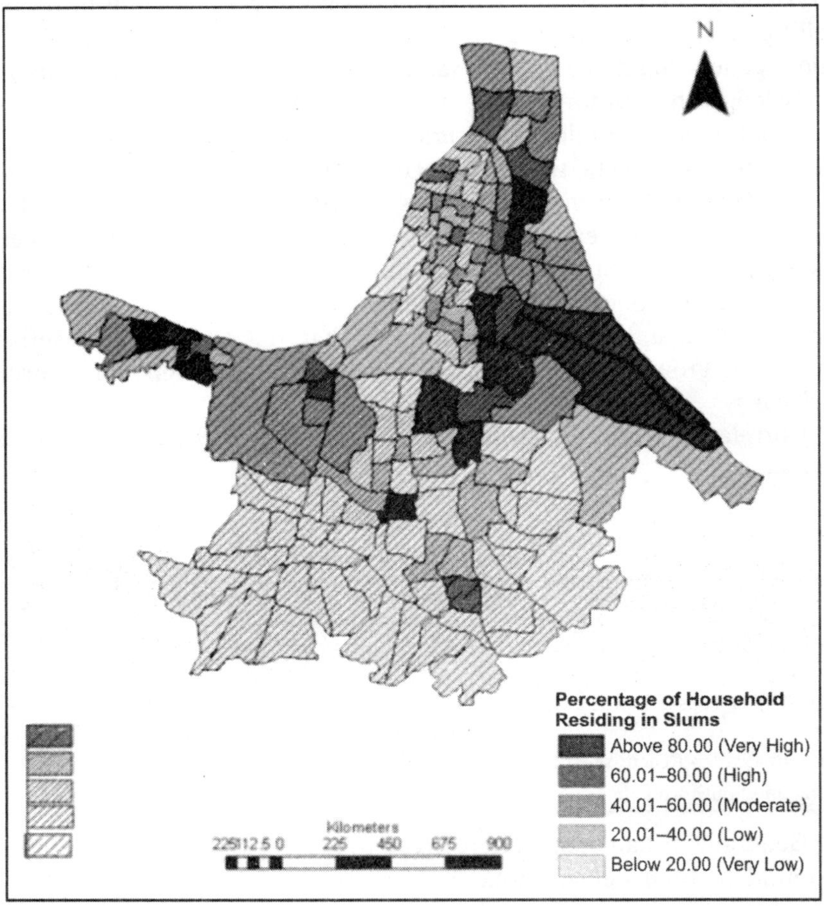

areas, located in the north-eastern periphery of Kolkata have low density, high population growth and highest percentage of population living in slums. On the other hand, Metiabruz-Garden Reach area in the west near the Kolkata port shows a completely different picture. Though 95 per cent of the total population of ward nos. 137 and 134 reside in slum colonies, these two wards have registered high density as well as high population growth during the last decade.

The wards located in the eastern and western peripheries of Kolkata do have more than 90 per cent of the total population residing in slums, but the nature of urban growth differs between these two parts. While the western periphery has recorded high growth rate as well as fairly high density, the eastern periphery has very high growth rate but very low density. On the basis of the size of slum population in each, wards located in Tangra, Tiljala and Topsia region (ward number 58, 65, 59, 66, and 67) and Narkeldanga area (ward 29) can be ranked as the top six slum wards in Kolkata.

Table 2

Relationship between Urban Growth, Density and Existence of Slums in Kolkata

Ward Number	Location	Rank in Percentage of Slum Population To Total Population	Urban Growth (2001)	Population Density (2001)	Rank by Size of Slum Population
58	Tangra-Tiljala	1st (99.98% population live in slums)	High	Very low	1st
29	Narkeldanga	2nd (98.8% population live in slums)	Low	Low	5th
137	Metiabruz	3rd (98.35% people live in slum)	High	Moderate	19th
134	Garden Reach, West Port	4th (97.85% population living in slums)	High	High	11th
65	Tiljala	5th (91.97% population live in slum)	Moderate	Low	2nd

Source: Census of India, 2001, Final Population Totals, West Bengal: Slum Population with Percentage of Slum Population to Total Population, Rank and Sex Ratio, West Bengal/Statutory Towns, 2001, Table 13.

Thus, it cannot be said that the wards with high density or the wards with high percentage of urban population tend to be slum locales. In Kolkata, though slum wards are found in the peripheral parts of the city where growth rate is high, the magnitude and dimensions of deprivation vary widely within each of these wards. Unless and until ward-wise variations in regard to access to various assets, amenities and services are analysed, one cannot gauge the depth of urban deprivation that cripples the area in manifold dimensions.

Intracity Variations in the Standard of Living

Standard of living is an important yardstick to measure the impact of urban growth on peoples' living environment; therefore, a composite index entitled as 'Index of Substandard Living' has been computed to assess ward level variations in standard of living:

Table 3

Indicators for Computing the Index of Substandard Living

Asset based Indicators	Housing Infrastructure based Indicators	Amenities and Basic Service based Indicators
Percentage of Households not having access to: • Television set, • Radio or Transistor • Telephone • Bicycle • Two wheelers (scooter, motor cycle, moped) • Four wheelers (car, jeep, van) • None of the specified assets.	Percentage of Households not having access to formal housing: • Household having lack of access to formal housing • Inadequate room	Percentage of Households having lack of access to: • Banking service • Electricity • Safe cooking fuel or LPG • Potable drinking water • Nearby source of drinking water

Figure 5
Index of Sub-Standard Living

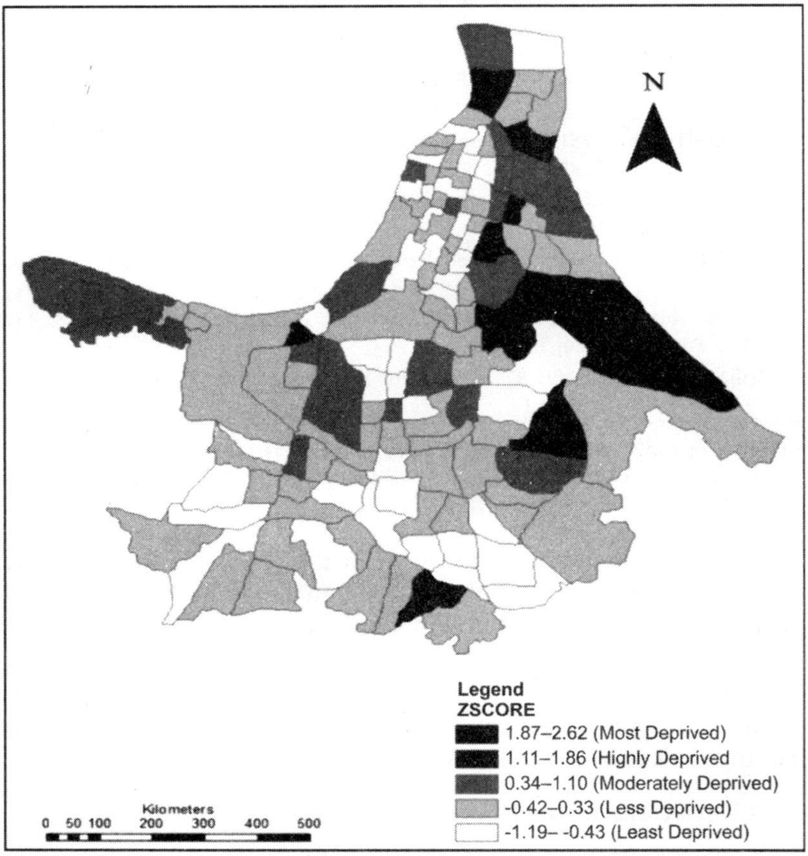

As illustrated in Figure 5 and Table 4, the highest level of deprivation is found in ward numbers 108 (2.62) and 109 (2.40). The next category, i.e. 'highly deprived' wards, are 57, 58, 29, 6, 13 and 36. These wards constitute the Tangra-Tiljala-Topsia region (57, 58, 108, and 109), and are situated on the eastern margin of Kolkata along the Eastern Metropolitan Bypass. Other wards constitute parts of Narkeldanga-Beliaghata region (ward 29), just adjacent to Tangra-Tiljala-Topsia region, Ultadanga-Maniktola area (ward 13) and part of Cossipore region (ward-6) in the extreme north. Ward number 79 in the south-west, embracing Khidirpore-Ekbalpore area also shows high level of deprivation. Though Garden Reach-Metiabruz region record for a very high percentage of household living in slums and a significant number of households not having access to various assets or amenities, wards in this area can however be termed as moderately deprived locales. Moderately deprived wards are also found in north Kolkata as well as in central Kolkata, but in the south they are very few in number except those located on the south-eastern fringe of Kolkata.

Table 4

Spatial Expression of Deprivation in Kolkata, 2001

Deprivation Index	*Score*	*Wards*	*Location*
Most deprived	1.87–2.62	110, 109	Eastern periphery, parts of Tiljala-Topsia-Kasba area
Highly deprived	1.11–1.86	58,57, 79,29, 13, 6, 36	North Tangra, Narkeldanga-Beliaghata, Ultadanga-Maniktola, Cossipore
Moderately deprived	0.34–1.10	1, 3,7,12, 14, 15, 21, 28, 31, 32, 39, 56, 59, 65, 80, 82,134, 135, 136, 137, 138, 139, 140, 141	Parts of Ultadanga, Cossipore, Tangra, Narkeldanga in north Kolkata Garden Reach Metiabruz, Ekbalpore area in south
Less deprived	–0.42 to 0.33	Wards are scattered in north, central and extreme southern part of Kolkata	
Least deprived	–1.93 to –.041	Central and south Kolkata	

Case Study: Slums of Kolkata

There are two broad categories of slums in Kolkata – slums that are officially recognized are called 'bustees'; and the large number of unauthorized squatter settlements that have sprung up by the side of canals (khaldhar), large drains, railway tracks/roads (jhupri) and on any vacant land/garbage dumps, known as udbastu. Living conditions in these shanties are the worst, being deprived of any basic amenities such as sanitation or water. They also live under the constant threat of eviction from civic authorities/lawful owners of land, etc. Lack of basic amenities makes the squatters to use any available space for easing themselves and the pollution and public nuisance due to this are quite high. The slums of Kolkata also can be divided into two groups, the older slums located in the heart of the city, some as old as 150 years (British period), and the recent slums mostly located in the outskirts of the city.

Table 5

Spatial Variations in Vulnerability in Slums of Kolkata 2011

Vulnerability Scores	*Slums*	*Location*	*Population Sub-groups/Communities*
Least Vulnerable (Below 0.10)			
Less Vulnerable (0.11–0.20)	Tollygunj	Southern Kolkata	East Bengal Refugees Hindus, General Caste
Moderately Vulnerable (0.21–0.30)	Chandni Chowk	Central Kolkata	Migrants from Bihar, UP, Odisha
Highly Vulnerable (0.31–0.40)			
Extremely Vulnerable (Above 0.40)	Dhapa, Garden Reach/Metiaburz	Eastern periphery, Western Kolkata	WB, N. India, Scheduled Caste (Dule, Bagdi, Chamars) Muslims from UP and Bihar

Source: Vulnerability Scores computed from field generated data, 2011.

Case I: Dhapa Slum in North Tangra (Ward 58)

This slum colony is situated on the north-eastern periphery of Kolkata, close to the Dhapa solid waste-disposal ground. Due its proximity to a waste-disposal ground, Dhapa slum is exposed to a multitude of environmental problems like bad odour, dust and smoke from nearby plastic and leather factories, lack of sanitation, extreme levels of groundwater contamination and other such health hazards. Slum dwellers here are highly vulnerable to various afflictions due to their unhealthy environment. The common characteristics of slum population characterized by illiteracy, poverty and unemployment adds to their vulnerability. Most residents here belong to the Scheduled Castes (Dule, Bagdi and Chamars) from West Bengal and other North Indian states. Currently rag-picking, personal services, factory work (plastic, wineries, etc.), rickshaw pulling and other types of informal activities are the common occupations here; mean income hovers around ₹ 7,000/month, women work participation is high, and family size is generally small in this slum.

Case II: Alagarah Mazdoor Lane Slum of Garden Reach/Metiaburz (Ward 80)

This slum is located near Kolkata port (West) and is inhabited by Muslims from Bihar and Uttar Pradesh. It was set up after 1971 (Liberation of Bangladesh). Illiteracy is high especially among women and the general education level is low. Men are mainly engaged in jari works and other low-paid jobs like rickshaw pulling, carrying loads in the port, truck driving and so on while the womenfolk stay at home and earn by making kite sticks. Average income here is ₹ 5,500/month per household or person. In addition, this slum is located in a crime and conflict prone zone, and social seclusion characterizes this slum. However, living condition and environment are not as bad as in Dhapa slum since the slum has underground drainage, good drinking water and other amenities.

Case III: Tollygunj Slum, South Kolkata (Ward 88)

Originated in 1960s as a refugee colony, the Tollygunj slum is now mainly inhabited by Bengali speaking upper caste Hindus. The level of education among the slum dwellers is found to be high and people here are mainly engaged in transport sector work, private formal jobs, petty business, construction work repairing works, etc. for their livelihood. There are also women who work as maids and nurses with an average income of ₹ 10,000/month. Living conditions are better here than other slums since the residents enjoy access to underground drainage, safe cooking fuel, good roads and safe drinking water. However, household congestion factor and room rent are high; buildings are old and dilapidated.

Case IV: Chandni Chawk Slum, Central Kolkata (Ward: 47)

Located in central Kolkata or core city, this slum is characterized by high room rent and congestion. People are generally recent migrants from Bihar,

UP, Odisha and other neighbouring states; they work in the nearby market area as shopkeepers, mechanics, porters, drivers and construction workers and the residents are economically better off compared to other slums, with average income of ₹ 15,000/month. Large and extended families, mess type accommodation and male dominated households characterize this slum, with very few inhabitants living with their families. Subtenancy is also common, and landlords let out space at exorbitant rent and live elsewhere in the city. People have access to all types of amenities and infrastructure but buildings are old and dilapidated.

Findings and Conclusion

Kolkata's urban growth and population density show an interesting spatial pattern: During the decade 1991-2001, growth rate was high in the south eastern part of the city especially in the wards adjacent to the Eastern Metropolitan bypass and southernmost part of the city. High density zones are also found in the extreme north, central Kolkata and few wards in the west near Garden Reach-Metiabruz area. Jadavpur area is the only region from south Kolkata which has recorded very high density in the decade under study. In case of Kolkata, population density and incidence of slums have an inverse relationship; largest concentration of slums is found in very low density areas. Wards where over three-fourths of the total households live in slums, are found in three locales, i.e. Cossipore-Chitpur-Belgachia region in the extreme north, Tangra-Tiljala-Narkeldanga region in the eastern periphery and Garden Reach-Metiabruz region in the extreme west near the port. Of these, Tangra-Tiljala-Narkeldanga contains the highest number of slum households in the city. This region constitutes the peri-urban interface of Kolkata and is characterized by high urban growth but very low density. The Index of Substandard Living computed for the entire ward population with the help of household amenities data provided by the Census of India reveals that the standard of living is very low in the wards lying in the north-eastern peripheral part of the city (Tangra-Tiljala-Narkeldanga). Therefore, north-eastern periphery of Kolkata needs special attention as this area is experiencing rapid urban growth and abject poverty, but has high potential for further development.

References

Bell, P.A., T.C. Greene, J.D. Fisher and A. Baum (2001). *Environmental Psychology*, Harcourt College Publishing, San Diego, California.

Crook, Nigel and Tim Dyson (1982). 'Urbanization in India: Results of the 1981 Census', *Population and Development Review*, 8(1): 145–51.

Dasgupta, Biplav (2000). 'Contrasting Urban Pattern in Punjab, West Bengal and Kerala', in A. Kundu (ed.), *Inequality, Mobility and Urbanization*, Manak Publications, New Delhi.

Department for International Development (2001). 'Meeting the Challenge of Poverty in Urban Areas', Strategy Paper, London.

Desai, R.J. and K. Sita (1990). 'Metropolitan Dominance in Maharashtra, 1971–1981', *Urban India*, X(1): 13–26.

Kar, N.R. (1962). 'Pattern of Urban Growth in Lower West Bengal (A Study in Regional Characteristics and Trend of Urbanization in and around Calcutta Metropolis)', *Geographical Review of India*, XXIV(3): 42–59.

Seamon, D. and R. Mugerauer (eds) (1985). *Dwelling, Place and Environment: Towards a Phenomenology of Person and World*, Martinus Nijhoff Publishers, Netherlands.

Sinha, V.N.P. (1969). 'Houses and House Types of the Chotanagpur Plateau', *Geographical Knowledge*, 2: 91.

Smith, D.M. (1973). *The Geography of Social Well-Being in the United States: An Introduction to Territorial Social Indicators*, McGraw-Hill, New York, 71, 85.

11

Impact of Urban Growth, Land Use Changes on Socio-Economic Vulnerability in the East Kolkata Wetland

An Assessment through Sustainable Livelihood Approach

Mala Mukherjee

India's urban transition is a historical phenomenon which has the potential to solve poverty and underemployment in rural areas and deliver a better standard of living to all Indian citizens. However, for achieving these goals India's urban development should be so customized as to meet the livelihood aspiration of the urban poor. 'Sustainable Livelihood Approach' (SLA) acknowledges economic vulnerability of the weaker sections of the society through the multifaceted dimensions of poverty which shows how the poor people develop diverse and changing livelihood portfolios to address their socio-economic vulnerability, which is not found equally among all sections of the society. Even within cities some areas especially the peri-urban areas witness a complex process of rapid urban growth and resultant environmental and social change which impacts peoples' livelihood opportunities unequally. Urban growth and the shift in land use pattern from rural to urban tend to benefit those who seek jobs in the non-agricultural sectors but deprive the people depending on primary activities. Therefore, through this approach, planned livelihood strategies can be developed which will help the urban poor to build up enough asset base and gain access to basic services and amenities for consumption. In this paper, socio-economic vulnerability of the residents of East Kolkata Wetlands has been addressed through the Sustainable Livelihood Approach (SLA). Just like other South Asian cities, Kolkata is often portrayed as an overcrowded, haphazardly grown and congested city with seemingly insurmountable problems of inadequate shelter, lack of clean water, inadequate infrastructure, filthy air, unemployment and underemployment. These deficiencies combined with inadequate resources, create a feeling of despair and hopelessness in the hapless residents in these settlements; these problems are more acute in the peripheral areas, especially in the north-eastern periphery, where most of the unauthorized slum settlements are on encroachments on the East Kolkata Wetlands.

Literature Review

Sustainable livelihood analyses (SLA) has now become the dominant approach in implementation of development interventions and several international agencies have been using this method since the 1990s; but the concept had remained vague and in rudimentary stage until the UK's Department for International Development (DFID) coined a systematic definition for this approach. The DFID defines sustainable livelihood analyses as: 'A livelihood comprises the capabilities, assets (stores, resources, claims and access) and activities required for a means of living; a livelihood is sustainable which can cope with and recover from stress and shocks, maintain or enhance its capabilities and assets, and provide sustainable livelihood opportunities for the next generation; and which contributes net benefits to other livelihoods at the local and global levels and in the short and long-term' (Chambers and Conway, 1992: 7).

'A livelihood is sustainable when it can cope with and recover from stresses and shocks and maintain or enhance its capabilities and assets both now and in the future, while not undermining the natural resource base'. SLA seeks to identify important assets in livelihood, their trends over time and space as well as the nature and impact of shocks or stress (both natural and manmade or socio-economic). SLA based policies are designed to address vulnerability by diversification of income streams. Thus, it is a systematic approach which can assess the issue of socio-economic vulnerability on the basis of the exposure of different groups to particular shocks, trends and seasonality and by analysing the sensitivity of their livelihood to these factors (Moser, 1996; Farrington, Ramasut and Walker et al., 2002). This approach places a special emphasis on 'access to' and 'control over' various assets; here assets can be classified as 'tangible' (physical assets which can be owned) and 'non-tangible' (social capital and legal frameworks which can help people to ensure their access to assets) assets (Chambers, 1995). Other international agencies like OXFAM, CARE and UNDP have classified assets as 'human', 'social', 'natural', 'physical', 'economic' and 'political'. 'Political capital' is the ability to influence political processes or decision-making process (Baumann and Sinha; 2001).

Many scholars have included labour, social infrastructure, housing, household relation and social capital in the list of assets (Moser, 1998). This approach can work at three levels (Farrington, Chapman and Slaymaker et al., 2001). The first one is the 'development objective level' which enhances the sustainability of peoples' livelihoods with particular focus on the livelihoods of the urban poor. The 'General Development Principles' state that all policies should be 'people centred', 'differentiated by recognising specific needs of different groups and areas', 'based on multi-level perspectives with micro-macro linkages', 'partnership between public-private and community sector', 'multi-dimensional concept of poverty' and should be based on holistic and dynamic principles (Carnery, 1998; Meikle et al., 2001).

The question of the applicability of SLA in the urban context has been replied by many scholars in many ways. Within cities, very different conditions exist in the peripheral areas or 'peri-urban' interface, which is defined as the meeting place of rural-urban activities, subject to environmental and social changes that represent livelihood opportunities, shocks and stress to the local population. Urbanization as a process has profound impact on peoples' livelihood especially in the peri-urban areas. A study of the urban fringes of Hubli-Dharwad city in Karnataka has revealed that urbanization has increased opportunity for employment over the years, but people especially women dependent on firewood collection and various other primary activities have lost jobs (DPU, 2001).

The literature reviewed in the paragraphs above forms the background for this study. A particular area of the East Kolkata Wetlands (Dhapa area Ward 58) has been selected as the study sample, as this ward has been witnessing rapid urban growth and change in land use pattern; for the same reason, this ward has witnessed livelihood vulnerabilities and further marginalization of the urban poor who were earlier dependent on fishing, farming and other primary activities.

Objectives

The objectives of this paper are the following:

1. To identify ward level variation in population growth, density, distribution of slum households, slum illiteracy and concentration of male non-workers in Kolkata with particular reference to East Kolkata Wetlands
2. To identify major shifts in land use pattern in East Kolkata Wetlands
3. To identify the nature of livelihood vulnerability of different households to the loss of livelihood and other socio-economic factors based on their exposure.

Data Sources and Methodologies

- For trend analyses, secondary data on population density, household density, population growth, percentage distribution of slum households, slum illiteracy, slum household size and percentage of male non-workers living in slums have been thematically mapped and analysed using ARC GIS software; from these analyses, socio-economic and demographic characteristics and trends have been obtained for the wards comprising East Kolkata Wetlands.
- Primary data collected from the field survey conducted during 17 September to 17 December 2011 from Dhapa settlement (ward 58) have been analysed using various statistical techniques (cross tabulation and PCA) to show 'access to' and 'control over' the following assets:
    1. Social capital (measuring social status through caste, religion and education level), human capital (family size, type and composition)

livelihood opportunities, change in occupation, control over working environment (daily duration of work, job satisfaction and chances of job loss), household income and expenditure, possession of voter card, ration card and access to formal credit by way of having bank account and insurance cover.

2. Construction of Composite Index (Livelihood Vulnerability Index) by Modified PCA with these indicators, vulnerable households have been categorized into five groups.
3. Listing of the occurrence of livelihood loss and its impact on individual households has been done through case studies.

Study Area and Research Problem

East Kolkata Wetlands form a part of the extensive inter-distribution of wetland regimes formed by the Gangetic delta (located in 22°0′27′ N. Latitude and 88°0′27′E Longitude). It consists of a complex system of natural and manmade wetlands lying east of Kolkata and covers 125 sq km. This area includes salt marshes, salt meadows, salt meltdown and sewage ponds. When Job Charnock laid the foundation of the Kolkata city on the levees of river Hooghly, the wetland covering the eastern fringes of the city was forested marshy area. The area was also called Salt Lake, serving as the backwater swamp and spill area of Bidyadhari River. Tidal effects of the Bay of Bengal made the water brackish or salty. Since early 15th century, the eastward shift of the course of river Hooghly has been bringing considerable changes in the process of delta formation in central and southern parts of Bengal. East Kolkata Wetlands constitutes a large system of marshes located in the peri-urban interface of Kolkata city. Proposal for converting the wetlands to accommodate the ever-expanding city of Kolkata was first made in 1830s but it was successfully implemented only in 1969 after the establishment of Bidhan Nagar Township, popularly known as Salt Lake City by reclaiming nearly 1,000 hectares of these lands.

A group of environmentalists had questioned the reclamation of the wetland for urban development in 1980s, and the government had initiated systematic research on the issues of the wetlands and its waste regulatory systems. The Ramsar Convention (2002) had designated it as a wetland of international importance. Later, in 2006 the 'East Kolkata Wetlands Management Authority' came into existence. Its main functions are the demarcation of the wetland boundaries, detecting changes in ecology and land uses, preventing unauthorized developmental projects, mining, quarrying, blasting and polluting activities and promoting researches on wetlands. Currently, a large number of low income households in this area are depending upon fishing and farming activities but there is hardly any initiative to protect their livelihood from the onslaught of rapid urbanization, nor are there any well-planned alternative livelihood strategies for those who stand to lose their jobs.

Discussions

As can be seen from the Ward map of Kolkata (Figure 1) urban growth is the highest in ward number 108 (shaded by black); wards 58 and 57 also have recorded impressive growth. These three wards comprise part of the East Kolkata Wetlands. Apart from this region, high urban growth is found in the south eastern and western peripheries of Kolkata.

Figure 1

Population Growth (1991–2001) (Kolkata Municipality)

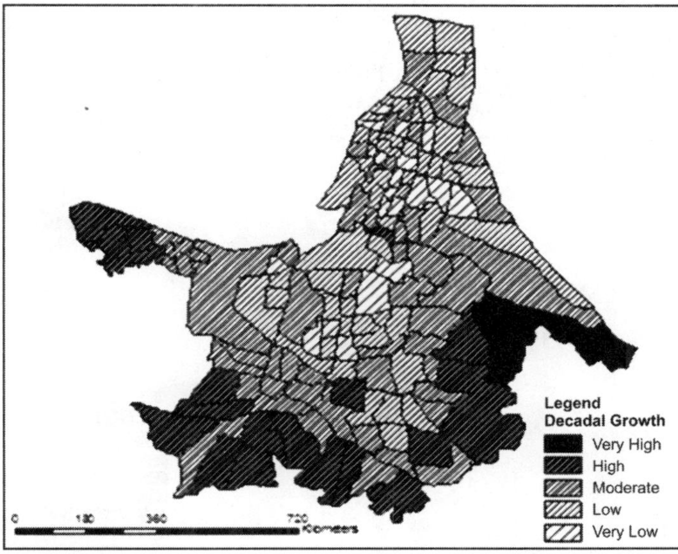

Source: Map prepared with ARC-GIS with the help of Census 2001 data.

As can also be seen the above map (Figure 2) the East Kolkata Wetlands mainly consists of agricultural lands, rural settlements, large water bodies and farms. It forms the immediate neighbourhood of Kolkata and provides fresh fruits, vegetables and fish to the city dwellers. Expansion of urban

Figure 2

Land Use Classification in East Kolkata Wetlands (EKW)

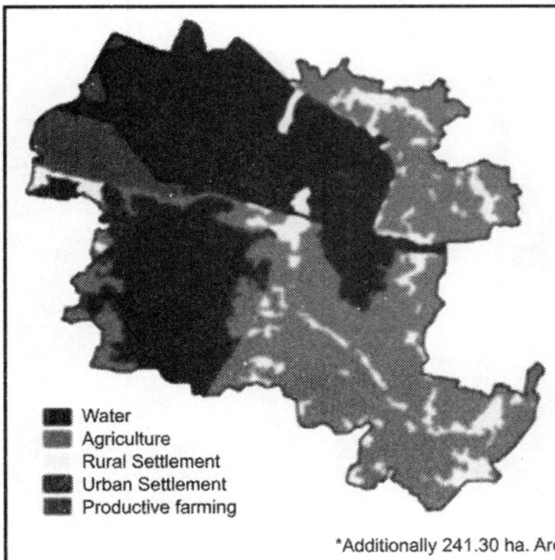

Land	Area
Water body	5,852.14 ha of which fish farming roughly constitutes about 3,898.70 ha. (45.93%)
Agriculture Land	Approximately 4,959.86 ha. (38.92%)
Garbage Disposal Site	602.78 ha. (4.73%)
Urban Settlement Area Rural Area	91.53 ha. (0.73%) 1234.99 ha. (9.69%)
Total Area	12500.00 ha.*

*Additionally 241.30 ha. Are being added to the system for making the system integral.

settlement to this area is by encroaching on agricultural lands and water bodies, and in the process pushing the poor people of the area further away from the city. The entire East Kolkata Wetlands is outside the limits of Kolkata Municipal Corporation's boundary, but ward number 58 (North Tangra) includes parts of this area (East Kolkata Wetlands) The main reason for identifying this area for this study is its specific location. As is evident from Figure 3, ward numbers 58, 57 and 108 show very low density.

Figure 3

Ward Number 57, 58 Shows Very Low Density

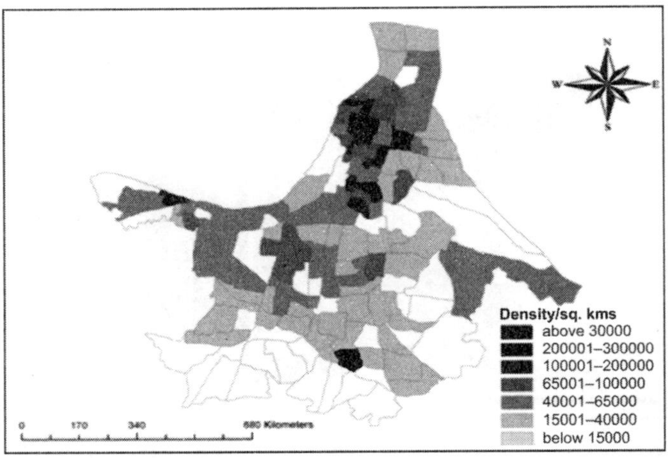

Source: Map prepared with ARC-GIS with the help of Census 2001 data.

Figure 4

Ward Level Variation in Percentage of Slum Households

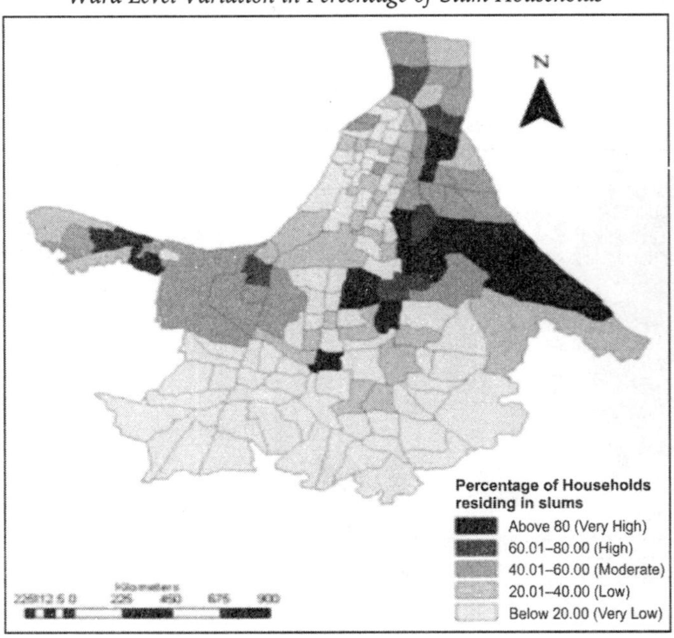

Figure 5

Scheduled Caste Population

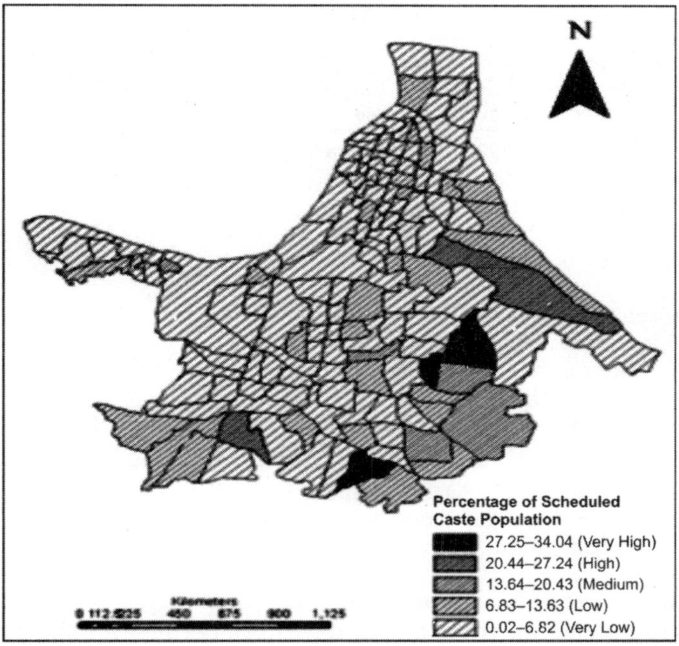

Figure 6

Showing Ward Level Variation in Percentage of Male Illiterates Living in Slums

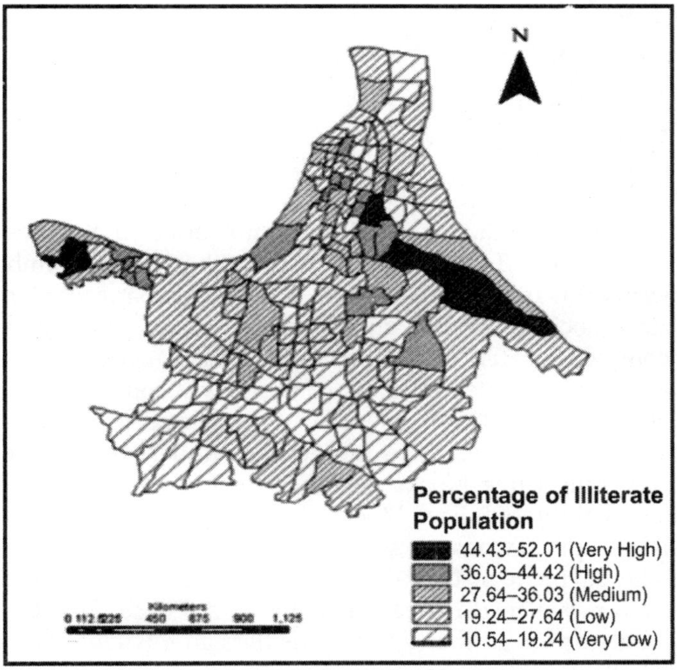

Source: Map prepared with ARC-GIS with the help of Census 2001 data.

Table 1

Relationships between Urban Growth, Density and Concentration of Slum Population in Kolkata's Top Five Selected Wards

Ward Number	Location	Rank in Percentage of Slum Population To Total Population	Urban Growth (2001)	Population Density (2001)	Rank by Size of Slum Population
58	Tangra-Tiljala (East Kolkata Wetland	1st(99.98%population live in slums)	High	Very low	1st
29	Narkeldanga (adjacent to EKW)	2nd(98.8% population live in slums)	Low	Low	5th
137	Metiabruz (Western side)	3rd (98.35% people live in slum)	High	Moderate	19th
134	Garden Reach, West Port	4th(97.85% population living in slums)	High	High	11th
65	Tiljala (part of EKW)	5th (91.97% population live in slum)	Moderate	Low	2nd

Source: Census of India, 2001, Final Population Totals, West Bengal: Slum Population with Percentage of Slum Population to Total Population, Rank and Sex Ratio, West Bengal/Statutory Towns, 2001, Table-13.

Ward numbers 58, 57 have the highest percentages of households living in slums; in Kolkata north eastern and western peripheries show the highest concentration of slums. North-eastern periphery which comprises Tangra, Tiljala, Kasba and Narkeldanga areas (part of East Kolkata Wetlands) contains the highest number of slum population. These wards also record highest percentage of scheduled caste population, high illiteracy and moderately high percentage of male non-workers.

Case Study of Dhapa Slum and Rajarghat North Tangra Housing Complex

Brief History

Tangra-Tiljala area contains the largest slum locale of Kolkata, and ward number 58 or North Tangra region records the largest number of slum dwellers within this region. It is also the most problematic ward in Kolkata in terms of low socio-economic development. Dhapa slum and Rajarghat Housing complex located in this ward have been chosen for the survey. Rajarghat housing complex consists of the newly constructed low income flats established by the Government of West Bengal in collaboration with Salim Group for accommodating slum dwellers under relocation from Dhapa slum. As yet, only three blocks have been completed and 67 households successfully rehabilitated. Each block has twenty flats, and one of the blocks is completely empty. Two years ago, some slum dwellers were allotted these flats after the payment of ₹ 10,000 only. Each flat costs ₹ 30,000, but the occupants can pay it in three easy installments. These flats are ownership flats, and residents are at liberty to sell the flats after paying the full amount, but currently flat allotment has been stopped due to administrative reasons. Each flat contains one bed room, separate kitchen, bathroom and attached balcony. All residents have separate electric metres and space for parking their vehicles. Though they have a private deep tube well and pump for water, the underground water of this region is yellowish and highly contaminated. Moreover, these flats are situated just near the Dhapa solid waste disposal ground and plastic factories. Thus, bad odour and smoke add to the air pollution. Residents are mainly rag pickers, rickshaw pullers, farmers and factory workers. Their socio-economic status is similar to those who live in the nearby slum (Dhapa slum).

Dhapa slum is located on the mound of garbage just opposite Rajarghat Housing Complex. This slum is characterized by narrow lanes, crowded interiors, 'Kacheha' houses made up of bamboo, plastic and other non-permanent materials and depicts a miserable environment. Most of the inhabitants here are poor migrants hailing from the different areas of Sundarban. This area is highly crime prone; environment is severely polluted and people are deprived of potable drinking water and other basic amenities. People living in this area have following characteristics:

Socio-Economic and Demographic Characteristics of the Respondents

Scope and applicability of the SL Approach in a particular area depends on the socio-economic and demographic characteristics of the households there; these characteristics can be expressed through variables like age-sex composition of the head of the household, family type, social background (caste, religion), migration status, educational level, income category, occupational characteristics and changes in livelihood.

1. *Age-Sex Structure:* Age and sex of the household head (mainly the main bread earner) determine economic potentiality of a household for recovering from any unforeseen catastrophes. In a patriarchal society, households headed by men in working age group are considered as economically sound; on the other hand female headed households and households headed by elderly or disabled persons are considered as economically vulnerable (see Table 2 and 3).

Table 2

Age Composition of the Household Heads

	21-35 years	*36-50 years*	*51-65 years*	*Above 65 years*
Rajarghat LIG Housing	18 (36)	17 (34)	10 (20)	5 (10)
Dhapa Slum	12 (24)	25 (54)	7 (14)	4 (8)

Table 3

Sex Composition of the Head of the Households

	Male	*Female*
Rajarghat LIG Housing	33 (66)	17 (34)
Dhapa Slum	37 (74)	13 (26)

Figures in parenthesis are in %

In this locality, most of the household heads are young and of working age group, and in this slum, 54 per cent of household heads are in the second age group (36–50 years) while in the LIG, 36 per cent and 34 per cent household heads are in the first and second age groups (21–35 years and 36–50 years) respectively. It is clear, therefore, that most of the surveyed households are headed by young people. This locality also has a significant number of female headed households (34% in the LIG and 26% in the slum).

2. *Family Type and Size:* In traditional Indian society, joint and extended families with more than one earning member are considered as financially secure. Nearly 50 per cent of all households (LIG and slum colonies together) are nuclear in nature; 32 and 40 per cent are joint families in the LIG and slum colonies respectively, and a significant number of single households are also found in the LIG as well as in the slum (see Table 4 and 5).

Table 4

Percentage of Households with Following Family Types

	Nuclear	*Joint*	*Extended*	*Single*
Rajarghat LIG Housing	26 (52)	16 (32)	0	7 (14)
Dhapa Slum	24 (48)	20 (40)	1 (2)	6 (12)

Figures in parenthesis are in %

Table 5

Percentage of Households Having Following Family Size

	Below 4	*5–8 persons*	*9–12 persons*
Rajarghat LIG Housing	28 (56)	22 (44)	0
Dhapa Slum	28 (56)	21 (42)	1 (2)

Figures in parenthesis are in %

Family size is generally small here; 56 per cent households have less than four members and rest have five to eight members. Therefore, family structure in this area also shows characteristic rural-urban interface with predominance of small or nuclear families along with the existence of a significant number of joint and medium size families.

3. *Social Background:* (i) Religion: Of the fifty households surveyed in Rajarghat LIG Housing colony, 49 (98%) are Hindus and only one household is Muslim; in the slum 47 (94%) of the total households surveyed are Hindus, and only 3 are Muslims.

(ii) Caste: Proportion of Scheduled Castes population is very high in this area; 90 per cent households in the LIG housing colony belong to SCs and the rest (10%) to the General category while 66 per cent households in the slums belong to SCs, 30 per cent to General and the rest to Scheduled Tribes. Among the SCs here, Dule or Baghdi community (a subcaste within SC) forms the majority.

(iii) Language: Bengali speaking population constitutes the majority of respondents (96% in LIG and 78% in the slum) and 22 per cent households in the slum speak Hindi. Rajarghat LIG Housing is mainly dominated by Bengali speaking households, but a significant number of Hindi speaking households are also found in the slum.

(iv) Migration Status: Migration to this area is mainly inter-district and not long distance; 98 per cent households in Rajarghat LIG Housing colony and 78 per cent households in the slum area are from South 24 Parganas which is the immediate adjacent district of EKW. In the slum, 14 per cent (7 households) are from Bihar and few are from Bangladesh. These households are living here for over twenty years, therefore they cannot be called fresh migrants anymore.

(v) Educational Level: Educational level determines livelihood potentiality of an individual; this area is mainly inhabited by illiterates and persons having very low educational level. Above 62 per cent respondents in the LIG and 72 per cent in the slum are totally illiterates; 9 per cent from both the habitations have completed Higher Secondary level. Only two persons are graduates in the slum colony and rest are just literates. Number of school dropout children is significantly high in this area. Dhapa LIG and slum colony have respectively 3 and 4 households having at least one child above the age five, not attending schools. Most of them have shown varied socio-economic reasons behind their not attending schools; these children help their parents in household work and in earning income.

Economic Status of the Respondents

(i) *Occupations:* Rag picking, factory work, domestic services, fishing and farming are the main occupations of the respondents; occupational structure is more or less same in both the slum and the LIG. About 26 per cent rag pickers living in the LIG were earlier fishermen or farmers; they lost their lands and water bodies at different points of time due to various developmental works while some sold their land for economic gain. These rag pickers work over 10 hours a day and sort out plastics from the nearby solid waste disposal ground.

Rajarghat Housing Complex/Dhapa LIG	Rag picker (26%), Factory worker (28%), and Rickshaw puller (12%), Fishing and Farming (10%), Casual Labourer (12%), Domestic helper (8%), shoemaking (2%), construction work (1%), Transport sector worker (1%)
Dhapa slum (North Tangra)	Domestic helper (14%), factory worker (16%), Construction worker (14%), Casual labourer (12%), Rag picker (10%), Fishing and farming (6%), Street vendor (4%), Rickshaw puller (4%), petty businessman (4%), Mechanic (2%), handicraft (4%)

(ii) *Monthly Income:* Over 34 per cent households surveyed earn below ₹ 5000 while 48 per cent earn ₹ 5000–10,000 per month. Only 16 per cent earn above ₹ 10,000, but not a single household is found to earn over ₹ 20,000 per month. Residents of Rajarghat housing complex also earn just like their slum counterparts. Here 50 per cent household earn below ₹ 5,000 and only 38 per cent earn between ₹ 10,000–15,000. Economic standard of slum and non-slum households are more or less the same here.

(iii) *Monthly Expenditure:* Dhapa slum and LIG colonies of North Tangra show that over 40 per cent households in both the locations spend less than ₹ 5,000 per month and over 50 per cent spend ₹ 5,000 to 10,000 per month. Very few can afford to spend more than ₹ 10,000. Thus, affordability of slum and non-slum households in Dhapa is more or less the same.

(iv) *Access to Formal Credit:* Only 42 per cent households living in Dhapa slum and 74 per cent households in the LIG housing have bank account (Table 6).

Table 6

Possession of Bank Account

	Yes	*No*
Rajarghat LIG Housing	37 (74.00)	13 (26.00)
Dhapa Slum	21 (42.00)	29 (58.00)

Figures in parentheses are in %

(v) *Access to Insurance and Identity Card:* Only 56 per cent LIG households and only 40 per cent slum households have access to insurance; in the slum colony, only 48 per cent households have both voter card and ration card. There are nine households in the slum who do not have any of these two cards. Lack of bank account, insurance cover, voter card and ration card is an indicator of one's high vulnerability as anyone who wish to access any governmental scheme or wants to avail subsidized loans, has to show identity proof (Table 7).

Table 7

Possession of Insurance

	Yes	*No*
Rajarghat LIG Housing	26 (56.00)	24 (48.00)
Dhapa Slum	20 (40.00)	30 (60.00)

Possession of Voter card/Ration Card

	Yes both	*None of the Two*	*Only Ration Card*	*Only Voter Card*
Rajarghat LIG Housing	35 (75.00)	1 (2.00)	5 (10.00)	9 (18.00)
Dhapa Slum	24 (48.00)	9 (18.00)	13 (26.00)	4 (8.00)

Figures in parentheses are in %

Livelihood Vulnerability Index

Principal Component Analyses is used in this study for the construction of Livelihood Vulnerability index. It reduces a large sets of variables thought to be associated with urban deprivation to a smaller number of sub sets or domains. Each observation is given a score on each factor selected for the particular indicator. The factor scores taken in combination are then used to represent aggregate dimensions of economic vulnerability. Through the following variables 'access to' and 'control over' certain asset bases have been measured:

Households Having 'Control Over'	*Households Having 'Access to'*
Social status (one's caste and religion, knowledge of local language), income and working environment (fixed working hours and job satisfaction).	Formal sector Employment, Voter Card, Ration Card, Bank Account, Insurance, Education

The General Deprivation Index is constructed using rescaled scores arising from the 'Principal Component Analyses' by rescaling follows equations:

S*ij = (Sij – minj)
(maxj-minj) ....equation no 1
(0= S*ij =1)

Sij is the factor score for locality 'i' on principal component j, maxj and minj are the highest and lowest factor scores on component j.

This equation produced rescaled factor scores in the range of zero to one and allowed the following equation to be used to develop a GDI:

GDIi = Sik*(1+?S*ij)

Tot_comp .... equation no-2 (0=GDIi =1)

Sik is the rescaled factor score of locality 'i' on component k which plays the primary role in deprivation, S*ij is the rescaled factor score of one of the component.

Tot_comp is total number of components. This produces a simple weighted index that accounts for the factors derived from the initial component analysis.

With these standardized and recoded indicators, Principal Component Analyses has been run in SPSS and five sets of components with factor scores derived. These factor scores are rescaled with the formula of

S*ij = (Sij – minj)

(maxj-minj) ....equation no-1

(0= S*ij =1)

Sij is the factor score for locality 'i' on principal component j, maxj and minj are the highest and lowest factor scores on component j.

Table 8

Livelihood Vulnerability Index (Percentage of Households in Different Vulnerability Groups)

Settlement	*Extremely Vulnerable (Above 0.80) (%)*	*n*	*Highly Vulnerable (0.61-0.80) (%)*	*n*	*Moderately Vulnerable (0.41-0.60) (%)*	*n*	*Less Vulnerable (0.21- 0.40) (%)*	*n*	*Least Vulnerable (%) (Below .20)*	*n*
Dhapa LIG	0.00	0	38.00	19	48.00	24	12.00	6	2.00	1
Dhapa Slum	8.00	4	56.00	28	28.00	14	6.00	3	2.00	1

Values of the GDI Score

Above 0.80: Extremely Vulnerable

0.61–0.80: Highly Vulnerable

0.41–0.60; Moderately Vulnerable

0.21–0.40: Less Vulnerable

Below .20: Least Vulnerable

Livelihood vulnerability varies across households: Thirty-eight per cent households in the LIG and 56 per cent households in the slum experience high vulnerability and 48 per cent LIG households and 28 per cent slum households experience moderate vulnerability. Four households in the slum colony come under the extremely vulnerable category; very few households come under less and least vulnerable categories. Therefore, within one and the same area and even within the same type of settlement, livelihood vulnerability varies across households depending on social, economic and demographic characteristics of the individual household (Table 8).

Livelihood Vulnerability Experienced by the Respondents

Statistical techniques alone cannot explain the real nature of economic vulnerability experienced by the poor households living in this area; whereas the following in depth interviews with farmers, fishermen and rag pickers highlight their real plight:

1. *Scope of the Application of Sustainable Livelihood Approach (SLA) in Dhapa:* Various policies and programmes have already been introduced in this area by way of environmental improvement, slum rehabilitation, monitoring of unauthorized constructions and promotion of awareness against the environmental degradation of the EKW; but none of them are based on SLA. The issue of livelihood vulnerability should be addressed in a different way through the following strategies:

> Coping Strategies or short term strategies should be based on providing gainful employment opportunity or alternative sources of livelihoods to those who stand to lose their livelihood options due to urban developmental projects. Enough low skilled jobs should be created in the nearby shopping complexes, recreation grounds and residential areas for the local people especially for women. There should be a concrete health care policy which will address the health vulnerability of those living near the solid waste disposal ground.
>
> Adaptive Strategies or long-term strategies should be based on environmental upgradation, effective implementation of slum rehabilitation and over all socio-economic development of the residents. The slum rehabilitation programme has already started and a few slum dwellers have been given one bedroom flats in Rajarghat LIG housing, but the number of flats are much less than the actual demand and moreover, flat allotment has been stopped due to some administrative problems.

Sumit Kumar Dalui (45) narrated his story of recent job loss and economic vulnerability. He had inherited a small piece of land from his ancestors and he earlier earned his livelihood by producing vegetables especially cabbages on his field adjacent to the Eastern Metropolitan Bypass. His wife and children used to sell the yield in the local market and earn income. Few years ago he noticed that productivity had remarkably declined. Therefore, he had to sell the land to a promoter at a nominal price; now he has nothing else to do except rag picking from the nearby solid waste disposal ground (locally called as 'Dhibi' or mound). He and his sons gather plastics, rubber and various other things from the garbage disposal ground; his wife works as a domestic help in the nearby multi-storeyed buildings and one of his daughter works as a beautician. He does not like his present livelihood, as it has no fixed working hours and is very unhygienic. He suffers from Eczema on both his hands due to contact with harmful elements while picking rags. He earns very little, i.e. around ₹ 5,000 per month from various sources and hence has to borrow money from friends to meet their daily needs. He has no idea when and how his economic hardship will be over, but still hopes that some government policies will give them an opportunity of a safe livelihood option in future.

Investment strategies should be based on securing more assets or substituting one asset by another asset (land and fisheries can be replaced by shops or rickshaws); those who are selling their lands should be encouraged to invest money in business ventures or in purchasing vans or rickshaws as these productive assets can enhance the household income. Introduction of collective supports like microfinancing, easy loans through self-help groups and external helps from various governmental and non-governmental organizations can reduce livelihood vulnerability.

Finally, all policies designed for this area should be based on *'Livelihood Promotion'* (through the generation of alternate sources of livelihoods), *'Livelihood Protection'* (maximum protection should be given to the households who depend on fishing and farming) and *'Livelihood Provisioning'* (already existing livelihood options should be made more gainful and safe). Household based strategies should not be neglected, because some households, especially female headed households are extremely vulnerable to change in livelihood. For example, a female headed household without any male member cannot opt for rickshaw pulling or other hard manual work; in such a situation, the household has to opt for domestic services, rag picking or street vending as occupation. Thus, household level variation in livelihood vulnerability should be addressed with special attention.

Devaki Mondal (45) a widow with four children narrated that her husband was a fisherman who caught fish from a nearby water body or 'Bheri'. East Kolkata Wetlands fisheries offer better fishing opportunity than any other place. Murky water and garbage help in tapping solar energy more efficiently than any other water bodies, and therefore time needed for fish spawns to mature is usually less (only 8 to 9 months) than in other areas. Recent encroachment of water bodies due to various developmental processes had compelled her husband to leave his earlier livelihood and opt rickshaw pulling as an alternative job. Unfortunately two years ago, he lost his life in a road accident and right now Devaki works as a maid servant and runs a petty shop in the nearby factory area. Her sons and daughters work as rag pickers; they want to go to school, but can't afford to do it.

Sureshwar Baghdi (58) hails from Malanchapur (a village in South Twenty Four Pargana). He was a fisherman and also had a piece of agricultural land in his native place but due to some economic hardship he had to sell it and came to Dhapa ten years back. He earlier worked in others' lands as a farmer, but recently the landowner had sold his land to a promoter for economic gain. Currently he is not able to work as a farmer, and so has taken to rag picking. He wishes to save some money for doing petty business. His wife and daughters also work as domestic helpers and in their leisure time they help him in plastic sorting from the garbage mound. One of his sons is a van rickshaw puller who delivers goods in the nearby leather factories. Gross income of the family hardly crosses ₹ 4,000 per month and they have no money to repair the small hut for the coming monsoon. He considers himself fortunate enough than his friend Vinay Mondal (55) who had lost his limbs due to an accident in an illegal plastic factory. Vinay was also a fisherman who had lost his job due to wetland encroachment. So, Sureshwar did not like to work in the nearby plastic factories.

Findings and Conclusion

East Kolkata Wetlands shows the typical problem of livelihood vulnerability due to rapid urban growth and land use changes. Wards located at the north-eastern periphery of Kolkata form a small part of EKW; these wards are characterized by high urban growth, low density, high percentage of slum population mainly of Scheduled Castes and high illiteracy. Dhapa area (ward number 58) forms a very small part of EKW, but this area falls under the administrative boundary of Kolkata Municipal Corporation; therefore, the impact of urban growth is clearly visible here. Besides, slum dwellers rehabilitation in low income flats is already going on in this area. It is found that, households living in both LIG and slum settlements have been facing livelihood vulnerability due to the encroachment of agricultural lands and fisheries as a result of which many of them are forced to opt for rag picking and other low yielding but risky jobs. Respondents are mainly from the poverty stricken villages of South Twenty Four Parganas and they mostly belong to Dule and Baghdi community (a sub-caste within Scheduled Castes population in West Bengal) whose ancestral occupation was fishing and farming. Factors like very low income, lack of access to formal credit, insurance cover, etc. due to lack of identity proof have made them extremely vulnerable to job loss. Though there is variation in vulnerability across the households, almost all the surveyed households come under the highly vulnerable and moderately vulnerable categories. Plight of the urban poor living in this area calls for direct governmental intervention based on Sustainable Livelihood Approach (SLA).

References

Baumann, P. and S. Sinha (2001). *Linking Development with Democratic Processes in India: Political Capital and Sustainable Livelihood Analyses*, Natural Resources Perspectives 68, Overseas Development Institute, London.

CARE International (2001). 'Participatory Livelihoods Assessment, Kosovo', Urban Briefing Notes, London.

Carney, D. (1998). *Sustainable Rural Livelihood*, Department for International Development, HMSO, London.

Chambers, R. and G.R. Conway (1992). 'Sustainable Rural Livelihoods: Practical Concepts for the 21st Century', IDS Discussion Paper No. 296, IDS, Brighton.

Chambers, R. (1995). 'Poverty and Livelihoods: Whose Reality Counts? Putting the Last First', *Environment and Urbanisation*, 7(1).

Development Planning Unit (DPU) (2001). 'Living between Rural and Urban Areas: Shaping Change for Improved Livelihoods and a Better Environment', Working Paper, Development Planning Unit, University College, London.

DFID (2001). 'Meeting the Challenge of Poverty in Urban Areas', Strategy Paper, Department for International Development, London.

Farrington, J., R. Chapman and T. Slaymaker (2001). 'Sustainable Livelihoods Approaches in Practice: Potentials and Constrains', paper prepared for the SIDA Poverty Workshop, Overseas Development Institute, London, 8 May.

Farrington, John, Tamsin Ramasut and Julian Walker (2002). 'Sustainable Livelihood Approaches to Urban Areas: General Lessons with Illustrations from Indian Cases', Working Paper 162, Overseas Development Institute, March.

Meikle, S., J. Walker and T. Ramasut (2001). 'Sustainable Urban Livelihoods: Concepts and Implications for Policy', Working Paper, Development Planning Unit, University College, London.

Moser, C. (1996). *Confronting Crisis: A Comparative Study of Household Responses to Poverty and Vulnerability in Four Urban Communities*, World Bank, Washington, D.C.

——. (1998). 'The Asset Vulnerability Framework: Reassessing Urban Poverty Reduction Strategies', *World Development*, 26(2).

UNDP (1998). 'Developing SL Indicators: Reviewing Lessons Learned and a Framework for Action', http://www.undp.org

12

Dynamics of Urban Growth, Resource Degradation and its Impact on Environment

Evidence in Million Plus Cities of India

C.M. Lakshmana

Urban growth is the rate of growth of urban population which is distinct from urbanization which is the process by which there occurs an increase in the proportion of population living in places classified as urban on account of movement of population from a rural to an urban area. On the other hand, urbanization or urban drift is the physical growth of urban areas as a result of rural migration and even movement of suburban masses into cities, particularly the larger ones. However, over a period of time, natural resource degradation due to development imperatives has been evident in India. For example, agricultural development during the green revolution era had over-exploited natural resources such as land and water in addition to consuming more energy. This apart, the construction boom both for residential and commercial use has been eating away useful agriculture land. Huge quantities of soil, forest and minerals are being used to construct our cities and to expand manufacturing, industry and residential estates. Demographic changes and the consequent demographic dividend have had its favourable impact on household income of middle class citizens of India. The increased earnings and bargaining power of middle class citizens of India have led to higher demand for consumer goods, especially electronic goods and motor vehicles. Air pollution caused by luxury goods and consumer durables, particularly motor vehicles is quite high in all major cities, and it is now considered as the fifth largest killer. Similarly, increased man-land ratio in the metro cities and class one cities directly account for significant amounts of land degradation, water and air pollution.

In view of this, the present study endeavours to assess the interrelationship between urban growth and resource degradation, and its overall impact on environment on one hand; and to highlight its impact on environment in million plus cities, with particular reference to urban growth and resultant resource degradation, on the other. As per 2001 census, the total number of UA/Towns in India is about 5,161 with a total population of 286.11 million. Of this, 441 class I cities account for about 63 per cent (178.22 million) of the total urban population (Table 1). The rest, i.e. about 37 per cent is distributed among other category of cities/towns (4,720). However, a deeper look at the picture shows that as of 2001, about 178.22 million people were living in 441 class I cities while about 107.98 million (61%) were living in 35 million plus cities. About 39 per cent (70.24 million) was residing in the remaining class I cities (406).

In this background, the study focuses its attention on the million plus cities in order to highlight resource degradation and the environmental decay particularly in these cities. In this context, it is imperative to sensitize researchers and policy makers about the priority areas of environmental research and urge them to come up with early, meaningful remedial action. There is need to increase awareness among decision makers, professionals and academics about the urgency of protecting environment and making the country's transformation sustainable and less injurious to human health and well-being.

Urban Growth at a Glance

The total urban area of India was 53,183 sq km in 1981, which increased to 78,163 sq km in 2001, the absolute increase in urban during the period being 24,981 sq km. However, the increased urban area in the total geographical area (32,87,263 sq km) was very marginal at the national level, i.e. 1.61 per cent in 1981; it increased to 2.37 per cent by 2001. However, the increase of urban growth in terms of area was quite significant for the period 1981–2001. The absolute increase in urban area during the period at the national level was 46.97 per cent. Interestingly, increased area in million plus cites was about 66 per cent which is higher than the national average, and also in excess by 20 per cent when compared to the overall increase at the national level. This particular aspect of urban transformation demonstrates how urban growth has led to diversion of agricultural land for expansion of our cities in terms of increased households, infrastructure and commercial use.

It is clear that the changed land use pattern is directly responsible for the evils like depletion of biodiversity, drying up water bodies, loss of greenery, all of which have serious bearing on human health and well-being. Rapid growth of population has also resulted in generation of huge quantities of waste, eco-degradation and eco-system imbalance.

Urban Growth in Terms of Area

The total urban land area of 35 million plus-cities of India was 7,448.75 sq km in 1981, which increased to 12,379.64 sq km by 2001. The absolute growth of urban area in terms of percentage in megacities like Delhi and Greater Mumbai had been declining over time and had reached the saturation level during the earlier decades. It is evident, therefore, that the growth rate of urban area has been coming down over time in general, but there has been a drastic increase of urban area in rest of the million plus-cities. What is noteworthy here is that the existence of saturation level population in Delhi, Mumbai, Kolkata and Chennai, and the consequent expansion of these cities during the earlier period had resulted only in average growth rate of area. As revealed by the 2011 census report, the dispersal of urban population especially in southern states of India during the period 1981–2011 has been significant; hence, the extent of expanded area in million plus-cities of southern states is also significant. However the relevant data is yet to be published by the census department. Therefore, the above inference cannot be final.

As presented in Appendix Table 1 (a), the cities of Surat, Nashik, Jaipur, Visakhapatnam, Lucknow, Hyderabad, Meerut, Ahmedabad, Asansol and Coimbatore were the top ten cities in regard to growth rate of area across million plus-cities during the period of 1981–2001, the growth rate being 53 to 80 per cent. The cities of Pune, Greater Mumbai, Vadodara, Kochi, Agra, Delhi, Rajkot, Bengaluru, Indore, Ludhiana, Madurai, Patna, Chennai, Kolkata and Amritsar come next in order in the matter of increase in growth rate of geographical area. However, increased area in terms of growth rate in two decades in these cities was lower than in the top ten cities; it ranged from 31 to 54 per cent.

The information contained in Appendix Table 1 (a) confirms the fact that by and large, increased urban area especially in million plus-cities and as well as in class one cities has been eating away useful agriculture land and hence this phenomenal growth has changed the entire natural landscape and land use pattern. Drastic reduction of flora and fauna, encroachment of lakes, drying up of water bodies, decline in biodiversity, etc. were the direct consequences of the changed land use pattern. The resultant eco-degradation and system imbalance in urban and semi-urban areas has seriously impacted human health and well-being. This important aspect has to be brought to the attention of policy makers, environmentalists and administrators in the country so that appropriate remedial measures figure in their policy formulations. In other words, there is an urgent need to change the environmental policy and associated guidelines to arrest resource degradation and the resulted damage on environment, human health and well-being.

Urban Growth in Terms of Population

During the decade of 1981–2001, Faridabad, Surat, Nashik, Ludhiana, Jaipur, Delhi, Visakhapatnam, Lucknow, Hyderabad and Pune were the ten cities at top positions in growth rate of population, where the increase ranged between 54 and 70 per cent. The cities of Rajkot, Bhopal, Meerut, Bengaluru, Vadodara, Indore, Agra, Ahmedabad, Vijayawada, Nagpur, Greater Mumbai, Asansol, Amritsar, Kanpur and Jamshedpur were next in order during the above two decades, the range of increase being 38 to 53 per cent. See Appendix Table 1 (b) for further details.

However, there has been significant imbalance between the growth in population and the expansion of geographical area in almost all the million

Table 1

Different Classes of Towns and their Population (in percentage in India)

Year	*Total UA and towns*	*Class I*	*% of Population*	*Class II*	*% of Population*	*Class III*	*% of Population*	*Class IV*	*% of Population*	*Class V*	*% of Population*	*Class VI*	*% of Population*
1961	26573	105	44.34	139	12.16	517	20.08	816	14.35	842	8.04	238	1.03
1971	3081	149	48.78	219	13.59	649	18.35	985	12.87	803	5.62	276	0.79
1981	3891	325	52.57	325	14.09	878	17.08	1240	11.24	900	4.34	324	0.68
1991	4615	322	56.67	421	13.33	1161	16.35	1451	9.77	971	3.43	289	0.45
2001	5161	441	62.29	496	12.04	1387	14.72	1564	7.90	1042	2.76	231	0.29
2011	5497	Not yet finalized											

Source: Census of India, 2001 (General Population Tables, Part II), Registrar General and Census Commissioner, New Delhi, India.

Note: Size of Population according to census classification: Class I town (1,00,000 and more)

Class II (50,000-1,00,000), Class III (20,000-50,000), Class IV (10,000-20,000), Class V (5,000-10,000), Class VI (less than 5,000) plus cities. As can be seen from Appendix Table 1(d), a similar trend can be observed in population density in these cities It means higher rate of population growth led to higher population density in these cities. Hence, increased man-land ratio is much higher in these cities compared to secondary and tertiary level cities. It indicates that pollution due to waste generation and use of resource has been the cause of air and water pollution.

Urban Growth in Terms of Households

The growth rate of number of households across million plus-cites is almost similar to the growth rate of population. As can be seen from Appendix Table 1(c), cities that are at the top in regard to growth rate of population are the ones that have registered the highest growth rate in the number of households. Increased growth rate of population among the top ten cities is more or less identical and ranged between 60 and 80 per cent. However, Ludhiana, Jaipur, Delhi, and Lucknow are exception in this sequence. It is fair to assume, therefore, that development imperatives in the past have led urbanization to reach saturation level in terms of residential area in these cities. However, these cities come next in order in terms of number of households. On the whole, cities that have registered higher rate of population growth are also the ones that have witnessed higher growth rate in number of households, but strangely, the growth rate of urban land area is lower than the rate of population growth as well as increase in number of households in these cities. It is clear from the above that urbanization in terms of increase in area is not in sync with the increase in number of households or population. It implies that there could be a more pressure on land and, therefore, more land degradation, air pollution and water pollution and resultant environmental degradation due to the waste emanating from this huge population.

Generally, adverse man-land ratio has been a fall out of population growth in all the million plus-cities. However a close examination of the sequence of events shows that the link between population growth and declining man-land ratio has been generally sequential in seven out of ten cities, the exceptions being Visakapatnam, Lucknow and Hyderabad where it has not been so. The expansion of area for the development of infrastructure in these cities may be behind the favourable man-land ratio. However diversion of huge tracts of agriculture land for infrastructure and residential development has caused to shrinkage of agricultural land in India which directly influenced the production of crops in the near future.

Urban Growth and Resource Degradation

Indeed, expansion of urban area for trade, commerce and manufacturing industry is behind both push and pull factors of migration in India. Further, higher the urbanization and urban growth, higher would be the diversion of land for non-agricultural use. By the same logic, huge urban population needs more water and sanitation facilities and it naturally entails overexploitation of resources like water, soil, minerals like sand and granite, etc. which are considered common property. As most of these activities are uncontrolled, the damage it could cause to the ecosystem is quite heavy. In addition to depletion of resources, environmental decay and its adverse effects on human health and well-being, such uncontrolled exploitation often leads to devastations like floods, droughts and landslides which mostly affect the rural populace.

Construction industry requires large quantities of wood for making bricks and most of the wood is sourced from natural forests or man-made agro-forests, both of which are not perennial. Indiscriminate felling of trees from forests as well as from revenue lands is threatening to destroy our tree-wealth. However, there is no proper accounting of this either by the department of agriculture or forest department. In this regard, an approximate calculation is made of resource depletion due to urban growth in the following lines:

It takes 450 gallons of water, 1500 no. of bricks and 5 lorry-loads of sand to construct a building with an area of 10 sq ft. Therefore, the construction of 10 million households in million plus-cities over a 20-year period must have used about 15,000 million of bricks, 5 million loads of sand and 4500 million gallon of water. Most of these natural resources, except perhaps water, are sourced from rural areas to take up construction in cities. Due to overexploitation, water table in many places has receded to below 2,000 to 3,000 ft and the available water is unfit for human consumption. This is a typical example of how urban growth has led to overexploitation of natural resources over time.

Besides this, the burgeoning middle class especially in urban areas are aggravating the problem by their unregulated consumption of higher per capita energy and generation of waste. Their higher purchasing power vis-a-vis rural population has certainly been giving rise to eco-degradation, ecosystem imbalance and thereby impacting human health and well-being. Outdoor air pollution is the fifth largest killer in India. Further, according to a study on waste generation in Bengaluru conducted by Gowri, Kulkarni, Vishnu Bajpai, Sun Sheg Han and Ramachandra, the average quantity of household waste generated is in the range of 87.9 gm/per/day to 156.0 gm/per/day.

In this regard, a rough calculation of the waste generated across million plus-cities during the period under review shows that in 1981, about 10.63 million households in million plus-cities generated about 1.65 million tonnes of solid waste per day; it increased to 3.28 million tonnes in 2001 by 2.10 million households. But the mechanism adopted to treat the waste so generated by the respective municipal bodies is archaic and unsuitable to handle such huge quantities of waste. The failure to treat/dispose solid waste properly reflects the ineffectiveness of our local bodies that are mandated with the task. As of now, about 80 per cent of generated waste is being directly dumped in the open landfills. Unscientifically dumped solid waste leeches out and pollutes groundwater in addition to emitting foul smell, causing mosquito menace, etc. This constitutes an important governance issue in urban India.

During rainy season, these problems get aggravated and make habitations near such dumps unfit for human life. This is one side of the story of resource degradation due to urban growth. There is another side to the story: congregation of rural migrants in cities sans adequate sanitation facilities has been directly causing land degradation and water and air pollution. For instance as per 2001 census, about 27 per cent of urban households do not have access to toilet facility, which results in open defecation on any available space and this is sure recipe for all undesirable consequences such as air and water pollution, worm infestation particularly in children, etc. The socio-psychological consequences of this demeaning situation is quite serious.

The burgeoning slum population in metropolitan cities is the main reason for the above malady. Rapid growth in the number of motor vehicles in the country in general and class I cities in particular has been causing air pollution which impacts human health and well-being. The number of registered motor vehicles in India increased by 100 times between 1951–2004; the poor quality of the public transport system has adverse consequences in that it forces people to make own transport arrangements by acquiring 2 and 4 wheelers, and the increased number of motor vehicles accentuate air pollution and affects human health and well-being (Ministry of Urban Development, 2011).

Resource Degradation and its Impact on Environment

Measuring environmental decay due to urbanization and its consequence for human health and well-being is a big task. However, keeping this in mind, the study has tried to sum up the issues by adopting an appropriate methodology. Firstly, the study uses the co-efficient of correlation technique in order to analyse environmental effects in million plus-cities. Secondly, the cities are classified into three groups as top ten, bottom ten and middle class cities, based on their growth rate of area, population and number of households.

Due to inconsistency of the sequential relationship of area, household and density among the cities, the study has taken into account top ten cities and middle class cities to measure environmental decay, linking physical growth of cities in terms of area, population, density and number of households. In order to measure the impact factor on environment due to urban growth, a consolidated statement has been prepared for 25 cities by using rank order sequence. The result is presented in Table 2. Impact factor on environment has been identified and grouped into three as (i) relatively high impact cities (ii) medium impact cities and (iii) relatively low impact cities, based on their physical growth in terms of area, population and number of households. Table 3 presents the relevant information.

The correlation analyses between growth of cities (by area) with growth of population as well as growth in number of households show a positive moderate relationship among them. Notably, the correlation coefficients between growth rate of area of cities and population growth rate is 0.41, and the value of correlation coefficient between growth rate of area of cities and household growth rate is 0.40 (both results are statistically significant at 0.05 levels but not added as table here). It means that an increase in the area of cities is accompanied by an increase in population and also an increase in the number of households.

Table 2

Consolidated Assessment of Environmental Effects in Million Plus Cities in India due to Urban Growth

S.No.	City	Ranks in Growth Rate of Population	Ranks in the Growth Rate of Area	Ranks in Increased Ratio of Population	Ranks in the Growth Rate of Households	Total
1	Faridabad (HAR)	1	10	7	1	19
2	Surat (GUJ)	2	9	6	3	20
3	Nashik (MH)	3	7	22	4	36
4	Ludhiana (PUNJ)	4	20	8	11	43
5	Jaipur (RAJ)	5	6	26	16	53
6	Delhi	6	16	3	14	39
7	Visakhapatnam (AP)	7	3	31	10	51
8	Lucknow (UP)	8	5	29	17	59
9	Hyderabad (AP)	9	2	35	8	54
10	Pune (MH)	10	11	21	7	49
11	Rajkot (GUJ)	11	17	10	6	44
12	Bhopal (MP)	12	32	12	13	69
13	Meerut (UP)	13	8	27	23	71
14	Bangalore (KA)	14	18	11	12	55
15	Vadodara (GUJ)	15	13	25	15	68
16	Indore (MP)	16	19	19	20	74
17	Agra (UP)	17	15	24	27	83
18	Ahmadabad (GUJ)	18	4	34	21	77
19	Vijayawada (AP)	19	11	2	19	51
20	Nagpur (MH)	20	31	4	24	79
21	Greater Mumbai (MH)	21	12	30	18	81
22	Asansol (WB)	22	1	32	5	60
23	Amritsar (PUNJ)	23	25	15	26	89
24	Kanpur (UP)	24	34	5	31	94
25	Jamshedpur (BIH)	25	12	13	28	78

Source: Arrived by the Author's Calculations used Census Data.

Table 3

Urban Growth Impact on Environment in Million Plus Cities in India

High Impact Cities (Ranks 20 to 40)	
1	Faridabad (HAR)
2	Surat (GUJ)
3	Nashik (MH)
4	Ludhiana (PUNJ)
5	Delhi
6	Pune (MH)
7	Rajkot (GUJ)

Cont'd...

...Cont'd

Medium (Ranks 41 to 60)	
1	Jaipur (RAJ)
2	Lucknow (UP)
3	Hyderabad (AP)
4	Bhopal (MP)
5	Meerut (UP)
6	Bangalore (KA)
7	Vadodara (GUJ)
8	Indore (MP)
9	Ahmadabad (GUJ)
10	Vijayawada (AP)
11	Asansol (WB)
12	Visakhapatnam (AP)
Average (Ranks 61 and above)	
1	Agra (UP)
2	Nagpur (MH)
3	Kanpur (UP)
4	Greater Mumbai (MH)
5	Jamshedpur (BIH)
6	Amritsar (PUNJ)

But it should be noted that the growth rate of population and households are relatively higher than the growth rate of area of cities. This abnormality has shown that the million plus-cities have already witnessed overloading of population with rapid increase of residential/commercial buildings. Increased man-land ratio is much higher in class I cities than any other cities. Further, increased activities such as trade and commerce under the globalization era and public necessities especially road transport – rapid growth of motor vehicles have led to increased road density.

Besides, the rapid growth of residential and commercial activities has led to overexploitation of the country's natural resource such as sand, mineral, water and soil, etc. As already stated earlier, these are the basic materials for construction industry. In this regard, an approximate calculation is made of resource depletion due to urban growth in the following paragraph:

Based on the index (see Table 3) prepared by the author, it can be seen that during the period under review the cities of Faridabad in Haryana, Surat in Gujarat, Nashik in Maharashtra, Ludhiana in Punjab, Delhi, Pune in Maharashtra and Rajkot in Gujarat were the high impact cities in so far as overexploitation and overuse of resources and resultant environmental effects are concerned. The cities of Jaipur in Rajasthan, Lucknow in UP, Hyderabad in Andhra Pradesh, Bhopal in Madhya Pradesh, Meerut in UP, Bengaluru in Karnataka, Vadodara in Gujarat, Indore in Madhya Pradesh, Ahmedabad in Gujarat, Vijayawada in Andhra Pradesh, Asansol in West

Bengal and Visakhapatnam in Andhra Pradesh fall in the second category where resource degradation and environmental decay were just below the first category.

However, the megacities of Chennai in Tamil Nadu, Greater Mumbai in Maharashtra, and Kolkata in West Bengal do not come under either high impact or medium impact category of cities. This is because these have already reached the saturation level in growth of area, population and number of households. However, it does not mean that these cities do not have any environmental challenges. These cities have already exploited natural resources to maximum limits in terms of residential and commercial construction in the earlier period itself. Hence, the threshold level of environmental degradation had already been reached in these cities much earlier. In recent decades, expectedly, urbanization has been spreading towards other cities, which is a welcome development. Though we need overall development, we also need to give top priority to protection of common property resource and avoid its degradation in order to make our lives comfortable. Every Indian citizen has an inherent duty to think and plan for healthy growth of cities, protect environment and ensure that developmental efforts are sustainable from the point of view of environment.

Summary and Conclusions

Indeed, the cities are the main drivers of economic development in any developing nation in the world. Unfortunately, the Indian experience, especially in million plus-cities has not been very positive; our growth has not been unaccompanied by resource depletion and environmental degradation. This has serious consequence for human health and well-being. The flip-side of development has been acute in class I cities than in other category of cities. Population growth has been higher than the growth rate of land area for want of a mechanism to balance man-land ratio. There has been significant inequality in urbanization process among cities/regions. In the past, resource degradation and related environmental burdens were much higher in the cities in north and west. This malady is now rapidly spreading to the southern region too. There is, therefore, urgent need to develop tier two and three cities by offering incentives to entrepreneurs (multinational companies (MNCs) in order to promote sustainable development in secondary and tertiary cities as this has the potential to arrest the migrants (both skilled and unskilled) into class I cities. Hence this is the right time to think about future growth of cities and make necessary policy initiatives in this regard in order to halt/reverse environmental damage in the country. There is also a felt need to change the existing policies to protect common goods resources especially, land, minerals and vegetation which are mainly affected by urban growth.

However, it is true that 'our urban cities' are indeed the 'engine of economic growth'. But, if we fail to develop secondary and tertiary level cities and discourage migration into million plus-cities, it will certainly have a negative impact on human health and well-being. As we have already seen, environmental degradation has reached its limits due to rapid urban growth and consequent resource depletion in class I cities in general and million plus-cities in particular.

References

Bhagat, R.B. (1992). 'Components of Urban Growth in India with Reference to Haryana: Findings from Recent Census', *Nagarlok*, 25(3): 10–14.

——. (2004). 'Dynamics of Urban Population Growth by Size Class of Towns and Cities in India', *Demography India*, 33(1): 33–47.

——. (2011). 'Urbanisation and Access to Basic Amenities in India', *Urban India: A Journal of the National Institute of Urban Affairs*, 31(1).

Bilsborrow, R. (1979). 'Population Pressures and Agricultural Development in Developing Countries: A Conceptual Framework and Recent Evidence', paper presented at Population Association of America (PAA) Annual Meeting.

Boserup, E. (1965). *The Conditions of Agricultural Growth*, Allen and Unwin, London.

——. (1981). *Population and Technological Change*, University or Chicago Press, Chicago.

——. (1990). *Economic and Demographic Relationships in Development* (edited by T. Paul Schultz), The Johns Hopkins University Press, Baltimore.

Davis, K. (1963). 'The Theory of Change and Response in Modern Demographic History', *Population Index*, 29(4): 345–66.

Dewaram, A.N. (2007). 'Population Growth and Environmental Degradation in India', *Asia Pacific Journal on Environment and Development*, 14(1): 41–63.

Duraiappah, A. (1996). 'Poverty and Environmental Degradation: A Literature Review and Analysis', CREED Working Paper 8, http://www.prem-online.org/archive/17/doc/creed08e.pdf

Durkheim, E. (1972). 'The Division of Labor, 1893', in A. Giddens (ed.), *Emile Durkheim: Selected Writings*, Cambridge University Press, New York.

Eakin, H. and T.M. Seldon (1995). 'Stroking the Fires? CO Emissions and Economic Growth', *Journal of Public Economics*, 57: 85–101.

Ehrlich, P. (1968). *The Population Bomb*, Ballantine, New York.

Ehrlich, P. and A. Ehrlich (1990). *The Population Explosion*, Simon and Schuster, New York.

Harte, J. (2007). 'Human Population as a Dynamic Factor in Environmental Degradation', *Population and Environment*, 28(45): 223–36.

Jodha, N.S. (1990). 'Depletion of Common Property Resources in India: Micro-level Evidence', *Population and Development Review*, 15: 261–84.

Kalipeni, E. (1992). 'Population Growth and Environmental Degradation in Malawi', *Africa Insight*, 22(4): 273–82. http://www.ncbi.nlm.nih.gov/pubmed.

Kawadia, Ganesh and Gunjan Malhotra (2007). 'Economic Development and Environmental Degradation in India', *Man and Development*, 29(3): 55–70.

Kulkarni, Gouri, Vishnu Bajpai, Sun Sheng Han and T.V. Ramachandra (1992). 'Population Growth, Internal Migration, and Environmental Degradation in Rural Areas of Developing Countries', *The European Journal of Population*, 8: 125–48.

——. (1989). 'The Effects of Population Growth and Agriculture in Guatemala', paper presented at Population Association of America (PAA) Annual Meeting.

——. (2012). 'Carbon Footprint of Municipal Solid Waste in Greater Bangalore', Conference Paper, LAKE 2012: National Conference on Conservation and Management of Wetland Ecosystems, School of Environmental Sciences, Mahatma Gandhi University, Kottayam, Kerala, November.

Kumar, P. (2001). 'Environmental Degradation in Rural Areas: Problems and Suggestions', *Yojana*, 45(10): 44–49.

Kundu, A. (1994). 'Pattern of Urbanization with Special Reference to Small and Medium Towns in India', in G.K. Chadha (ed.), *Sectoral Issues in the Indian Economy*, Har-Anand Publications, New Delhi.

Lakshmana, C.M. (2008). 'Effects of Population Growth on Environmental Degradation: With Reference to India', *Demography India*, 37(1): 63–79.

Lee, R. (1986). 'Malthus and Baserup: A Dynamic Synthesis,' in D. Colman and R. Schofield (eds), *The State of Population Theory*, Basil Blackwell, London, 96–130.

Marx, K. and F. Engels (1989). 'The German Ideology, 1846', in C.L. Arthur (ed.), *The German Ideology: Part One with Selections from Parts Two and Three and Supplementary Texts*, International Publishers, New York.

Ministry of Urban Development (2011). *Report on Indian Urban Infrastructure and Services*, Government of India, New Delhi.

Paul, S.R. (2009). 'Rapid Population Growth and Environmental Degradation: Ultimate versus Proximate Factors', http://www.journal.cambridge.org /production/action.

Registrar General and Census Commissioner, Census of India 1981, Town Directory, Series 1, India, Part X-A (i), New Delhi, 1988.

Registrar General and Census Commissioner, Census of India 1991, Primary Census Abstract, Series 1, India, Vol. 1, Part II-B (i), New Delhi, 1995.

Registrar General and Census Commissioner, Census of India 2001, General Population Tables (Table A-4), Part-II, New Delhi, 2007.

Scott, R., H. Jikum and Z. Linxiu (1997). 'Poverty, Population and Environmental Degradation in China', *Elsevier Science*, 22(3): 229–51.

Shafix, Bandhyopadhyay S. (1992). *Economic Growth and Environmental Quality: Time Series and Cross Country Evidence*, World Bank, Washington, D.C.

Sharma, P.D. (2008). 'Population Growth and Environmental Degradation', http://safeenvirionment.worldpress.com

——. (2012). 'Urbanization, Migration and Sustainable Development: Status and Concerns', conference paper presented in the Prelude conference on Urban Governance, Development and Service Delivery organized by the Centre for Political Institutions, Governance and Development, ISEC, Bangalore, 1 September.

United Nations (1997). Glossary of Environment Statistics in Methods, Series F.67, New York.

Urban India (2011). Evidence, www.autumnworldwide

World Bank (2004). *Sustaining Forests*, The International Bank for Reconstruction and Development, Washington, D.C.

Appendix Table 1(a)

Growth Rate of Area Across Million Plus-Cities in India (1981–2001)

Top Ten Cities		
1	Asansol (WB)	
2	Hyderabad (AP)	
3	Coimbatore (TN)	
4	Visakhapatnam (AP)	
5	Ahmedabad (GUJ)	(Growth rate range between 53 per cent to 79 per cent)
6	Lucknow (UP)	
7	Jaipur (RAJ)	
8	Nashik (MH)	
9	Meerut (UP)	
10	Surat (GUJ)	
Bottom Ten Cities		
1	Faridabad (HAR)	
2	Dhanbad (JHAR)	
3	Vijayawada (AP)	
4	Jamshedpur (BIH)	
5	Varanasi (UP)	(Growth rate range between around one per cent to 20 per cent)
6	Nagpur (MH)	
7	Bhopal (MP)	
8	Allahabad (UP)	
9	Kanpur (UP)	
10	Jabalpur (MP)	Negative growth with minus 12 per cent
Middle Cities		
1	Pune (MH)	
2	Greater Mumbai (MH)	
3	Vadodara (GUJ)	
4	Kochi (KER)	
5	Agra (UP)	
6	Delhi	
7	Rajkot (GUJ)	(Growth rate range between 31 per cent to 54 per cent)
8	Bangalore (KA)	
9	Indore (MP)	
10	Ludhiana (PUNJ)	
11	Madurai (TN)	
12	Patna (BIH)	
13	Chennai (TN)	
14	Kolkata (WB)	
15	Amritsar (PUNJ)	

Appendix Table 1(b)

Growth Rate of Population Across Million Plus-Cities in India (1981–2001)

Top Ten Cities		
1	Faridabad (HAR)	
2	Surat (GUJ)	
3	Nashik (MH)	
4	Ludhiana (PUNJ)	
5	Jaipur (RAJ)	(Growth rate range between 54% to 69%)
6	Delhi	
7	Visakhapatnam (AP)	
8	Lucknow (UP)	
9	Hyderabad (AP)	
10	Pune (MH)	
Bottom Ten Cites		
1	Allahabad (UP)	
2	Kochi (KER)	
3	Coimbatore (TN)	
4	Chennai (TN)	
5	Dhanbad (JHAR)	(Growth rate range between 25% to 37%)
6	Varanasi (UP)	
7	Patna (BIH)	
8	Jabalpur (MP)	
9	Kolkata (WB)	
10	Madurai (TN)	
Middle Cities		
1	Rajkot (GUJ)	
2	Bhopal (MP)	
3	Meerut (UP)	
4	Bengaluru (KA)	
5	Vadodara (GUJ)	
6	Indore (MP)	
7	Agra (UP)	(Growth rate range between 38% to 53%)
8	Ahmedabad (GUJ)	
9	Vijayawada (AP)	
10	Nagpur (MH)	
11	Greater Mumbai (MH)	
12	Asansol (WB)	
13	Amritsar (PUNJ)	
14	Kanpur (UP)	
15	Jamshedpur (BIH)	

Appendix Table 1(c)

Growth Rate of Households Across Million Plus-Cities in India (1981–2001)

Top Ten Cities		
1	Faridabad (HAR)	
2	Patna (BIH)	
3	Surat (GUJ)	
4	Nashik (MH)	
5	Asansol (WB)	(Growth rate range between 60% to 88%)
6	Rajkot (GUJ)	
7	Pune (MH)	
8	Hyderabad (AP)	
9	Kochi (KER)	
10	Visakhapatnam (AP)	
Bottom Ten Cites		
1	Amritsar (PUNJ)	
2	Agra (UP)	
3	Jamshedpur (BIH)	
4	Madurai (TN)	
5	Kolkata (WB)	(Growth rate range between 44% to 59%)
6	Kanpur (UP)	
7	Jabalpur (MP)	
8	Allahabad (UP)	
9	Dhanbad (JHAR)	
10	Varanasi (UP)	
Middle Cities		
1	Ludhiana (PUNJ)	
2	Bengaluru (KA)	
3	Bhopal (MP)	
4	Delhi	
5	Vadodara (GUJ)	
6	Jaipur (RAJ)	
7	Lucknow (UP)	(Growth rate range between 25% to 43%)
8	Greater Mumbai (MH)	
9	Vijayawada (AP)	
10	Indore (MP)	
11	Ahmedabad (GUJ)	
12	Coimbatore (TN)	
13	Meerut (UP)	
14	Nagpur (MH)	
15	Chennai (TN)	

Appendix Table 1(d)

Increased Man-Land Ratio Across Million Plus-Cities in India (1981–2001)

Top Ten Cities		
1	Allahabad (UP)	
2	Vijayawada (AP)	
3	Delhi	
4	Nagpur (MH)	
5	Kanpur (UP)	(Increased Ratio range between 139 to 213)
6	Surat (GUJ)	
7	Faridabad (HAR)	
8	Ludhiana (PUNJ)	
9	Varanasi (UP)	
10	Rajkot (GUJ)	
Bottom Ten Cites		
1	Jaipur (RAJ)	
2	Meerut (UP)	
3	Kochi (KER)	
4	Lucknow (UP)	
5	Greater Mumbai (MH)	(Increased Ratio range between minus 403 to minus 2)
6	Visakhapatnam (AP)	
7	Asansol (WB)	
8	Coimbatore (TN)	
9	Ahmedabad (GUJ)	
10	Hyderabad (AP)	
Middle Cities		
1	Bengaluru (KA)	
2	Bhopal (MP)	
3	Jamshedpur (BIH)	
4	Patna (BIH)	
5	Amritsar (PUNJ)	
6	Jabalpur (MP)	
7	Kolkata (WB)	(Increased Ratio range between 9 to 129)
8	Chennai (TN)	
9	Indore (MP)	
10	Dhanbad (JHAR)	
11	Pune (MH)	
12	Nashik (MH)	
13	Madurai (TN)	
14	Agra (UP)	
15	Vadodara (GUJ)	

Index